My Montana Birds

My Montana Birds

By Gary Swant

Published By: Gary Swant
GoBirdMontana, LLLP
800 St Marys • Deer Lodge, Mt 59722
www.gobirdmontana.org
Email: birdmt@charter.net
406-691-0368

ISBN: 979-880-210-9908

Editing, Design and Production by:
Dale Swant
Pleasant Valley Publishing
Davenport, Washington

Cover image from the author's collection.

Library of Congress Control Number: 2021901687

Printed in the United States of America

COPYRIGHT © 2021: All Rights Reserved. No portion of this book in whole or part may be reproduced, stored in a retrieval system, or transmitted in any form or by any means—electronic, mechanical, photocopy, recording, or any other—except for brief quotation in printed reviews, without the prior written permission of the author.

Table of Contents

Dedication 5
About The Author 6
Purpose Of This Book 7
Classification & Nomenclature 8
Birding Ethics 9
Montana Birding, A Year Around Experience 12
New Resource For Birders 15
eBird-The Future of Birding 17
Getting Started At Bird Watching 20

BIRD FAMILIES IN TAXANOMIC ORDER
CLEMENTS/CORNELL 2019

For both beginners and advanced birders with common names in parenthesis.

Anatidae *(Geese & Ducks)* 23
Phasiandae *(Grouse)* 42
Podicipedidae *(Grebes)* 46
Columbidae *(Doves)* 50
Caprimulgide *(Nighthawk)* 52
Trochilidae *(Hummingbirds)* 54
Rallidae *(Rails)* 58
Gruidae *(Cranes)* 62
Recurvirostridae *(Avocot/Stilt)* 64
Charadriidae *(Plovers)* 66
Scolopacidae *(Shorebirds)* 70
Stercorariidae *(Jaegers)* 76
Laridae *(Gulls)* 78
Gaviidae *(Loons)* 86
Phalacrocoracidae *(Cormorant)* 89
Pelecanidae *(Pelican)* 91
Ardeidae *(Herons)* 93
Threskiornithidae *(Ibis)* 98
Cathartidae *(Vultures)* 101
Pandionidae *(Osprey)* 105
Accipitridae *(Hawks)* 107
Strigidae *(Owls)* 117
Alcedinidae *(Kingfisher)* 134

Picidae *(Woodpeckers)* 136
Falconidae *(Falcons)* 142
Tyrannidae *(Flycatchers)* 149
Vireonidae *(Vireos)* 152
Laniidae *(Shrikes)* 154
Corvidae *(Crows/Jays)* 156
Paridae *(Chickadees)* 166
Alaudidae *(Lark)* 170
Hirundinidae *(Swallows)* 172
Bombycillidae *(Waxwings)* 175
Sittidae *(Nuthatchs)* 177
Certhiidae *(Brown Creeper)* 179
Polioptilidae *(Gnatcatcher)* 181
Troglodytidae *(Wrens)* 183
Mimidae *(Thrashers)* 189
Sturnidae *(European Starling)* 193
Cinclidae *(Dipper)* 195
Turdidae *(Thrushes)* 197
Fringillidae *(Finches)* 204
Calcariidae *(Longspars)* 215
Passerellidae *(Sparrows)* 217
Icteridae *(Blackbirds)* 229
Cardinalidae *(Tanagers)* 241

Official List of Montana Birds 248
Alphabetical List of Birds Described In This Book 255
Index of Bird Families by Species 257
List of Birds Found By Lewis & Clark 260
Glossary of Birding Terms 266

Dedication

As I thought about who to dedicate this collection of bird stories to I immediately thought of two people who have been important in my pursuit of all things birds.

First is my wife, Laura Lee of more than 55 years of marriage. She has always been interested in my passion for birds, thus her interest in birding. When I retired from teaching we looked at each other and said, "The kids are raised, what do we do now?" I replied, "When the nest is empty—go birding!"

Indeed we have. We have birded together in 34 countries and territories and six continents. She drew the line at going to the 7th continent with me, Antarctica. She just wasn't interested in the waves and swells of the Drake Passage for 72 hours both going and coming. She is not as serious a birder as I am, but she has an impressive life list and hangs in there most of the time. Only once did she complain. We were going across a large lake in a small open boat that was clearly overloaded. Waves were coming over the bow of the boat and two Malagasies were in the back furiously bailing water over the side to keep us afloat. She looked at them and emphatically said, "You have pushed me about as far as I want to go."

The second is my grandson Caleb Lashway. I have nine grandchildren and he is the only one who really took to birds; and he did so by age two. He and I have birded in several countries around the world, and he currently works with me as a bird guide and avian researcher and business partner in our company *GoBirdMontana, LLLP*. Without his interest in birding I would have had to end my professional birding career and company. He does much of the field work, with good ears, and I do the office work, with not so good ears.

Thank you for allowing me to share my passion for birds with you. ♦

About The Author

Whenever I pick up a book, I look at the title first, the credentials, then the experience of the author to see if the two match. If they do, I consider the book, if not, I don't.

I'm a native Montanan, born in Deer Lodge where I currently reside. I've lived my entire life in the state of Montana. I hold a Bachelor's Degree in Education with an emphasis on Biology, and a Master's of Education with an emphasis on Environmental Education. I taught Biology and Field Ecology in Deer Lodge for 25 years plus numerous summer session environmental graduate courses for Montana State University, University of Montana and Montana School of Technology.

AUTHOR GARY SWANT

During those years I was fortunate to receive the Outstanding Biology Teacher of the Year award in 1971, Presidential Award for Excellence in Science Teaching in Montana in 1986, and the Montana Environmental Educator of the Year award in 1993.

Since 2014 I've written newspaper columns on bird species and bird issues for a number of Montana newspapers including the Silver State Post (Deer Lodge), Phillipsburg Mail, Bitterroot Star (Hamilton Valley), Madisonian (Ennis) and Lee Newspaper's in Butte (Montana Standard) and Helena (Independent Record).

In 2018 and 2019 I received First Place for Outdoor Writing in small Montana newspapers.

In 2005 I formed *GoBirdMontana, LLC* as a bird guide service and avian field research organization. I was recognized for this work in 2016 with the Montana Audubon Citizen Scientist of the Year Award, and the Montana Chapter of the Wildlife Society, Conservation Award in 2018.

In addition, I have worked with state, federal, and private industry doing field avian research. Currently I am vice-chair of the Berkeley Pit Waterfowl Mitigation Advisory Board. Where we are actively seeking solutions to waterfowl mortality issues at the Berkeley Pit in Butte for Montana Resources and Atlantic Richfield. ♦

Purpose of This Book

As mentioned on the previous page, for many years I have been writing articles for newspapers in Western Montana. I wrote about birds that interest me. I also wrote about birds I managed to shoot a decent photograph of in the wild. In all, I have articles on 115 of Montana's 442 species as of August, 2021. Most articles reference the Upper Clark Fork Valley where I live, but the birds featured exist in Western Montana and many parts of Eastern Montana as well.

Birds are one of the most difficult wildlife subjects to photograph. They are generally small, quick, skittish, and have a limb between themselves and your camera. It takes many hours and hundreds of shots to get a few pictures that illustrate a bird well. All of the photographs in this book were taken by the author unless otherwise noted.

When I meet people on the street they often tell me how much they enjoyed my articles and that I should write a book using my articles so folks could have them in one volume. This book is my attempt to do so.

My articles were not scientific monologues of the species of Montana, others have already done that. Nor does it cover all 442 species known to occur in Montana. It is a volume of *My Montana Birds* that I have enjoyed enough to write about.

There were two other individuals that passed through Montana in 1805 that wrote about the birds they saw. They traveled up the Missouri and Jefferson Rivers and crossed the Bitterroot Mountain range into Idaho. They returned in July, 1806 and split up, some going north to the Marias River and the other group going south along the Yellowstone. They took meticulous notes on their travels which included a list of birds that they saw. Those two were Lewis and Clark.

Of course there was no Montana, or Montana territory, they were traversing the Louisiana Territory in anticipation of finding the Northwest Water Passage to the Pacific Ocean from the Dakotas; which turned out to be myth. Some of their bird descriptions were vague and there is dispute as to what they actually saw. I thought that my readers might be interested in what they saw and compare to the species that I have written about. Several species that they recorded had never been described before their journey. Appendix D is a list of the birds they saw on their Journey of Discovery. Appendix A is a list of the Birds of Montana as of July, 2021 and is the order of birds in this book.

If you purchased this book, I assume that you are interested in birds. I hope you will use my book to interest your children or grandchildren to enjoy birds. Perhaps you can read about a specific bird and then go and see if you can find that bird around Montana's lakes, streams, ponds, forests and by-ways. Young people need to get re-introduced to the great outdoors. They need to learn life doesn't have to be spent in virtual reality, but can be lived in real time; hearing, feeling, smelling and being seduced by *Mother Nature*. ♦

Classification & Nomenclature

On many occasions, when teaching a beginning birding class, students are overwhelmed by the seemingly disorder of bird names on a checklist and in field guides. They often say something like, "Why can't the birds just be in alphabetical order, I could find them a lot easier."

At first, this seems to make sense, but birds are organized by family groups that share certain physical and biological characteristics. For decades checklists and field guides changed little in the sequence of listing birds. This was due to the sequence of bird families based on morphological features such as toe arrangement, beak types, and feather tracts to name a few.

With the advent of DNA sequencing in the last several decades, science has a totally new understanding of the relationship of the major lineages of birds. This has caused the positioning of many families within the genetic sequence to change. As an example, in my Fourth edition of National Geographics' *Birds of North America* (1987) loons are listed first. In the 7th Edition (2017) geese are listed first, and loons are placed after waterfowl, game birds, grebes, pigeons, cuckoos, goatsuckers, swifts, hummingbirds, rails, cranes, shorebirds, jaegers, auks - murre - puffins, gulls, terns, and tropical birds. No doubt, family orders will change again, as better understanding of the DNA sequencing improves. In addition, the order of species within a family has changed.

Each species has a two part scientific name composed of a capitalized genus followed by a small letter species. This scientific name is unique to each species. Efforts are being made to standardize the English common name worldwide. As an example, the magpie is in the family Corvidae. The standardized English name is Black-Billed Magpie, and the scientific name is *Pica hudsonia*.

There are 85 families of birds in North America with 1,023 species. Not all families occur in all areas. If you learn the characteristics of the families in your area and their location in your field guide, bird identification become much easier.

In this book, species are organized by Clement-Cornell—2019 taxonomy. ♦

Birding Ethics

It seems prudent that you should start reading about birds with an article that I wrote about birding ethics when in the field. Let's start with understanding the basics of ethical birding and then get into the *My Montana Birds*.

When I first starting birding in 1970, birding was very low tech. Basically, you had a field guide, a pair of binoculars, and if you had the financial resources maybe a scope and tripod. There were not a lot of us out there watching birds either.

My how things have changed!. The first significant change was the number of birders. Today there are many. Why? Baby boomers started to retire, people were retiring earlier, and the internet allowed people to work from home and adjust their work schedule around recreational opportunities.

Secondly, people who retire early or are working from home have more discretionary funds than in the past. I first noticed this change when birders began to carry SLR cameras with long lenses and were getting good pictures. In a few years these cameras were replaced with Digital SLR and high quality "Point & Shoot" cameras. In the past an exceptional bird picture was a rarity and taken by the professionals. Today, excellent bird pictures are being taken every day.

NIKON 750 CAMERA WITH 500 MM LENS

Cameras today are really computers that do much of the work for you and the resolution or pixels are as high as 48 megabites. It is not uncommon to see birders packing cameras costing three to five thousand dollars. The internet has many sites where birders can post and view images. As an example, on Facebook there are a number of Montana birding sites. Montana Birding has 5,778 members as of 2020, and most post bird pictures. Montana Rare Bird Alert has 973 members, and a picture is necessary to post there. The national "What's this Bird" Facebook page has 23,503 members and is totally based on photographs.

Another area of improvement in birding is bird songs. When I first started birding I had a set of wooden whistles designed to imitate bird songs. Obviously, the number of whistles you

NOTE PAD OPENED to a field guide program paired with a bluetooth speaker.

could take to the field was limited. This was replaced with six cassette tapes of the birds of North America. You had to pack a bulky tape player to the field, use the right tape, fast-forward to the correct footage, and play. Next came the "Walkman" with all of the songs on a single CD. The problem with this was you had to punch a button a number of times to get to the correct track and hold a wired speaker in your hand. Today most birders use an App on their phone, and a "Bluetooth" wireless speaker clipped to their vest. You simply type in the species name and not only do you get the song, but most Apps have photos, maps and facts about the species.

NOTE PAD OPENED to eBird checklist.

The opportunity for abusing birds with all of this technology is tremendous. Some try to get the perfect picture by getting to close to birds and cause stress or scare birds off the nest, or spook a bird out of the area before others have the opportunity to view the bird.

Playback has always been controversial. Birds respond to a call because it agitates a bird into thinking it is responding to the call of another bird. This is especially true when birds are competing for a mate during breeding or protecting a territory. Birds can also be driven off a nest by the call of a predator bird.

SPOTTING SCOPE mounted on a tripod.

SMART PHONE attached to spotting scope.

Better optics also adds to stress on birds. As optics improve their light gathering ability has increased. This enables longer viewing times in the field or viewing in less than ideal conditions such as low light during a storm or at sunset. The result is that more birders are watching birds for longer periods of time for more days a year. The cumulative effect of all of this change in birding could take its toll.

Admittedly, this may not be as big of a problem in Montana. I rarely encounter birders in the field. If I use playback on a species it may be the only time in the year that this bird responds to artificial songs. In other areas of the country this is not the case. I have been in areas where hundreds of birders frequent an area weekly and playback abuse would undoubtedly take its toll. Heavily birdied areas often have rules against playing songs and calls.

The American Birding Association (ABA) has attempted to mitigate this issue with a Code of Birding Ethics. I thought it might be useful to inform you of their efforts. We all make mistakes in the field out of enthusiasm for getting a good look at a bird. Hopefully you might remember what the ABA stresses in their Ethics Code when those moments happen.

SPOTTING SCOPE mounted on a car window.

RESPECT AND PROMOTE BIRDS AND THEIR ENVIRONMENTS

From a practical perspective promote birding by keeping cats and other domestic animals indoors or controlled, reduce window strikes, and plant native landscaping when possible. Some may want to financially support conservation of birds.

Avoid stressing birds by being cautious around active nests, display and feeding sites. Limit the use of recordings particularly in heavily birded areas, with species that are rare, or species that are threatened or endangered. Exercise restraint when photographing, recording or approaching birds.

When you are out birding, minimize habitat disturbance. Be aware of how your vehicle can leave tracks in the soil.

Respect and promote the birding community and its individual members. Be a role model for others, bird and report your sightings with integrity and honesty. Respect the rights and skill levels of fellow birders, as well as others participating in other outdoor activities in the same areas.

Share bird observations with others, unless it would harm a sensitive or threatened species.

If you observe unethical birding behavior, be sensitive and respectful, and try to resolve the issue in a positive manner. Always teach by example, especially if you are a group leader.

RESPECT AND PROMOTE THE BIRDING COMMUNITY AND ITS MEMBERS

Never enter private property without the landowner's permission. Many popular birding areas may have additional regulations governing birding activities. Be aware of these regulations that protect sensitive areas, the use of audio, putting up feeding stations and photography.

Adapted from the ABA Code of Birding Ethics, v.2.1 Nov. 2019

You can obtain the complete Code of Ethics by going to www.aba.org, click on "About" and then "Ethics".

I hope you will read this code occasionally and promote and practice ethical birding. Unethical birding can end opportunities to enjoy birding and the great outdoors for all of us who live here in Montana and elsewhere. ♦

Montana Birding
A Year Around Experience

Montana is an outstanding place to go bird watching. It is a destination area for many birders to obtain life birds and rarities. What makes Montana a great place to bird is its size. From East to West it is more than 850 miles wide and some 300 miles North to South. Within this vast land area are a variety of habitats providing homes for a lot of bird species. One of Montana's most unique habitats is the alpine tundra zone above timberline. These are found in Glacier National Park, the Beartooth, Flint Creek, Pintlar, Highland and Pioneer Mountain ranges. Alpine tundra gives the opportunity to find White-tailed Ptarmigan, Rosy-finches, and American Pipit. Just below this alpine zone one often finds Chestnut-back and Boreal Chickadees in Northwest Montana. Eastern Montana has extensive native prairie which provides some of the best opportunities for rare grassland birds such as Thick-billed, and Chestnut-collared Longspur, Baird's, Le Conte's and Nelson's Sparrows. Montana is rich in public lands and offers more than 80 state parks, 60 state Wildlife Management Areas and 22 National Wildlife Refuges with unparalleled birding in a variety of habitats.

NORTHERN PYGMY OWL

Birding at Warm Springs, Freezout, Bowdoin and other wetlands offer 41 shorebird species during spring and fall migration.

Montana has an impressive 442 avian species on the "state checklist" as of July 2021. No individual has seen all 442 species. As of August 2021 on eBird the top two birders (myself and Dan Casey) have 378 species each. Only 45 birders have seen over 300 species within our borders. While only 8 birders have an eBird list for every county in the state. I hold the state record for the most species seen in a single year (328) which I set in 2007. (See One Man's Quest to List 300 Different Species in 365 Days, page 16, Montana Outdoors, May-June 2008).

Many bird species leave the state in September and October and don't return until April and May. So what is the opportunity to see winter birds in Montana? Let's look at the facts. Of the 442 species seen in Montana, approximately 108 have been seen 20 times or less, and a number have only been seen once. In an average year, all the birders in Montana combined see about 350 species. The average birder sees between 200 and 225 birds a year. When I set the state record in 2007,

I traveled 24,000 miles and spent 151 days in the field. Few will bird that hard in a year.

A bird is considered to have "overwintered" in Montana if it is regularly seen between December 15 and February 15. If a bird is only seen once between those dates it is considered observed, but not overwintering. The official number of birds that have been seen in the winter in Montana is 220, but the numbers that officially overwinter are 176. Approximately, 40% of the total birds seen in the state overwinter. The average overwintering number seen by most serious birders is between 120 and 140 species.

There are nine species found in Montana only in the winter. You will not see them here in the summer. These species include; Rough-legged Hawk, Gyrfalcon, Snowy Owl, Northern Shrike, American Tree Sparrow, Lapland Longspur, Snow Bunting, Common and Hoary Redpoll. Of these species, Rough-legged Hawk, Northern Shrike, and American Tree Sparrow are common. The remainder can be a challenge to find. The Lapland Longspur, Snow Bunting and Redpolls are best found after a heavy snow fall that concentrates species in plowed fields and along riparian areas. A few Gyrfalcons are in the state every year along the highline. Several of these species are irruptive, meaning they occur in large numbers in one year and few are seen other years. Data from the Warm Springs Christmas Bird Counts, illustrates the irruptive nature of the Common Redpoll. In 2000 we had no Redpolls on the CBC count, in 2001 we had 869, again in 2002 none. Between 2000 and 2010 there were four years with none, and six years with sightings.

SNOWY OWL

The Snowy Owl can be irruptive. In years when rodent populations are sparse in Canada. Many migrate south into Montana looking for rodents. The Flathead Valley had a large irruption where I viewed 15 Snowy Owls feeding on voles in a field near Polson.

So where do you look for birds in winter? Watch backyard bird feeders. Putting out black sunflower seeds, not millet or millet/sunflower mixes, gives the best chance for a variety of birds species. Millet draws House Sparrows which discourages other species from using feeders. Add a thistle feeder, suet and water greatly enhances the number of species possible. Place feeders near shrubs such as juniper that gives protection and increases the number of species using a feeder.

Winter species you can expect to see at feeders are; American Goldfinch, Pine Siskin, Common Redpoll, House Finch, American Tree Sparrow, Eurasian-collared Dove, Bohemian Waxwing, Red-breasted, White-breasted, & Pygmy Nuthatches, Black-capped & Mountain Chickadees, Hairy & Downy Woodpeckers and Northern Flicker. It is not uncommon to attract Northern Pygmy Owls, and Sharp-shinned Hawks for a meal of feeder birds. If you are in the right habitat, scattering seed on the ground can draw in Wild Turkey, California Quail, and Gray Partridge.

Other good areas to observe birds in the winter are areas of open water in lakes and streams for 30 overwintering species of waterfowl. Wherever waterfowl are concentrated there is a good chance that Bald Eagles, Golden Eagles, Northern Harriers, and possibly Gyrfalcons will be working the area for a meal. Winters also bring gull rarities, such as Iceland and Lesser Black-backed to major rivers such as the Yellowstone and Missouri.

Hedge rows, particularly with mature Junipers, and grassy fields near hedgerows, typically have several species of owls. Of Montana's 15 Owl species, 13 overwinter, and the other two, Flammulated and Barn have been reported in the winter. Walking down a hedgerow or Juniper stand can produce a Great Horned, Snowy, Northern Pygmy, Long, and Short-eared Owls. One of Montana's rarest owls, the Great Gray can often be seen in the winter feeding in mountain meadows along the forest edge.

Learn to bird year around, not just in warm weather. Winter provides just as many opportunities as summer. You will be surprised how many you will find. Why not make a list of how many you see between December 15 and February 15? Make a goal of seeing 75% of Montana's overwintering species. If you get that many, you will have a lot of fun, a lot of outdoor time and memories of winter birds.

I know football is a great indoor winter sport, but so is getting outdoors and enjoying one of Montana's most watchable wildlife – Birds.

Appendix A has the official list of all of the birds of Montana. Note how many you see in the winter verses summer. ♦

BIRDING THE PRAIRIE GRASSLANDS ON A MONTANA RESERVATION.

New Resource For Birders

Montana is a reasonably good place to bird with 442 species (2021) found within our borders. There are no endemics (found only in Montana) species, but we have a number of birds that folks do travel to the state to find. These include prairie species such Thick-billed, and Chestnut-collared Longspurs, as well as alpine species such a Gray-crowned and Black Rosy-Finch. I was surprised in 2018 when I led a tour of serious birders for the Western Field Ornithologist convention in Billings, how few had seen the Black Rosy-Finch. Also, many go to Glacier Park for a chance to see a White-tailed Ptarmigan, or Northern Hawk Owl.

Locally in the Upper Clark Fork valley, I have had numerous calls to guide birders for the Great Gray Owl, and to find Sagebrush Sparrow, and Gray Flycatcher in the Bannack area.

Typically, Montana is not a birding destination for birding tour companies as is Texas with 640 species, Arizona with 505 species, or countries like Ecuador, the size of Nevada, with 1,576 species and eight endemics!

Consequently, few books have been written on Montana birds. There are several field guides of the common birds of Montana, but they don't cover all of Montana's species, and enviably you find a bird that is not in the guide. This is especially frustrating to new birders, who are unfamiliar with Montana's avian species.

In terms of North American field guides I use and would recommend the *Sibley Guide to Birds* second edition, 2014, and National Geographic's *Field Guide to the Birds of North America*, 7th edition. Neither guide is arranged in the latest American Ornithological Societies' taxonomic order, because it is changing almost yearly.

Specifically, with Montana in mind, one older book that is useful is Terry McEneaney's *The Birder's Guide to Montana*. It is useful, but a little dated as the copyright by Falcon Press is 1993.

The resource that I use the most is P.D. Skar's *Montana Bird Distribution*, 7th Edition, 2012. This reference lists all of Montana's species, and their distribution on a coded Latilong map of the state. In addition, the time of year they occur is shown on a bar graph, and the number of records on file with the Montana Natural Heritage Programs database is noted. The 7th edition only lists 427 species, as that was the number seen in the state at the time of publication. Thus, the current edition is getting a little dated, but you can access the database by

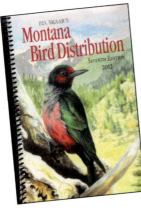

going to the Montana Natural History Program's website at http://mtnhp.org/mtbird/ and print out the current map for each species and access observation data. Every 5 to 10 years that data base is published in a book for easy access while in the field. I am not aware of the future publication date for the 8th Edition, but I imagine it is still a few years out.

What is exciting for me, as an avid birder is the latest Montana resource, *Birds of Montana*, 2016, by Jeffery S. Marks, Paul Hendricks, and Daniel Casey, all with strong roots in Montana. The book was sponsored by Montana Audubon and proceeds from sales go to Montana Audubon.

This is no light weight book, it weighs five pounds with 659 pages! Within its pages are an extensive review of the status, distribution and abundance, ecology and conservation of all of Montana's avian species at the time of publication.

The first chapter is on the geography, topography, and habitats of Montana's landscape and is essential information to understanding the distribution of Montana's birds. This is followed by 20 pages of the History of Montana Ornithology and is fascinating reading. The final preliminary chapter discusses bird conservation within the state, the agencies, and organizations that are dedicated to the long term health and survival of Montana's birds through habitat protection and enhancement.

The remainder of the book is dedicated to the species accounts of the current 433 species (2016) found within the borders of our great state. Each account describes the field marks and distribution of the species, subspecies if there are any, current status and occurrence within the state, including records of interest, habitat preference, and conservation of the species. A final section of each species account introduces you to any historical notes and information about the species that is of interest to ornithologists and birders alike.

Accounts are detailed enough to give researchers valuable information and insights, as well as readable by novices, backyard birder, and serious birders.

No one would pack this well researched volume to the field, but I can see many who enjoy birds reading a few accounts each winter evening as the snow blows and the wind howls, and we dream about spring migration.

These authors have done outstanding work in the writing of *Birds Of Montana* and it will be a source of enjoyable reading and knowledge to many in and out of the state of Montana.

If your interest in birds, draws you to know more about our Montana avian friends, you should consider adding this fine volume to your library. You will most likely find yourself as you read telling others, "Did you know such and such about any of a number of different species."

Birds of Montana can be purchased through American Birding Association sales at Buteo Books on the web at http://www.buteobooks.com/abasales.html or at the Montana Audubon Office in Helena.

Good reading and birding this fall and winter. ♦

eBird-The Future of Birding

I want to share with you the most exciting and relevant new development in Birding: eBird. eBird is a web-based program as well as an App for mobile devices. The phone App is simply a field version of the web-based program.

I used to keep hand written notes in the field on bird observations and then enter those notes into my computer with a program called Birdbase. I now use Birder's Diary which allows you to directly input your eBird data into your computer  so I have access to my personal data. This allows for far fewer errors and takes very little time to do. One of the advantages of eBird is the data is automatically shared with birders and scientist around the world.

The advantage of the eBird App is that I no longer have to make field notes on observations, and then enter the data in eBird at home. In the past, depending on how busy I was, I sometimes entered the data the same day, but often I would get a backlog of field notes, and would go several days before I entered the data. With the phone App, I have been able to enter the data in the field, and it is automatically entered in the eBird database. I have also gotten more specific on where my observations are made. I used to do one list for the entire day. As an example; the Upper Clark Valley. Now I start a new list, every five miles of observations, making the data much more site specific.

eBird allows you to do the following: record the birds you see in the field, keep track of your bird lists, share your sightings with others, explore graphs and maps on the trends in bird species, and contribute to science and conservation.

If you want to add the App to your mobile device go to your App Store and type in eBird. You will see NA (North America) as a free App. To use Asia, Europe, Africa, South America, etc. you will need to download additional lists (packs). You probably should familiarize yourself with North America, before you download other 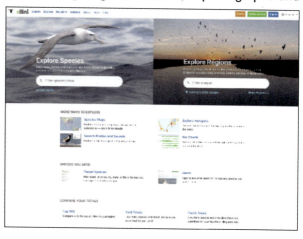 eBird packs. You should also access the web version at home and register both, that way your mobile App and web-based eBird will communicate seamlessly.

I use the PC and iPhone version. I do all of my field work on the iPhone and then study and manipulate the data and print out reports on my PC. The important thing to remember is that all of the data that you enter with your phone or tablet is automatically placed in your personal database and is accessible on online.

One change I have recently made in the way I use eBird is switching from my iPhone to a data line connected to an android tablet. The advantage for me is that the screen is larger, it is easier to see, and the keyboard fits my hands better. I purchased a mini-pad so it is not too large and still usable in the field. In addition, I downloaded four field guides to the tablet so I have everything in one unit. The tablet is bluetooth enabled so I can use an external wireless speaker for playing bird songs from the field guides.

How many birders are using eBird? Currently nearly a million users, who have posted from 2,774,557 locations, and 900 million bird observations as of mid 2020. This provides for an incredible database for you to explore.

So how do you use the program? When you are in the field, open the program, and tap "Submit Sighting". It then brings up a list of birds for the area you are in, based on input from others for that date.

Next you enter the number of birds for each species that you see. Once you are done you click "stop" and check if it is a complete checklist or not and the number of people in your party. The App has kept track of the distance you traveled and the time. The App then brings up a list of recent locations you have birded, or you can go to a map and pinpoint the location.

You now click "Submit" the list. If you have no phone connection click "Save" and then submit it later. You also have the option of sharing the list with others through email.

There are constant upgrades to the App and the current program may be different than what I have described.

When you are home using your computer, you have lots of options as to what to do with your field data. On the eBird home page click "My Data", and a screen will come up with "Your bird Statistics" and "Your Lists". Under your list you can either click on "Life" or "Year list" and that list will appear on the screen with the birds in taxonomic order. To the right of the species name will be the date you first saw the species and the location. If you click on the species a list will appear of every location you have seen the species in a given year, and if you click on the location, every species seen at that location will appear. All lists are printable.

The other option is to click on "Explore Data". On this page you can get a list of species for any region you type in. Another option is a Map of the US with dots for all of the sightings for a particular species. On this option you can select the date and get real time data on the migration of a species in the spring or fall. You can also select line or bar graphs for a particular species, at a given location during a calendar year.

A fun option on this page is the "Top 100" for a location and year. It is interesting to see how many species you have seen compared to others in an area for a particular year.

There are many other ways to use eBird besides those I have described. I encourage you to explore eBird for yourself and begin to enter your observations. Using eBird, will make you a better birder. Its free, it's fun, and you will be contributing significant data, used by scientists to study population trends and migrations.

As with the App, the current eBird program for PC and Apple may be different than what I have described. I have included several screen shots from the eBird website to give you an idea of what they offer. ♦

THE AUTHOR WITH WIFE LAURA LEE EXPLORING ST. PAUL ISLAND, ALASKA FOR BIRDS.

Getting Started At Birdwatching

You wouldn't be reading this book if you weren't at least casually interested in birds. You might be a person who has never been on a bird walk or looked at a bird through a pair of binoculars but would like to start. So let's start at the beginning.

Birding is one of the fastest growing outdoor hobbies in America and Montana. A recent study showed Montana has more birders than any other state. Why is this true? Birds are easily the most watchable wildlife there is and the variety of birds is spectacular with 442 species observed in Montana. Some call themselves birders if they put out a feeder and watch birds through a window. I am assuming that a birder is someone who leaves home and deliberately goes to an area to specifically look for birds.

Birding can become very addictive, as my wife well knows. I bird about 100 days a year and drive around 10,000 miles a year doing just that. You don't have to be that serious, but a couple of outings a month will provide you with an active hobby. It gets you out into nature and perhaps into areas you have never explored.

So what do you need to get started? First of all you need a quality pair of binoculars. I have seen beginners using $50.00 binoculars and they quickly become discouraged. You simply don't see the details of the bird with poor quality optics. Don't be tempted to dust off grandpa's old binoculars and go look for birds. Advances in binoculars over the past few decades have been remarkable in close focusing and lens coatings have significantly increased light gathering and clarity.

You don't have to spend $2,500.00 or more as I have either. Fortunately, there are several models of binoculars in the $400 to $600.00 range that are excellent. Choose a "roof" model (two straight barrels) they are easy to use, resistant to misalignment of barrels, and light weight. The "roof" models prisms direct the light in a straight path allowing for a more compact and lighter binocular with a brighter image. The older "poro" designed binoculars use prisms that bend the light several times resulting in the eye piece and lens not in a straight line and a dimmer image. The "poro" construction also makes the design larger and heavier than "roof" models.

When purchasing binoculars understand the numbers. The first number is the power compared to the unaided eye. The second number is the size of the objective lens; the lens opposite the eye piece. The larger this number the more light the binoculars will gather. The down size is the larger the second number the bigger and heavier the binocular. The key is to get the right power and light gathering for your use of the binoculars.

If your hands and arms are steady purchase a 10 x 42 model. The higher the power the more magnification and unstableness in holding them to your eyes for long periods of time. A 42 mm lens is adequate for light gathering and keeps the overall weight of the binoculars down. If you are a little shaky buy 8.5 by 42 or 7 by 42 models.

When you get your binoculars practice finding objects through your binoculars. Many beginners cannot find a bird that is being pointed out to them because they are not used to looking through binoculars. You should be able to instinctively bring binoculars to your eyes and see what you are looking at. To learn to do so practice with a branch on a tree. Stare at it with you naked eye, then slowly lift the binoculars into place without taking your eyes off the branch and see if it is in view through the binoculars.

Many beginning birders complain of a sore neck from carrying binoculars after several hours. Some of this soreness is from cocking your head upward when viewing a bird, but much of it is the weight of the binoculars on your neck. Consider buying a shoulder strap for better weight distribution instead of the neck strap that comes with your binoculars. With shoulder straps the weight of the binoculars is shifted from your neck to your shoulders. I often wear my binoculars all day and forget I have them on because the weight is distributed to my body, not my neck.

So how much should you spend? As much as you can afford. If you are on a limited budget you should be able to find good binoculars in the $400 to $600 range. Better quality binoculars range from $2,500 to $3,000 and they both can be 10 x 42 binoculars.

What then is the difference between a $500 and $3,000 pair of binoculars? To start with is construction. High end binoculars are rugged, will take abuse and not get out of alignment between the two barrels. High end binos are waterproof, fog proof, not just water resistant. The real difference is in the lens coatings. Coatings are applied to reduce the reflection of light at the glass surface which allows more light to pass through the lens. The coatings effectively increase transmission of light. This is observed as an increase in the brightness, contrast, and color fidelity of the images. High end binos have higher quality coatings which make a difference is what you can see at dusk, dawn and inclement weather.

IMPORTANT TO KEEP LENSES CLEAN

This is why it is so important how you clean your binos. Always blow the lens off first to remove dust particles that can scratch the lens when you wipe the lens. Some lens cleaners actually degrade the coatings. Hand sanitizers especially degrade coatings. Swarovski, makers of one of the top brands of high end binos, recommend spraying your binos with Simple Green and then wiping clean with a cloth designed for binoculars.

The final difference is the guarantee. Better brands have lifetime warantees against all kinds of damage. I once drove over a pair with my truck damaging them greatly. I called rather apologetic asking how much it was going to cost to repair the binnoculars. There was no charge; they were simply warranted for a lifetime. Another important consideration is where the repair shop is located. An American based repair facility will have a shorter turnaround time than one overseas.

One other thing to consider. It's great to look on the Internet at models and prices. I would not recommend that you purchase a pair without first having them in hand. Two different brands of equal quality binos might not fit your hands or eye position on your head. Don't purchase a pair without using them for an hour or so in and out of the store.

Other than all this, purchasing the right pair of binoculars is an easy task, I wished. If you do purchase a pair, enjoy your new binoculars, they can be a life time purchase. I purchased my first pair of 10 x 42 SLC Swarovski binos more than 25 years ago. They perform today as well as did when I bought them. I did purchase a pair of 10 x 42 EL Swarovski binos a couple of years ago, only because the new coatings are better, and the close focus is greatly improved. ♦

Family Anatidae

Snow Goose 24
Ross's Goose 26
Trumpeter Swan 27
Tundra Swan 27
Wood Duck 29
Baikal Teal 30
Blue-Winged Teal 32
Eurasian Wigeon 33
Harlequin Duck 33
Surf Scoter 35
White-winged Scoter 37
Stejneger's Scoter 38
Black Scoter 39
Long-Tail Duck 39
Common Goldeneye 40
Barrow's Goldeneye 41

SNOW GOOSE

White Geese were in the news in Butte on November 26, 2016 with the tragic death of nearly 3,000 birds out of the 60,000 that landed in the Berkeley Pit.

Fortunately, Montana Resources (MR) and AR/BP have been implementing recommendations from the Berkeley Pit Waterfowl Mitigation Advisory Board of which I am a member. Newly implemented recommendations have been a series of propane cannons around the perimeter of the pit that fire randomly, and the installation of several "wailers". Wailers are electronic sound devices which emit loud distress calls of waterfowl, and calls of predators such as Peregrine Falcons. This combination seems to be working well, as well as the direct hazing of birds that land on the water with rifle shots near them. Other methods that are being tested are laser beams, a remotely operated hydroplane, pyrogenic explosions, and high intensity search lights.

SNOW GOOSE

In the five years since that event there have been a few incidents with one to three thousand birds in the pit, but no significant loss of birds. In fact, our hazing efforts have had over a 99 percent success rate. We have learned how to haze birds off the water successfully.

Montana Resources and Atlantic Richfield have learned so much since that fall's "perfect storm" conditions that caused the event to happen.

We now monitor white geese in the Upper Clark Fork Drainage March through December as well as acquire information on their movements several hundred miles both North and South of the pit. We are prepared days ahead of geese and other waterfowl coming into the Summit Valley and the Berkeley Pit. White geese typically show early in March at the Warm Springs WMA. Small numbers continue through mid-April with each weekly survey of the WMA and other ponds in the Upper Clark Fork Valley. It is very unusual to see white geese past the end of April. Typically numbers observed have been from a single bird to 200 to 1,000 in a flock.

As we witnessed in the fall of 2016 migration numbers can be large in comparison to spring. On the infamous November night the estimation of white geese flying over the Berkeley Pit was between 60 and 90 thousand with 30,000 landing in the pit. Of those 30,000 that landed 3,000 died over the next couple of days.

Why do we use the term white geese? There are actually two species within the group, white geese. The more abundant species in our valley and Montana is the Lesser Snow Goose or just Snow Goose. The other is the Ross's Goose which looks very similar superficially.

The Snow Goose has two sub-species. The one we have locally is the Lesser

SNOW GEESE

Snow Goose, *Chen caerulescens* and the other is the Greater Snow Goose, Chen c. atlanticus. The Greater has a length of 31 inches, wingspan of 56 inches and weighs 7.4 pounds. In comparison the Lesser has a length of 28 inches, wingspan of 53 inches and weighs 5.3 pounds. The greater breeds in Northwest Greenland and winters in northeast Mexico. Their migration pathway is Eastern North America. The lesser breeds in Alaska and Siberia and winters in California and Gulf Coast. Lesser's have four migration paths across North America from the West Coast to the East Coast.

The Greater Snow goose is an all-white bird with black wing tips. I have never seen one. The Lesser Snow Goose is also most often all white with black wing tips, but there is dark morph as well which can look like a different species; in the past called the Blue Goose. The Lesser also has a "wedged-shaped" head, showing various degrees of tan color with an obvious "grin patch" (black area on lower bill). The base of the bill is strongly curved. All of these traits can be seen on the photo of the Lesser Snow Goose.

In comparison, the Ross's Goose is rather small weighing only 2.7 pounds, a length of 23 inches and a wingspan of 45 inches. Additionally, the head is round rather than wedged shape, the bill is short and stubby, lacks the "grin patch", and the base of the bill is straight rather than curved.

Most of the white geese that fly through the Clark Fork Valley are Lesser Snow Geese. As March becomes April, the number of Ross's increases, but never exceeds the number of Lesser. Just the opposite happens at Freezeout, where Montana experiences most of the white geese migration. By mid to late April it is not uncommon for most of the white geese to be Ross's.

We hope that the Berkeley Pit never experiences another "perfect storm" landing of large numbers of white geese at the pit. But I can assure you, Montana Resources and Atlantic Richfield have taken the problem seriously, and with the help of the Advisory Council are better equipped to prevent birds from landing. New hazing techniques are showing that they are better at getting birds back off the water in a shorter period of time as well.

Looking back on this event, we now know what triggered the 2016 event. We

ROSS'S GOOSE

had warm weather in southern Alberta that allowed the white geese to stay and feed in grain fields into late November. This is several weeks later than normal. Then the last week of November an Arctic front occurred that caused the birds to begin to move South. However, cold weather had also frozen all of the open water at Freezout, the Helena Valley, and the Upper Clark Fork Drainage, including Warm Springs WMA. The birds had nowhere to land and kept coming south. Exhaustion and dehydration was beginning to effect the birds when they reached the Summit Valley and the Berkeley Pit. There they meet a strong south wind and snow storm that blew the birds towards the ground. The only open water was the pit and they landed.

ROSS'S GOOSE

Being dehydrated, they gulped water and their lactic acid cramped muscles were too tired to continue flying. We are fortunate more did not die over the next three days.

The "perfect storm" conditions may never happen again, they haven't for five years. If it does happen we think we have learned enough about deterrents and hazing that mortality will be significantly less. We are not anxious to test our theories, but we are prepared to do so if needed. ♦

BERKLEY PIT

Photo by Mark Mariano

TRUMPETER SWAN

I had just spent 20 minutes watching a group of 11 Tundra Swans when a person called and asked if I had seen the Trumpeter Swans in the same pond. I asked when they had seen them. It was just a few minutes before I was watching the same white swans, which were not Trumpeter but Tundra Swans. They are hard to tell apart without some experience and studying their field marks.

This got me to thinking that I should write an article on how to identify Tundra verses Trumpeter Swans.

First of all, most people can identify large white water birds as swans, not Snow Geese or Ross's Geese. After that it gets a little difficult. I even have to spend a little time, once in a while and check the field guide to make sure that my first impression is correct. I been known to get the ID wrong as well.

TRUMPETER SWAN

Let's begin with the Trumpeter Swan. Trumpeters were so rare a few decades ago that the joke was, "If it has a band on its neck it's a Trumpeter, if not, it's a Tundra." Fortunately, Trumpeter Swans have rebounded in the last 50 years and it is not unusual to see them today. I remember my first sighting. I hiked several miles into a remote lake in Yellowstone Park and was thrilled with finding four Trumpeter Swans, two adults and two signets. There have been a high number of Trumpeters wintering in the Upper Clark Fork Drainage in recent years. We documented 27 Trumpeters and 2 Tundra in open water on December 9, 2020.

The call of the Trumpeter is very diagnostic and as their name suggests they sound like a trumpet being blown. Tundra Swans produce more of a whistling sound, thus the older name Whistling Swan.

TUNDRA SWAN

Physical traits are a little more difficult. I first look at the head. If the top of the head and bill are in a continuous slope it is a Trumpeter. If you get a frontal view the base of the bill is pointed at the center. Additionally, the side of the bill from the eye to the lower mandible is a straight line. Overall, Trumpeters are larger with an 80 inch wingspan, compared to a 66 inch

TRUMPETER SWAN IN FLIGHT

wingspan in the Tundra. Trumpeters weigh 23 pounds verses 14.4 in the Tundra. Size is often difficult to ascertain, especially through binoculars or a spotting scope. Size is a good way to separate the two species in a mixed species flock. In side profile the Trumpeter has an evenly round back when the wings are folded and the Tundra has a more peaked back.

The bill of the Tundra ends abruptly at the base and the head is rounded so that the bill and head do not form a continuous smooth line. The base of the bill has a rounder border rather than the pointed center of the Trumpeter. Often Tundra Swans show a lot of yellow on the bill. Trumpeters tend only to have limited yellow on the lower mandible and never on the upper portion of the bill near the base.

This may all sound like a lot to keep track of when birding. If you look at both species over time you will get an innate sense for these two species and identification will come easily and quickly. I hope this has helped. Now go to the field and separate these two species. You'll feel good about your birding skills and build your confidence by doing this. ♦

WOOD DUCK

In my opinion, the Wood Duck is the most beautiful of all of the waterfowl. In fact, the unique patterns and colors of this species rival nearly all of North America's birds. I can't help admire this species every time I see it. Nature out did itself with this one.

Wood Ducks are not abundant in the Upper Clark Fork Valley, like Mallards or American Wigeon, but they are common, breeding in secluded ponds and marshes. A few winter in the warmer areas of Montana, but most winter in the Southeast US and along the Pacific Coast.

Breeding adult males are stunning with an almost improbable array of colors, distinguishing this

WOOD DUCKS

duck from all others. In silhouette this species is small, shows a stubby bill, crested head, and long squared off tail. They weigh 1.3 pounds compared to the more common 2.4 pound Mallard. The array of colors begins with the bill. It is a combination of reddish orange at the base and lower mandible, white above and black tipped. The head is round with a drooping green crest outlined in white. There is a bright white "chin-strap" below the red eye with dark iris extending to the neck. The remainder of the head is dark. The chest is slate brown with white spots. The flank is yellow to light tan separated from the breast by a perpendicular white bar. The back and raised long tail are dark with a streak of white extending onto the tail.

Females and immatures are muted gray brown with blue and green highlights on the wing. The most distinguishing field mark is a large white teardrop surrounding the eye.

Wood Ducks are usually found in small groups, and do not mix with other species. They prefer areas that are sheltered with overhanging branches reaching the water, creating dark and secretive areas. They are most at home in swamps rather than open water in large ponds and lakes. They have the unique habit of perching in trees, often high above the water. They are surprisingly nimble as they walk along tree branches. They prefer natural tree cavities or nest boxes that are close to the water for incubating eggs.

If you have not observed a Wood Duck take the time to search secluded ponds with vegetation that reaches out over the water. ♦

BAIKAL TEAL

BAIKAL TEAL   *Photo by feathercollector*

    In December of 2012 I wrote about the Harris's Hawk that was identified in the Flathead Valley. The species had never been seen in Montana before but had been reported in Idaho and Wyoming. Some of these rare sightings are accepted by State Rare Bird Committees and others are not. The problem with the Harris's Hawk is it is a sedimentary species of the Southwest and is unlikely to have flown this far north. The more likely scenario is that it was an escapee from a falconer living in Montana or Idaho. No one stepped forward to claim the bird and it shows no physical marks (leg bands or jeers) to indicate that it was a captive bird. The bird has survived the winter and is currently in the Lolo/Hamilton valley.

    The debate rages if it came here on its own. It can only be counted as a Montana species if it came here on its own and survives without artificial feeding. It has met one requirement but the source of origin is still unknown.

    On April 27, 2013, Radd Icenoggle, of Lolo, was birding the McClay Flats area southwest of Missoula in search of a Western Screech Owl that had been reported. He was walking a ditch bank and noticed two Wood Ducks and an additional male bird with strange plumage. He immediately identified it as a Baikal Teal and got off several shots with his camera before it lifted off and disappeared.

    The Baikal Teal is not even found in most North American field guides that I use. When included the range is described as a very rare Asian species, primarily in the fall in the Western Aleutian Islands. Radd was able to identify the bird because of its unique plumage as you can see in the photograph at the left.

There is no other North American duck with similar plumage. The breeding male has a striking green nape with yellow and black neck and throat. The crown is dark and the breast is light brown with dark spots. The gray sides are set off front and rear with white bars. The wings show considerable white. This species breeds in the forests of Siberia and migrates to South Korea, Japan and Eastern China to winter. The global population was threatened by hunting in the 1980s with less than 100,000 individuals. Today the population is about 1.07 million.

I heard about the teal in the late evening on April 27th and was in Missoula by 8:00 AM the next morning. While driving to Missoula my wife called to report that another person had spotted the bird around 7:00 am. I found the bird at 8:15, and was especially impressed at the remoteness of the spot where it was found. I have birded McClay Flat many times, but never along the vegetated ditch bank in the southeast corner of the area. Had Radd not been looking for a reported Western Screech Owl, the bird may have gone unseen.

How did this Eastern Asia species end up in Missoula? The most likely explanation is that consistent storms with strong easterly winds blew it west. How many of these rarities go unnoticed? No one really knows. I am sure it happens. Of Montana's 442 official birds, 108 have been seen less than 20 times, and 24 have been only seen once. I have been fortunate to see 7 of those 24. There are others rarities out there; it just takes a knowledgeable birder in the field at the right time and place.

The teal remained in the area from April 27th to May 14th. Hundreds attempted to see the bird, half of them were successful. It took my grandson six trips to see it, fortunately he lived in Missoula.

Others traveled long distances from other states and did not see it. It was in a ditch and not always visible and on private property not accessible to the public. It was best observed with a scope from a public road across the field and above the ditch.

When a rarity is reported most ask a few questions before chasing it. What is the chance that it will stay put long enough to see it? Should I wait a day and make sure it is staying and risk missing a one day phenomena? Do I have the time and the money to chase it? Is it really a countable rarity or an exotic escapee?

My experience has taught me to go as soon as you hear about the bird and answer the questions later. I missed one rarity by a day because I was sick and left a day late. Looking back, I could have been sick in the car as well as in bed, and I would have one more bird on my Montana list. Oh well, life will go on with only 378 Montana species instead of 379. Isn't birding great! ♦

BLUE-WINGED TEAL

Southwest Montana is a great place to observe waterfowl. The best places to look are Racetrack Pond, Warm Springs Wildlife Management Area, Clark Canyon Reservoir, Georgetown and Silver Lakes.

BLUE-WINGED TEAL

I have observed four species of geese, two species of swans, and 25 species of ducks in these water features. In addition, I have observed 34 species of shorebirds and waders.

In this article I want to talk about three of the less common waterfowl seen in Southwest Montana.

The first is the Blue-winged Teal. Statewide this bird is rather common with 2,400 observations recorded with the Montana Natural Heritage Program (MNHP) as of August, 2021. It is the last waterfowl species to occur in the valley with my first sighting on May 14th. In contrast, the first sighting for the Northern Pintail was March 5th. Blue-winged teal are easily recognized by the "half-moon" crescent behind the bill in the male in breeding plumage. Females and non-breeding males look alike with a much less prominent crescent in the male and only white at the base of the bill joining the white throat in the female. I typically see between 100 and 200 individuals per summer, which is not a lot, compared to other waterfowl species but they do breed in the Upper Clark Fork Drainage. ♦

EURASIAN WIGEON

The second waterfowl is the Eurasian Wigeon. This species is nearly identical to the more common American Wigeon that I typically find by the thousands locally in spring migration. The male American has a pinkish brown body, white or buffy forehead, and green swath through the eye. The European Wigeon has a pale gray body, dark rufous head and buffy forehead. The MNHP has had only 195 sightings for this species in Montana. I typically get one or two sightings a year in the Upper Clark Fork Drainage. They are an early spring migrant and you do not typically see them locally in the fall. The earliest I have seen one is February 10th. As the name implies they are a European species. Evidently individuals mingle with American Wigeons in spring migration and are accidental in North America. ♦

EURASIAN WIGEON

HARLEQUIN DUCK

Harlequin Ducks have been extremely difficult for me to photograph and get a decent photograph. The picture with this article is the best I ever got and it's far from good. Typically, they are far out in the river and not easy to get close to very often. Secondly, they tend to be in rapids and perhaps the humidity and spray in the air makes it difficult for my camera to lock the focus on the bird.

Harlequins are perhaps the most unique species of duck we have in Montana. There are 39 duck species in North America. Yet only one duck in the genus *Histrionicus*. That in itself is a clue that they are different. Their plumage is unlike any other duck. They are small, 1.3 pounds, (Mallard 2.4 pounds). Their necks appear swollen, the head is round and appears to lean forward. The bill is small and the tail is long. Overall, they are gray with an intricate pattern of white lines and circles. The flank is chestnut as

HARLEQUIN DUCKS ON A ROCK MIDSTREAM

well as a chestnut streak below a white line on the crown of the head. The overall look is rather like a clown's costume. Females are drab brown with a round white spot on the neck and a white crescent mark below the eye. A pair are sitting on a rock in the photo on the previous page.

Their vocalization is unique as well with a *"squeak"* reminiscent of a mouse. Some have nicknamed them sea-mouse.

Distribution is not widespread in Montana. They are found in the western third of the state. They breed and forage in mountainous streams that are clear, fast flowing water and rapids. The easiest places to see them is in Glacier Park along McDonald Creek and along the Yellowstone River in Yellowstone Park. During migration you might encounter them along many streams in Western Montana. I observed them once in the Clark Fork River at Bearmouth near Missoula. However, nearly all of the direct breeding records are from the Northwest corner of Montana.

HARLEQUIN DUCK

Adults and first year juveniles winter along the Pacific coastal waters in rafts of 10 to 50 often associating with other species such as scoters. Males arrive at the breeding grounds in Montana in late April and early May followed by females a few weeks later. Young appear by late June to early July. Males migrate back to coastal waters by early June and females and juvenile linger into late August and early September.

If you are fortunate to come upon Harlequins on rapid water their behavior is fascinating. I have watched them floating in quiet pools of water below rapids and then abruptly fly to the head of the rapids and careen down through the rapids back to the quiet pools of water. It would appear they are playing since they repeat the process over and over. Perhaps I was watching juveniles learning to navigate rapids which is their preferred habitat.

They also appear less cautious than other waterfowl and will allow you to observe them as long as you don't get too close. They are not like other ducks that explode off the water in quick flight the moment they see you.

Harlequins feed by diving in rough water feeding off crustaceans and aquatic insects. When not feeding you will often see them sitting on the rocks that form the rapids.

You might think, because of their remote mountain stream habitat, the number of observations is low. It is not. This duck has been recorded 3,602 times in Montana. Compare that with the White-winged Scoter with only 105 observations. The difference is that this species occurs in both Yellowstone and Glacier Park in a fairly small area and can be easily observed and reported.

Harlequin Ducks are a SOS (Species of Concern) in Montana. The population

Harlequin Duck   *Histrionicus histrionicus*

is fairly stable, but because their habitat is so limited, environmental degradation of those areas could endanger breeding success. Fortunately most populations in Montana are in Glacier and Yellowstone Parks with protected environments. A lot is not yet known about this species and are monitored and studied in Glacier Park extensively.

Fall is not the time to see this species since they migrate to Pacific Coastal waters and stay there until spring. If you have not seen the species plan a trip to Glacier next spring. Look on eBird or contact the park for the best times and locations. I find them yearly along McDonald Creek below Avalanche Creek or in Avalanche Creek itself. If you want to see the colorful male go in May, otherwise juveniles can be seen most of the summer. ♦

Surf Scoter   *Melanitta perspicillata*

SURF SCOTER

To see all the waterfowl migrating through Montana you need to wait until October to get the last three all in the same genus *Melanitta*; the scoters.

All three breed in Canada, Alaska and Arctic regions on freshwater ponds and lakes. They migrate south in October and November and winter along both coasts in ocean waters. We only see them as fall migrants in our area.

The casual birder may never see any of these rare fall migrant scoters. Most sightings are found west of the divide and a good portion of these sightings come from the Upper Clark Fork Drainage at Warm Springs WMA, Silver Lake, Georgetown Lake, and East Fork Reservoir. The general explanation for this is scoters like deep water where they dive for mollusks and snails.

Scoters typically stage for 7 to 10 days for rest and rebuilding of fat reserves before continuing to the coast. They are typically in small groups of five

FEMALE SURF SCOTER

or less but 2020 was an exception. I saw groups of 11 and on 10/21/20 we recorded 33 Surf Scoters, an all time high record.

The Stejneger's has been seen once, Black has been recorded 23 times, White-winged 105 times and Surf 108 times across Montana. The fall of 2018 was outstanding for viewing scoters in the Upper Clark Fork Drainage. In the fall of 2019 I observed the Black three times (all the same bird), October 8, 11 and 30th.

My other two sightings were in October of 2011 and October of 2012. I observed the White-winged Scoter four times in 2018; October 15, 20, 30th and November 6th. In the past I had seen it 18 times in Montana. The Surf Scoter, being the most common in Montana, gave me 31 sightings in the past. In 2019 I saw Surf Scoters eighteen additional times. Of my 49 sightings 18 percent were in 2019! My first sighting was on October 8, then 11, 20, and 30th. Each of these sightings I believe to be different individuals due to location and date.

MALE SURF SCOTER

Then the strangest thing happened. On November 3, 2018 I found a female Surf Scoter at AR Pond 2 at the Warm Springs WMA. Water in this pond is no more than 12 feet deep. So much for Surf Scoters needing deep water bodies. On the 6th of November I saw the same individual in the same area associated with American Coots. I continued to see this individual 4 more times, in the same area, associated with American Coots in a small area of open water surrounded by ice. Posting these sightings to eBird, I got a notice that the sighting of a Surf Scoter was infrequent past November 15th and RARE after the first of December. This individual bird stayed in the same location for 46 days!

There are three previous December records for the Surf Scoter in Montana,. December 10, at Lee Metcalf NWR, December 17, at the Great Falls CBC, and December 23, at the Bighorn River CBC. Only two records are in the spring in May; all of the rest of the records are September through December with the most in October.

Unfortunately the last time I saw the Surf Scoter was December 18. This was just five days short of the latest state record but was the second latest sighting for December.

Scoters are easily distinguished from other ducks as their bills are much heavier constructed and shaped differently than other ducks. Males and females differ substantially in all three species. Males of all three species are also easily told apart. The Surf, pictured with this article has a multicolored bill and bright white head patches. The White-winged is black, with a yellow bill and a white "comma" patch below the eye. The Stejneger's is difficult to tell from the white-winged and was split from the white-winged in 2019. Distinguishing field marks are white or very pale gray eyes and a distinctive white mark under the eye. The bill is uniquely shaped with red, yellow and orange markings and a large black basal knob. The Black is all black with a yellow knob on the bill. Males of these four species are beautiful birds and always bring excitement the first time you see them each fall.

Females look more alike, but with a little effort you can distinguish them. Surf females are brownish-black with a vertical white patch at the base of the bill and a whitish patch near the back of the neck. The female White-winged shows extensive white between the eye and bill and the white secondary wing feathers are visible. Female Stejneger's are medium brown, with large white wing patches, vari-

Surf Scoter   *Melanitta perspicillata*

able amounts of white and gray on the cheeks and between the eyes. Their bills are dark olive-brown and lack the basal knob; eyes are dark brown to black. Black females show a dark cap and clean pale white cheek reminding you of a female Ruddy Duck.

If you are interested in seeing scoters, Silver Lake west of Anaconda is the most reliable place to find them. Begin making trips to Silver Lake about the second week of October and continue doing so until the lake freezes over.

Park on the dam with your car facing south and glass the water along the dam. They are often far out so a scope is advisable. If you do this once a week you will be sure and see Surf and most likely White-winged. If you are really lucky you may even see a Black Scoter.

Be sure to have your field guide with you so you can distinguish females and juveniles. They are much more common than males in our area in the fall. ♦

White-Winged Scoter   *Melanitta deglandi*

WHITE-WINGED SCOTER

Waterfowl are some of the more familiar birds that people are aware of in nature. There is hardly a person who doesn't know what a Mallard looks like and the it's familiar *"Quack, Quack"*. Others species that are familiar to most are the Canada Goose, Snow Goose and the Northern Pintail.

In all, 34 species of waterfowl are found in Southwest Montana and 39 species have been recorded statewide. Those not seen in Southwest Montana include, Brant, Mute Swan, American Black Duck, Gargeny and Tufted Duck. All of these birds have only been seen a few times.

There are four species of waterfowl in Montana that most folks are not familiar with and they are the Scoters, Surf, White-winged, Stejneger's and Black.

MALE WHITE-WINGED SCOTER

One of the reasons that folks are unfamiliar with Scoters is that they are typically only late fall migrants in Montana. I don't even start looking for them until October. The earliest date I have for a Surf is September 28, for White-winged – September 24, and Black – October 8. Another limiting factor to their familiarity is that in our area I have only seen Surf and White-Winged in four locations: Warm Springs WMA, Silver Lake, Georgetown Lake and East Fork Reservoir. I have only seen Black in three locations; Warm Springs WMA, Silver Lake and East Fork Reservoir. You simply don't see them in very many places.

The reason is that Scoters prefer deep water, feeding on mollusks, snails and other shellfish. Therefore most of my observations have been at Silver Lake which is quite deep.

White-Winged Scoter   *Melanitta deglandi*

Surf is seen most often followed by White-Winged and then Black in the Upper Clark Fork Valley and the state. The Montana Natural Heritage website shows 108 sight records for Surf, 105 for White-winged, 1 for Stejneger's, and 23 for Black Scoter.

I have never been particularly successful is photographing these species as they tend to be far from shore, in rough wavy water and dive frequently; often being underwater more than on the surface. They also have a tendency to pop up far from where they dove.

Each fall I am seeing more Scoters in the Upper Clark Fork Basin. I now see an average of 15 Surf and seven White-Winged Scoters annually. I don't see a Black Scoter annually, but have seen eight in the last decade.

In 2016 I found White-Winged Scoters at Warm Springs ARCO Pond 2 in calm water no more than 30 feet from shore. I got the best pictures that I have ever taken. In fact, the Montana Natural Heritage program used my pictures for the web based Montana Animal Field Guide.

So how do you tell these species apart? The Surf Scoter male's breeding plumage is dark with white on the back of the neck and forehead and a large thick multicolored bill showing white, yellow and a black spot. Females are browner with a light whitish patch on the side of the neck and a vertical white patch behind the bill.

White-Winged males, are also dark often showing white wing bars and a "comma" below the eye. The bill is longer and thinner than the Surf and yellow near the tip. Females are browner with an oval white patch behind the bill. ♦

Stejneger's Scoter   *Melanitta stejnegeri*

STEJNEGER'S SCOTER

Stejneger's Scoter is difficult to tell apart from the White-Winged Scoter. There are a number characteristics the Stejneger's Scoter that separates it from White-Winged. Males of the White-Winged Scoter have browner flanks, dark yellow coloration on most of the bill and a less tall bill knob. Stejneger's Scoter has a very tall knob at the base of its mostly orange-yellow bill. Females of both species are identical in the field.

You should not expect to see Stejneger's Scoter. Stejneger's breed in Eastern Asia and winters off the coast of China, the Korean Peninsula and Japan. It is accidental in North America and the only record for this species in Montana was seen in 2015. ♦

STEJNEGER'S SCOTER   *Photo by Bob Martinka*

BLACK SCOTER

The Black Scoter male is all black with a yellow knob at the base of the bill in the breeding male and the female is browner with a large whitish cheek patch. The bill appears long and thin in the female and not as long in the male because of the yellow knob.

As mentioned earlier, the White-Winged pictures are the best I have ever taken. So far I have not gotten a picture of a Black Scoter; but there is always next year.

BLACK SCOTER *Photo by BJ Worth*

Next fall if you are interested in seeing these species make a few trips to Silver Lake and look along the west shore near the dam in October and November before the lake freezes and you will most likely see one or both of these species. It is the most reliable place in Montana for Scoters

Foremost it will be a state bird if not a life-bird for many of you. ♦

LONG-TAILED DUCK

The last species is the Long-tailed Duck, formerly called Old Squaw. Males in breeding plumage are obvious with long tail and black and white contrasting colors. The picture that I took is of the winter plumage. Breeding plumage is more black on the chest and head, with brown back, rather than the white back of the winter plumage. This species has been recorded in Montana 147 times. Locally I have seen them at the Warm Springs WMA, Racetrack Pond and Silver Lake for a total of 14 times since 2007. Most of these sightings were in the fall. This species is so rare locally that I had not seen one between 2016 and 2020 and none since.

LONG-TAIL DUCK

You may never see a Long-tailed Duck, or Eurasian Wigeon, but certainly if you look in shallow ponds with emerging vegetation in late May and June you will find the Blue-Winged Teal. ♦

COMMON GOLDENEYE

As Winter approaches the number of waterfowl species in the Upper Clark Fork Drainage drops rather quickly. During summer months you can expect to see as many as 34 species of waterfowl in the drainage. Five are rather rare, Greater White-fronted Goose, Harlequin Duck, Eurasian Wigeon, White-winged Scoter, and Black Scoter; but that still leaves you 29 common species.

FEMALE COMMON GOLDENEYE

In 2018, I was fortunate to see 32 of the 34 species in the valley. The only two that I missed were the Greater White-fronted Goose and the Harlequin Duck.

During the winter months the number of waterfowl species you can find is no more than ten or twelve. I went out today (12/05/18) to see what I could find and I located twelve waterfowl species. All you need to do is find a little open water and sit a while and see what shows.

So what water is open in the winter? The most dependable site is the North Dutchman Pond northwest of Anaconda. The reason for this is the water comes up out of the ground in that area and is rather warm. This pond stays open except in the coldest of our winter weather. Another area that usually has a little open water is AR Pond 2, and AR Pond 1 at the Warm Springs Wildlife Management Area. The open areas are where water currents flow from one pond to another.

The final area for watching waterfowl is along the Clark Fork River, or any free flowing stream, such as Flint Creek. I'm always surprised how many waterfowl use the back water areas of open streams.

So what were the species I saw on that winter day in 2018? Three of the species were in good numbers, 121

MALE COMMON GOLDENEYE

Canada Geese, 61 Mallards and 224 Common Goldeneye. All of the others were less than 10 individuals and included Snow Goose, Trumpeter Swan, Northern Shoveler, Gadwall, Ring-necked Duck, Green-winged Teal, Lesser Scaup, Surf Scoter and American Coot.

The Surf Scoter is the latest sighting I have had for that species in our area,

Common Goldeneye   *Bucephala clangula*

and eBird listed the sighting as RARE for that time of year. That's the beauty of going out, you never know what you might see, or what record you might break for either early arrival, late departure or just being in an area.

The most plentiful of the species today was the Common Goldeneye. They are not difficult to identify, but there is another species that looks a lot like them, the Barrow's Goldeneye. ♦

Barrow's Goldeneye   *Bucephala islandica*

BARROW''S GOLDENEYE

MALE AND FEMALE BARROW'S GOLDENEYE

Barrow's do stay late into the fall in the Upper Clark Fork drainage, but typically don't overwinter.

The Common Goldeneye males appear as a black and white duck from a distance. The head is actually greenish-black with a yellow eye. The Barrow's head look similar to the Common except for some subtle differences beyond this article. Their head color can appear bluish, greenish or black depending on the angle of the sun reflecting off their head feathers. The best way to tell them apart is the white patch on the side of the head. In the male Common Goldeneye, the patch is oval shaped and in the Barrow's the white patch is crescent shaped. You can clearly see the difference in the photos on these pages.

Females look a great deal alike as well. The difference is that Common Goldeneye has a black bill fading to yellow near the tip. The Barrow's has an all yellow bill. Again, you can see that in the pictures.

On several occasions I have seen adult males that were clearly hybrids from the interbreeding of the two species. In this case the white patch is an oblong circle rather than a crescent or circle. The head color is maroon, rather than the greenish black of the two distinct species.

I encourage you to get out in winter to see how many waterfowl species you can find. It might surprise you how abundant they are in most drainages of Western Montana. ♦

Family Phasianidae

Spruce Grouse 42
Dusky Grouse 43
Gray Partridge.. 44

Spruce Grouse   *Canachites canadensis*

SPRUCE GROUSE

I grew up hunting blue grouse and fool's hens, but neither of those names are official names today. The fool's hen is actually a Spruce Grouse and what was the blue grouse was split a few years ago into Dusky and Sooty Grouse. Dusky is the interior species and Sooty is the coastal species of Washington and Oregon. I am sure for many hunters they will remain "Blue Grouse" for decades to come.

There are 12 game birds in Montana and 21 in North America. In the 1920-1960 period it is was popular to introduce exotic game birds to North America. They included Chukar, Gray Partridge, California Quail, Himalayan Snowcock and Ring-necked Pheasant. Others were introduced but never established populations. Three exotics that exist in Montana today are the Chukar in small numbers, Gray Partridge and Ring-necked Pheasant.

This article is about the native Spruce Grouse of most of Canada, Northern Idaho, and

SPRUCE GROUSE

Western Montana. The United State's population of this species was considered a separate species from the Canadian population and called the Franklin's Grouse until the middle of the 20th century. There are now two recognized sub-species the Franklin's and Taiga. Even today you hear all three names for this species; Fool's Hen, Franklin's Grouse and the official name; Spruce Grouse.

I have encountered this species many times in the mountains of the Upper Clark Fork Valley on wetter north facing slopes that typically have an under story of Beargrass and Dwarf Huckleberry. Spruce Grouse are a boreal species that can be found in wetter areas that are much like the coniferous forest of Canada. ♦

Dusky Grouse   *Dendragapus obscurus*

DUSKY GROUSE

The number of Dusky Grouse sightings reported to the Montana Natural Heritage data base is 1,088, nearly twice that of the 591 records for the Spruce Grouse. Densities for both species may be close to the same, but Spruce Grouse habitat is general less accessible and more remote than that of the Dusky.

Telling a Spruce Grouse from a Dusky is not difficult. The Spruce is less than half the weight of the Dusky at one pound compared to 2.3 pounds for the Dusky. Male Spruce appear overall to be rather dark with a black neck with white spots on a dark breast. The back is dark without white spots. Tail is short with white tips on the upper tail feathers. The white tipped feathers show conspicuously when the tail is fanned during mating displays. If you encounter the Taiga sub-species or race, tail feathers are black with rufous-brown tips. The head has a red eye comb above a yellow-brown eye. Females are browner than males and the breast has horizontal black bars rather than white spots.

DUSKY GROUSE - *Taiga sub-species*

The majority of the Spruce Grouse diet is made up of conifer needles which some say, "taints the flavor and are less preferred than the Dusky Grouse". In the fall of the year I have observed both species eating dwarf huckleberry and chasing and consuming insects; especially grasshoppers.

It is hard to go out and find any of our grouse species other than looking for them in proper habitat. Driving roads or walking trails in the early morning or late evening increases your chances of seeing these beautiful game birds.

Take a walk in proper habitat and see if you can find one. ♦

GRAY PARTRIDGE

Gallinaceous or "Chicken-like" birds include Turkeys, Pheasants, Grouse, Partridge and Old World Quail. There are 22 gallinaceous species in North America, of which several have been introduced from Europe and Asia. Twelve are found on Montana's official species list. The California Quail common in the Hamilton Valley was not recognized on the Montana list until just recently. In order to qualify a species must reproduce successfully without artificial means of support. Four species; the California Quail, Gray Partridge, Ring-necked Pheasant and Chukar have been successfully introduced into Montana.

GRAY PARTRIDGE

The White-tailed Ptarmigan is found in Glacier Park with a single report of a Willow Ptarmigan in the same area. Sharp-tailed Grouse are an Eastern Montana species with small numbers in the Helena Valley. There is only one recognized Chukar population in the state near Bridger but I have seen Chukers South of Dillon. There is debate as to the origin of the Dillon Chukers. Greater Sage Grouse are sage dependent and the closest ones I have seen to the Upper Clark Fork Valley are near Bannack. Most Greater Sage Grouse are east of the Continental Divide. Greater Prairie-Chickens are locally extinct as they were found in Sheridan County 150 years ago. Ring-necked Pheasants are uncommon in the Upper Clark Fork due to the lack of adequate winter cover. In the mountains surrounding our valley we have Dusky (Blue), Spruce and Ruffed Grouse. Attempts to re-establish Wild Turkeys in the Upper Clark Fork Drainage have had limited success but statewide they have been successful.

Gray Partridge are common in the Upper Clark Fork year around and I have seen an increasing number the last few

GRAY PARTRIDGE

winters. Gray Partridge, often called Hungarian Partridge, or "Huns", were introduced from Europe in the early 1900s into Montana. In the Upper Clark Fork Valley bottom lands they are the only reliable "upland game bird" one will see and the only winter species. Gray Partridge are found in small coveys in agricultural fields and pastures. At our home which is found on the edge of agricultural grasslands we see them often.

They are non-migratory and winter well here but not in large numbers. They have a preference for the edges of plowed fields with tall grass cover. Most years we only see one to two coveys with less than 15 birds. They defend themselves by the entire flock exploding into "cackling" short distance flights.

Field marks are a plump-body, grayish-brown overall look, an orange face, gray finely barred neck with chestnut barred gray flanks. Males have a dark belly patch.

To observe them in the Upper Clark Fork Valley and Western Montana drive agricultural roads near grain fields. Once you see them, stop and observe quickly, because they take flight fast. ♦

A BIRDING ADVENTURE WITH MT KILIMANJARO IN THE BACKGROUND

Family Podicipedidae

Horned Grebe..46
Red-Necked Grebe 47
Eared Grebe 49

Horned Grebe　　　　　　　　　　　　　　　　　　*Podiceps auritus*

HORNED GREBE

Sexes in the Horned Grebes look alike. They can be distinguished from Eared by a rufous thick neck and solid rather than wispy yellow ear patch on a flat-topped head. The back is dome shaped, dark and the feathers are white edged giving a scaly appearance. The dark bill is short, straight and yellow tipped. The head often appears swollen. Non-breeding plumage is mostly gray and white with dark above the eye and an all white neck. I typically see Horned Grebes in fall migration, in non-breeding plumage. I have seen them in breeding plumage, but they only stage for a very short period and move on to the breeding grounds in Northern Canada and Alaska. There are a few records of breeders in Southern Canada and extreme Northern Montana. They winter in protected coastal inlets and bays. They are not especially social, occurring as individuals to a few if there is abundant food. They sit low in the water and dive constantly.

HORNED GREBE

In the fall make it a goal to see both of these species in our area. ♦

RED-NECKED GREBE

Grebes are rather common and all six species are seen in the Upper Clark Fork Valley and Western Montana. The Clark's Grebe is rare and only seen by a few birders every year west of the Continental Divide. The Horned Grebe is transient in spring and fall and breeds in Canada and Alaska, with a few breeding in Northeast Montana. The other four all breed in our area. The Western and Pied-billed Grebes breed in small numbers and two to four hundred Eared Grebes nest at the Warm Springs WMA.

The Red-necked Grebe, this article's featured bird, is of local concern as numbers are decreasing in Montana. Local breeding populations exist at Georgetown Lake and Warm Springs WMA. There are approximately 30 breeding pair at Warm Springs and at least that many at Georgetown Lake.

RED-NECKED GREBE

Red-necked Grebes can easily be distinguished from other grebes in breeding plumage. They are a rather large grebe with a thick rufous neck, whitish cheek, black cap, and large bill with yellow on the lower mandible. Sexes are alike. Winter plumage is gray with white neck crescent. Chicks as shown in this picture have the black and white striped head that many grebe species juveniles show. Older juveniles look similar to winter plumage adults.

Red-necks are usually silent except during the breeding season. Their breeding call is frequent, loud, and carries across the water for long distances. It is described as a loud repeated *"Krik Kirk"* followed by a braying reminiscent of a gull call. Once you learn their call it is unforgettable and an enjoyable spring wetland sound.

Precopulation courtship behavior is an extensive, "water ballet" which creates strong pair bonding. Nests are a collection of floating vegetation anchored to emerging vegetation and built by both parents. I have seen them on the nest as early as mid-May and as late as mid-July. Red-necked Grebes are colonial breeders and often breed near gull colonies. It is thought that gulls provide sentry protection. Striped headed chicks are able to swim and dive from birth, but are often seen riding on their parents backs, especially when frightened. Predators include

RED-NECKED GREBE ON NEST

large fish, herons, mink and raccoons.

The greatest threat to Red-neck Grebes is human disturbance during early chick development. Nests and chicks can be abandoned with too much disturbance. That is perhaps the reason that populations seem to be decreasing at Georgetown Lake and increasing at Warm Springs WMA. Summer boating is increasing at Georgetown Lake exponentially.

As you bird aquatic environments this summer see how many of Montana's grebe species you can identify. With a little effort you can find five of Montana's six species rather easily. ♦

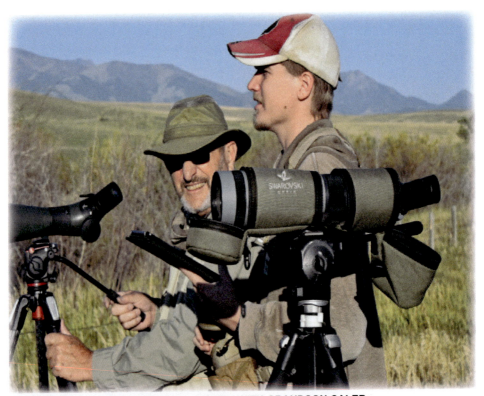

AUTHOR TAKING ENNIS LAKE BIRD SURVEY WITH GRANDSON CALEB.

EARED GREBE

There are six species of grebes in Montana. All six can be found in the Upper Clark Fork Drainage. Two species that are very similar in appearance are the Western and Clark's Grebes. I have seen the Clark's Grebe less than a dozen times in our area since 2005. The Western Grebe is common. The Pied-billed Grebe is uncommon, illusive and not often seen; but often heard. The Red-necked Grebe is abundant locally with 5,400 observations statewide. The two species I want to inform you about here are the Horned and Eared Grebes. The Eared is abundant and the Horned is a spring and fall migrant. Superficially they are similar and novices often misidentify them. They share small size, red eyes and short pointed bills.

EARED GREBE

Let's look at the Eared Grebe first. The sexes look alike. In breeding plumage the long skinny neck is black and the head is slightly peaked with wispy yellow ear tufts. The black of the neck extends onto the back. The sides are rusty brown. There is a slight upturn to the dark bill. The rear appears cropped and they ride high in the water. In non-breeding adults the dark head cap extends over the eye and the wispy yellow plumes disappear. A white crescent lies behind the eye and the chest and flanks are whitish. The neck is dusky rather than black and the bill is lighter in color.

Eared Grebes are social birds and a successful colonial breeder across most of Montana in shallow freshwater lakes, ponds and marshes. Typically there are upward to 400 breeding pair at Warm Springs WMA. Fall migration finds most of them in coastal waters along the Pacific Coast from Washington to the Gulf of Mexico. ♦

Family Columbidae

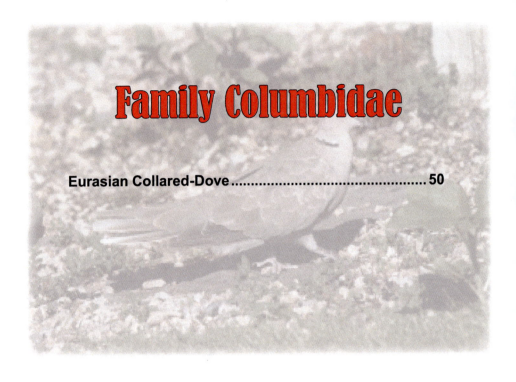

Eurasian Collared-Dove 50

Eurasian Collared-Dove   *Streptopelia decaocto*

EURASIAN COLLARED-DOVE

I frequently get calls about birds that folks see in their backyards. One of the birds I often get calls on is the "Ringed Turtle-Dove." There are six species of pigeons and doves identified in Montana. The Ringed Turtle-Dove is not one of them! However its image is found in most field guides, and looks a lot like the Eurasian Collared-Dove folks see, thus the confusion. The Eurasian Collared-Dove is so new to North America it was not found in field guides published prior to 2003. Ringed Turtle-Doves are escapees from pet stores in Southern Tier States and there have been no self-sustaining populations reported.

EURASIAN COLLARED-DOVE

Eurasian Collared-Doves are native to Asia and since 1930 they have expanded their range into Europe. I saw my first specimen in England in January 2001. The species was introduced in the mid-1970s in Florida. They rapidly spread across America. My first Montana Eurasian Collared-Dove was in May of 2003 in Malta. In May of 2006 I recorded two in Deer Lodge. They quickly increased locally and 86 were counted on the 2008 Christmas Bird Count in the Deer Lodge Valley. Since then we have them in the hundreds on most counts. The rate of their expansion has been most amazing with sightings now in Alaska during summer months! Numbers do seem to diminish in winters that have extended periods of cold (Below 0 degrees Fahrenheit), but they still remain in Montana.

There is no evidence they compete with other species of doves such as the more familiar Mourning Dove and Rock Pigeon. They seem to be filling an unoccupied niche between these two species. If you want to observe them in your yard scatter cracked corn or grain on the ground under your black sunflower feeders. They are primarily ground feeders

In comparison with the native Mourning Dove the Eurasian Collared-Dove is a larger bodied, much paler gray in color, lacks black spots on their wings, and has a distinctive black band "collar" on the back of the neck in adults. Juveniles lack the black band. Their call is a *"Cooo cup coo"*, which is much different than the Mourning Dove's mournful call.

Just to make things interesting, in August of 2009 a Band-tailed Pigeon showed up in Elliston and stayed for nearly three weeks. That species has only been seen 28 times in Montana through 2021 and made for quite a stir among those who chase birds.

Remember birds are Montana's most watchable wildlife and a great way to connect kids to the outdoors and environmental issues. ♦

BIRDING IN THE ECUADORAN RAIN FOREST

Family Caprimulgidae

Common Nighthawk..52

Common Nighthawk   *Chordeiles minor*

COMMON NIGHTHAWK

There are three species of nighthawks found in North America; the Common, Antillean and Lesser. The Antillean is only found in the southern tip of Florida as it is a common species in the Caribbean islands of Cuba and Jamaica. The Lesser is found in Southern Texas west to California and south to Mexico.

COMMON NIGHTHAWK

Common Nighthawks summer in all of the continental United States and winters in much of South America. In migration it flies through Central America and Mexico, not across the open water of the Gulf of Mexico into the continental United States and Canada. Only the Common Nighthawk is found in Montana and they are one of the latest spring migrants to come to West-

Common Nighthawk — *Chordeiles minor*

ern Montana. My first sighting of the Common Nighthawk is May 25, much later than all other migrants.

So why are they so late in coming? They are totally dependent on flying insects for food, especially flying ants, and must wait until there is an ample food source before mating and raising their young. They are found statewide with only a few direct evidences of breeding sites, and a lot of probable breeding sites. Common Nighthawks are listed as transient for our valley but I suspect that is because no one has found a nest yet.

COMMON NIGHTHAWK

Common Nighthawks are found fairly often over water and streams in small numbers until late August. They are not common, but given the right circumstances numbers can be impressive. A number of years ago there was a hatch of flying ants coming out of the ground at our home just north of Deer Lodge. Within minutes there were swarms of flying ants over our fields. In less than five minutes there were 50 to 75 nighthawks flying through the swarm feeding. It was obvious to me that one nighthawk had come upon the swarm and communicated with others to come to the feast.

Nighthawks are in the family *Caprimulidae* or Goatsuckers. They feed by frantic flight on falcon shaped long pointed angled back wings. They either see an insect from a perch and "hawk" it or fly directly into swarms of insects with their mouth wide open. Note the wing bars and white chin patch in the flight photo.

Most of their feeding in flight takes place at dawn or dusk but they will occasionally hunt over water midday. They perch in the daytime lengthwise along tree limbs or on the ground. They are very cryptically colored and when nesting or resting are hard to see as they blend in with the bark of a limb or exposed soil. While resting in the daytime they are in a near turbid state and can easily be approached without taking flight.

In flight they are easy to identify by white wing bars on the lower side of the wing and a white tail bar.

If you are interested in seeing this unique migrant from South America drive along valley streams near dusk in late June through August and you will most likely see them. ♦

Family Trochilidae

Anna's Hummingbird 54
Calliope Hummingbird 56
Rufous Hummingbird 57

Anna's Hummingbird   *Calypte anna*

ANNA'S HUMMINGBIRD

    Fall is a great time to be out birding as it is the time of year when you can get rarities. Many birds are in migration along the Pacific Coast and occasionally a storm will push a species inland, or they are juveniles that just get lost and we end up with a rare species in Western Montana. It has happened to me twice during October and is the subject of this article.

    Everyone knows what a hummingbird is although they may not know which one they see. There are twenty species of hummingbirds observed in North America according to the *National Geographic Birds of North America, 7th Edition*. In Montana birders have documented seven species. I have a birding trip planned to Ecuador where there are 131 documented species. If birders there can learn all of those, we should be able to learn the identification of Montana's seven species. In Southwest Montana we

ANNA'S HUMMINGBIRD

typically see three hummingbird species. The two most common are the Calliope and the Rufous. In addition, birders will occasionally see a Black-chinned Hummingbird.

We left our hummingbird feeder up longer in the fall of 2019 than usual. While we were eating lunch a large hummingbird showed up at the feeder. I instantly knew what it was, not because of its features, but I knew that in the late fall Anna's Hummingbird occasionally show up in Montana. From September 29 through October 23 a juvenile Anna's Hummingbird came daily to our feeder. They don't show often as there have only been 38 sighting for this bird in Montana. In addition, looking at the records for Montana there has never been a sighting in the Upper Clark Fork Valley. Of course, I have never left my feeder up in October either.

ANNA'S HUMMINGBIRD

The Anna's is a common hummingbird of other areas. It is a year around resident of the Pacific coast in British Columbia, Washington, Oregon and California. Some migrate from the coast and winter in northern Mexico. This is probably how one ends up in Western Montana. They begin their migration in British Columbia and drift inland.

Anna's are noticeably larger than the other three species found locally. They weigh .15 ounces, compared to .1 ounce for the more familiar bright green Calliope. When you first see the Anna's they appear stockier than most hummingbirds with a short bill compared to their body size. They appear more grayish green than bright green like the Calliope and show no rufous coloring. The male has a bright red crown and head when the sun angle is right and the female shows a red central patch on a white throat. The only hummer it could be confused with is the Black-chinned, but they are much grayer in appearance.

The one that I photographed with this article is a male. The sun angle was not right to show the red on the throat and head in this picture but we did observe that trait while watching it.

People ask me how often do you go birding? My answer is I am always birding, and that is how you find rarities such as this Anna's Hummingbird. Keep your eyes looking, you never know what you might just see. ♦

CALLIOPE HUMMINGBIRD

As I sit down to write this I have 12 hummingbirds at the feeder on the back of the house and another six or so on the front porch. It is a little hard to tell the actual number as they are coming and going so fast I can barely count individuals. A typical individual visits your feeder every 30 minutes, and then is catching insects the rest of the time. A good rule of thumb is to count the total number you see at any one time and multiple by 10 to get the actual number using your feeder in a day.

CALLIOPE HUMMINGBIRD

Folks, year after year, ask me what happened to the hummers this year, I don't have any? I find that I really don't see a lot of them until mid-July when the young of the year begin flying. Up until then the parents are busy feeding the young high protein insects and you just don't observe them. The backyard feeder frenzy typically lasts from mid-July until well into mid to late August. We are currently re-filling our feeders every other day.

Our formula is to boil water and pour four parts hot water to one part sugar. Do not add dye, it is unnecessary and probably unhealthy. There are a variety of feeders and we have tried several but like the large flat bottom ones as there seems to be more room for birds, thus reducing their aggressive behavior while feeding.

Two species are common in the Upper Clark Fork Valley, and one is occasional. The two common ones are the Calliope and the Rufous, with an occasional sighting of a Black-chinned. Other hummers observed in Montana are Ruby-throated, Anna's, Costa's and Broad-tailed.

RUFOUS HUMMINGBIRD

The Calliope and Rufous can be easily separated at your feeders. The Calliope is our smallest hummingbird weighing only .1 ounce (2.7 grams), with a length of 3.25 inches. The Rufous weighs .12 ounces (3.4 grams) and a length of 3.75 inches.

The Calliope has an overall greenish look in males, females and juveniles. The tail is short, and the wings reach just beyond the tail when the bird is perched. The tail is square at the end

Calliope Hummingbird   *Selasphorus calliope*

and shows black feathers with white tips. The bill is short and thin.

    Males Calliope are distinguished from females by streaked rosy feathers on the neck, called a gorget. The gorget appears to flash as its changes the angle of the sun reflecting off its rosy feathers in flight. Females show very subdued lines in the throat.

Rufous Hummingbird   *Selasphorus rufus*

RUFUS HUMMINGBIRD

    The Rufous Hummingbird has an orange-rufous appearance. Upon close inspection other colors became apparent. The wings are shorter and the tail extends beyond the wings, which is the opposite of the Calliope. The wings show green and brown coloration. Some (5 percent) also show a green back.

RUFOUS HUMMINGBIRD

    Males Calliope are distinguished from females by a solid orange-red throat, compared to an orange-red central spot in the female. In flight when the tail is spread there is rufous at the base of the feathers, then black, ending in white tips in the outer tail feathers.

    Hummers can become extremely tame. The other day they were landing on the feeder as I hung it on the hook under the eve. They didn't even wait for me to leave!

    Photographing hummers is challenging and fun. You need a well lit area to hang your feeder, then use a high shutter speed of 1/2000 of a second or more. You will also need an "extreme" flash card that can keep up with the camera's ability to shoot frames. With my camera (Nikon D750) I can shoot seven frames a second. As they come in to feed, start shooting as many frames as you can. The auto focus will not lock on with many of your photos, but just keep shooting. One out 30 or so will be in focus. Be thankful you are not shooting film, you couldn't afford it.

    Have fun and see what kind of photos you can produce. A good photo is very rewarding. ♦

Family Rallidae

Sora..58
American Coot...60

Sora   *Porzana carolina*

SORA

The rail family has nine members in North America with five species having been seen in Montana. There are three that are common and all three breed in Western Montana. The most common of the three is the American Coot which is the only local rail that is not secretive. Many inexperienced birders think coots are

a member of the duck family. American Coots are the most abundant species of rail in most waterways. In spring counts I often tally six to eight thousand individual coots with only one or two other rails individuals. For me the most elusive of the rails in our valley is the Virginia Rail. The Sora is elusive, but common in most local marsh lands and typically more vocal than Virginia Rails, but still rarely seen.

Sora are bulky, pear shaped birds with a bright yellow, candy corn shaped bill. They have a small head, and thick neck with a pointed tail that is often

SORA

cocked upward. Their legs are relatively long for their size. They weigh 2.6 ounces with a wingspan of 14 inches. They arrive here in the spring in May.

Coloration is cryptic with warm browns above and gray on the face and breast. They show a distinctive black face mask as well as white under the tail.

Many of you have no doubt heard Sora, as their call carries well, but probably did not realize what you were hearing. It was just one of those strange marsh sounds that one hears now and again. The song is a long, high, squealing whinny descending and slowing at the end. Both sexes call and once you have learned their song it is unlikely you will forget it.

I see Sora regularly between late May to September in marshy areas in much of Western Montana. If you go to one of these areas and sit you will most likely encounter one or at least hear one. They respond to electronic calls and a car engine starting up.

When feeding they are methodical walkers typically with their head down and crouched. They are most often on the edge between open water and emergent vegetation making them hard to see.

Many birders have North America's bird songs on portable devices such as an notepad or phone. If you use external speakers and play their song they are very responsive. If present, they usually call back. If they don't respond often they are moving through the marsh towards what they think is another Sora. I have had them approach as close as two feet. As always be conservative in the use of electronic calls as they can stress birds or cause them to abandon an area.

In summer take a few hours and bird a marsh and listen for the long descending *"Ker-wee Ker-wee"* whiny call of the marsh. The Sora I photographed for this article was at Arrowstone Park just south of Deer Lodge. ♦

A FRUSTRATING DAY BIRDING DURING MY PANAMA ADVENTURE IN 2019.

AMERICAN COOT

I know that for many birders an American Coot is not a very exciting bird. However, coots are a unique species. I have had a number of beginning birders ask about the all dark duck with the white bill. The assumption is that if it is swimming around in the water, about the size of a duck, and definitely not a goose, it must be a duck. In this case it is not a duck but rather a rail.

AMERICAN COOT

Rails are typically secretive marsh birds, and difficult to see. Rails are more often heard than seen. That holds true for the other two rails that breed in Western Montana; the Virginia Rail and Sora.

There are nine rail species in North America and five species found in Montana. The American Coot is the most common and found statewide. The Yellow Rail and the Common Gallinule are extremely rare with only 20 sightings for Yellow Rail and one for the Common Gallinule. Virginia Rail is uncommon with 374 sightings and Sora are common in proper habitat with 1,449 sightings. Both Sora and Virginia Rail are found in the Upper Clark Fork and Flint Creek Valleys. The most reliable area for these two species is the Dutchman Wetlands northeast of Anaconda.

Coots have a blackish head and neck with a red eye, slate gray body, and a distinctive white bill not flattened like a duck bill. They also show a divided white patch under the tail that shows well when they dive and dabble for food. The feet are lobed, not webbed, and yellow. Sexes are identical.

Their flight from the water is labored and they tend to run along the surface until airborne with their large feet trailing behind a very short tail. The young are distinctive among waterfowl chicks. In the downy stage they are black bodied with hairy orange-red feathers on the head and shoulders.

RAFT OF AMERICAN COOTS

American Coot — *Fulica americana*

American Coots can be found in large numbers during spring and fall migration especially at Warm Springs WMA and Georgetown Lake West of Anaconda. Throughout the summer months at Warm Springs WMA there are around 300 breeding pair. The graph with this article tracks the number of American Coots in surveys I have conducted from 2011 through 2020. The blue line shows the average number for each week March through November. Typically, Warm Springs WMA gets between 8,000 and 9,000 spring migrants. Fall migrants average 35,000 individuals with a historic peak of 65,000 in 2018. That is a lot of coots! The 2020 counts are in red on the graph. The spring population in 2020 was above average and the Fall population appears to be tracking the 10 year average.

It is estimated that there are 6 million American Coots in North American. Fifty-seven thousand breed in Montana, and 2.2 million migrate through Montana from Canada in the fall. Thirty-five thousand coots in weekly counts at Warm Springs translates into about 250,000 American Coots migrating through the Upper Clark Fork drainage. Nearly 13 percent of all coots in in the US migrate through the Clark Fork drainage.

In the past there were also large numbers of American Coots at Georgetown Lake in the fall. However, the past several falls have not shown more than 5,000-6,000 thousand staging birds. They peaked at just under 14,000 in 2020.

Coots that are seen in the spring breed and summer in Western Canadian Providences and migrate south to Texas, New Mexico, Arizona and California. Their staging, resting and feeding is around 3-5 days locally before flying further south.

The number of Bald Eagles also increases at Warm Spring WMA along with the coots as they feed on them. Coots float in large groups called rafts. Bald Eagles fly over the rafts, panicking them, and then grab a vulnerable coot with their talons. They take the coot to swallow water and hold them under until they drown. Eagles feeding on coots is especially common after ice forms and coots are forced into smaller and smaller areas. Eagles simply walk up to the edge of the ice, grab a coot in its talons and drag it onto the ice and eat the breast muscles. I have also seen coots frozen into the ice with the eagles feeding on the trapped birds.

If you are in the Warm Springs WMA area in May or September through October take some time and drive around the WMA and observe this annual explosion of spring and fall rails. Enjoy! ♦

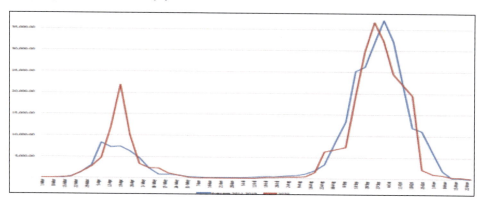

Family Gruidae

Sandhill Crane 62

Sandhill Crane *Antigone canadensis*

SANDHILL CRANE

Sandhill Cranes are one of the largest birds in Montana with a wingspan of 77 inches and weighing 10.6 pounds. These birds are unmistakable with their long legs, all reddish-brown body, red crown and dagger like beak. As their feathers wear they take on a rusty or fawn color, causing birders to occasionally mistake them for a deer standing in a field. Sexes look alike with males slightly larger. In silhouette they appear short necked, small headed and bottom heavy. They can often be seen in large numbers in fields where they feed on small rodents, amphibians and invertebrates.

They breed along rivers and wet meadows. Their long slightly descending rolling bugle call can be heard for a mile or more in the stillness of morning. I often hear their loud resonating call from my home in early morning.

Sandhills have one of the most unique mating behaviors of all Montana's birds. They pair bond by display dancing. As you watch it appears to be

SANDHILL CRANE

a choreographed complex duet of jumping, spinning and wing flapping that can leave you spell bound. Females give a more rapid and higher pitched call than males during courtship dances.

They first show in Western Montana in late April to early May after wintering in New Mexico, Texas and Mexico. They can often be seen in groups of 100s to 1000s in both migration and wintering flocks. Along the Pratt River in Nebraska upward to 10,000 can be seen in migrating flocks. In our area numbers are rarely above 100 during migration with many pair remaining in the valley to breed in wet meadows and hay lands.

Those that breed locally are Greater Sandhill Cranes. The Lesser Sandhill Crane is a subspecies that migrates further north to Northern Canada and Alaska. Lesser Sandhill Cranes are smaller at 7.3 pounds and stand 5 to 6 inches shorter in height. I have only observed Lesser Sandhill Cranes in our valley once in the spring of 2012. There were four Lesser with a group of 25 to 30 Greater in a wet meadow at the Warm Springs WMA near Anaconda.

If you go out to observe this species do so in the early morning and you will most often hear them before you see them. If you observe them in late June through August you have the opportunity to see their young called colts. I usually see a single colt with the parents, but it is not uncommon to see two.

Sandhill Cranes are one of the most observable "large" birds in Western Montana if you search proper habitat. Be sure and take a camera as their size makes it easy to get good photographs. With today's modern cameras that take 4-8 frames per second, you can get some interesting action pictures. Be sure to use a shutter speed of 1/1000 or higher or the image will be blurred. If you are lucky you might see them dance. ♦

BIRDING iN ANTARCTICA

Family Recurvirostridae

Black-necked Stilt 64
American Avocet 65

Black-necked Stilt *Himantopus mexicanus*

BLACK-NECKED STILT

The Black-necked Stilt has a length of 14 inches, wingspan of 29 inches and weighs six ounces. Historically it is transient to our area and breeds only occasionally in Montana. In the summer of 2014 the first breeding record for our valley occurred. Three chicks from a single nest successfully fledged from the Job Corps ponds at Warm Springs WMA.

BLACK-NECKED STILT

This species shows a black back and wings. The black extends up the back of the neck and over the crown of the head through the red eye. The bill is straight and legs are pinkish red. I see a few each year in our valley compared to several hundred American Avocets.

It's January, and I am dreaming of May and the return of the shorebirds as I look out on the snow covered landscape. I guess having stayed in Deer Lodge all of my life I appreciate each season, but I do look forward to spring birding and especially those challenging and beautiful shorebirds. I hope you will plan to get out in nature more this spring than in the past. We are becoming a nation of people who are losing contact with nature in preference to electronic gadgets. I for one am planning to reverse this trend in my life. Hope to see you out there somewhere watching birds. ♦

American Avocet *Recurvirostra americana*

AMERICAN AVOCET

As I sit at my computer in the short days of winter I am thinking about the beauty of shorebirds. Shorebird is a general term for 62 species in North America. They are small to medium-size birds with thin bills and long legs relative to their body size. They typically forage on open shorelines and wet grasslands. Forty-one species have been found in Montana with thirteen breeding in the state. I have been fortunate to see all forty-one species in Montana.

AMERICAN AVOCET

In the Upper Clark Fork Valley at the Warm Springs Wildlife Management Area I have observed 29 species. Of these, seven breed locally and the remainder migrate further north. Migrating shorebirds do not stay in our valley long in the spring as they are in a hurry to get to their breeding grounds. However, in the fall migrants returning south will linger longer and provide good viewing. Adults return south before juveniles. Spring migration is from late April through May and fall migration from mid-August through September.

The six shorebirds that breed at Warm Springs WMA are Killdeer, Black-necked Stilt, American Avocet, Spotted Sandpiper, Long-billed Curlew, Wilson's Snipe and Wilson's Phalarope. In my opinion, the two most beautiful shorebirds in our valley; are the American Avocet and the Black-necked Stilt.

The American Avocet is large with a length of 18 inches, and wingspan of 31 inches, weighing 11 ounces. This species is recognized by its unique upturned slim bill, long neck and legs. The breeding males and females have an orange-buff neck and head. The male's bill is straighter than that of the female, otherwise they look alike. Wings and body show a striking black and white pattern. Non-breeding adults show a pale gray head. Juveniles have a slight orange head.

I have seen up to 120 at a time during spring migration at Warm Springs WMA. Typically, twenty pair breed locally on shallow ponds in the valley. Avocets can reliably be seen May through August in the Ducks Unlimited Ponds of the Warm Springs WMA. ♦

Family Charadriidae

Black-bellied Plover 66
American Golden-Plover 67
Killdeer 69

Black-bellied Plover   *Pluvialis squatarola*

BLACK-BELLIED PLOVER

There are seven plover species found in Montana which are part of a larger group of birds collectively known as shorebirds.

Some are rather common and others are not. The most common and familiar to almost everyone is the Killdeer with 8,858 records with the Montana Natural Heritage Program. Mountain Plover, a unique upland grassland species dependent on arid bare ground in central Montana, has been recorded 3,926 times. Piping Plover only breeds in the Northeast corner of Montana. They are fairly easy to find, though rare, and many birders go to see this species to add to their life list, thus 1,327 observations. The Semi-palmated Plover is found statewide but not often

BLACK-BELLIED PLOVER IN SPRING PLUMAGE

seen with 312 observations, and the rarest, Snowy Plover has only been seen 11 times which is not enough to show a state distribution pattern.

That leaves two species which are uncommon but I see both of them annually on local mudflats. The Black-bellied Plover has 270 observations and the American Golden-Plover has 105 observations. Both species have been seen across the state in proper habitats.

I am fascinated by these two species because I have to work hard to find them and their spring and fall plumages are so different. I rarely see either of these species in the spring.

The Black-bellied Plover's migration route is along the West Coast of North America with few straying inland. The American Golden-Plover's migration route is from North Dakota south in a straight line to the Gulf of Mexico, then most of the Eastern United States. Of the 12 sightings I have for the American Golden Plover in our area 11 have been in the fall. For the Black-bellied Plover only seven of the 28 sightings have been in the spring.

The Black-bellied Plover is the larger of the two at eight ounces verses five ounces for the American Golden-Plover. Wingspan is 29 inches in the Black-bellied and 24 inches in the American Golden Plover.

BLACK-BELLIED PLOVER IN FALL PLUMAGE

In flight the Black-bellied shows a black armpit in all plumages the American Golden does not.

The breeding plumage in the Black-bellied has a black face, neck and belly, but the vent area is white. The back is white with black spotting, the back of the neck, and cap are white and the bill is large and heavy. Most of the world's birders only see the Black-bellied in non-breeding or fall plumage and it is known as the Gray Plover. We are fortunate in Montana to see both spring and fall plumage. ♦

AMERICAN GOLDEN-PLOVER

AMERICAN-GOLDEN PLOVER

The American Golden looks petite compared to the Black-bellied with a shorter, thinner bill. The neck, throat, belly and vent are black. The back is a golden colored with black spots that extends up the back of the neck forming a cap. Spring plumage is just a striking as that of the Black-bellied Plover. Unfortunately, I have yet to get a spring breeding plumage picture of an American Golden Plover.

Fall plumages are more difficult to separate and I do it by overall size and bill. The bill is petite in the golden compared to the Black-bellied. The Black-bellied is grayer overall than the American-Golden. The two plumages are so different novices often have trouble realizing these are the same species as the spring versions.

Why the huge difference in plumage? Spring plumage in males is typically brighter than females and plays a role in mate selection by females. Those with the brightest plumage may have better genes to give to offspring for their survival. It's a little like the bull elk that wins fall sparing indicating better genes. The victor gets the harem, mates with the cows, and passes his superior genes to the offspring. ♦

KILLDEER

Killdeer utilize mud flats, shallow water and marshes. There they probe for a variety of invertebrates including insect larva, worms and soft bodied animals. Most shorebirds are in the family Scolopacidae, except for Plovers which are in the family Charadriidae.

Eleven plovers are found in North America and seven in Montana. Four are found in Western Montana valleys. They are the Black-bellied Plover, American-Golden Plover, Semipalmated Plover and Killdeer. The first three plovers are found locally during spring and fall migration only. They breed in Northern Alaska, Canada and the Arctic Circle. Spring migration "staging" for food is brief as they are biologically driven to get to the breeding grounds and nest early to increase chick survival.

KILLDEER

Fall migration adult plovers begin to arrive in Western Montana by late August and juveniles in mid-September and October. Fall migration staging is longer with individual birds remaining for up to 10 days.

A limited number of Killdeer remain in Western Montana and breed although most migrate further north. Fall migration can have large numbers of Killdeer on local mudflats and are a combination of local breeders and migrants. A few Killdeer do remain and overwinter in warmer climes with open water statewide, but rarely in the Flint Creek or Clark Fork Valleys. Only the Bitterroot Valley has confirmed overwintering status. In a recent fall survey at Warm Springs I counted 52 Killdeer feeding and taking on reserves for their long flight south to warmer climates. Killdeer winter along our southern coastal waters in Mexico, Central and South America. Killdeer is the only plover that breeds statewide with a few overwintering.

The most noticeable field mark of the Killdeer is the two black bands across the breast. The overall pattern of this 9-11 inch plover is brown above and white below. The head pattern shows a brown cap with a black forehead band which goes through the eye. There is also a blackish-brown band that extends from the base of the bill to the back of the neck. The orbital eye ring is red. The legs are as long as the tail. In flight, and sometimes when standing, they show rusty upper tail feathers and rump. Sexes appear the same.

Their call is a shrill *"kill-dee" or "fill-dee"*, thus the name Killdeer.

Killdeer are noted for a conspicuous distraction display when a predator or a person approaches. The adult drags a wing as is if it is broken, fans the rusty tail, and loudly calls to get attention as it runs away from its nest or chicks. The bird manages to just stay ahead of the intruder. When the intruder is no longer a threat the bird miraculously recovers and flies off calling loudly. To me the call is implying; "The jokes on you!" ♦

Family Scolopacidae

Dunlin 70
Wilson's Snipe 72
Lesser Yellowlegs 73
Greater Yellowlegs 74
Red Phalarope 75

Dunlin *Calidris alpina*

DUNLIN

    I probably said it before, but the fun thing about birding is finding the unexpected. That is what happened on April 30, 2019 on the south end of AR Pond 3 at Warm Springs Wildlife Management Area. I found a Dunlin in full breeding plumage. What a unique and beautiful plumage this bird has. I was fortunate to get a good picture of this species feeding.

DUNLIN

    I don't have a picture of the non-breeding or winter plumage for the Dunlin. The plumage is much different. The bird's black belly is white, the black speckled lines of the chest are light brown and the russet red color of the back and sides is replaced with a dull gray color. If you didn't realize that the breeding plumage in this species is very different than the non-breeding plumage you might not realize that you were looking at the same species.

The Dunlin is not common in Montana with only 212 sightings. Most observations are in May with a few more sightings August through September. Number of sightings has been decreasing since 2015 with a high of 17 sightings that year. Then nine in 2018, five in 2019 and none since. Sightings are scattered throughout the state.

Breeding occurs in the Arctic and northern coastal regions of Alaska east to the Hudson Bay and on to the eastern coast of Greenland. My 2019 Dunlin "staged" (rested and regained strength by feeding) for about a week before continuing north.

They winter in coastal areas of southern Alaska all the way to Baja and central Mexico.

I have two additional records for this species in the Upper Clark Fork Drainage. One was a breeding male on 04/16/16 and a non-breeding plumage individual on 08/27/14. All three sightings were at Warm Springs Wildlife Management Area.

Dunlin's are a medium sized shorebird at 8 ½ inches. The familiar Killdeer is 10 ½ inches in length. In addition to the black belly and rufous red back and sides, Dunlins can be distinguished from other shorebirds by a long bill that is curved at the tip and stout black legs. The body is stocky and the head is round. In flight the center of the rump is dark contrasting with the whitish edges.

Dunlins often mix with other shorebirds and the day I photographed this one it was with three Semi-palmated Plovers.

They inhabit mudflats both in migration and on breeding grounds and feed by walking several steps, then making an exploratory probe with their bill. If they sense an invertebrate they plunge their bill completely into the mud to the base of the bill.

Their call is a short, high pitched *"trill"*. They are a nervous shorebird taking flight at the slightest sense of danger, but often return to the very spot they took flight from in the first place.

Seeing shorebirds both spring and fall totally depends on the presence of mudflats or water over mud less than two inches deep. Some springs, due to high water, there are few mudflats locally and seeing a variety of shorebirds is a challenge. Fall's migration opportunities to see a number of shorebird species is totally dependent on water flows over the summer. If by mid-August water levels over traditional mudflats is still high, chances of seeing shorebirds is low. They will just continue flying south until they do find a suitable mudflat. This is very stressful on the metabolism of birds. As fat reserves are depleted they begin to metabolize muscle cells reducing their ability to fly long distances. Estimated mortality for migration is around 8-12%, but probably increases with fewer places to stop and "stage". ♦

WILSON'S SNIPE

I often chuckle when a young person asks if someone wants to go snipe hunting. They have in mind a practical joke by giving someone an impossible task of running around the woods at night, carrying a bag and flashlight, trying to catch a snipe. The jokester typically doesn't realize we really do have snipes in Montana, at least in the summer, in large numbers and a few wintering in warm waters.

The Wilson's Snipe, formerly called Common Snipe, is a late arriving shorebird that breeds across Montana and is quite common. My earliest record for this species is April 5th and latest October 17th. In a recent CBC on January 1, 2020 a single adult was seen in a warm water creek west of Anaconda.

WILSON'S SNIPE

Wilson's Snipes are distinctive in shape, rather stocky, heavy bodied, short legged and long billed. Superficially they look like an American Woodcock only half the weight. American Woodcocks are rare in Montana with only four records for the entire state.

Wilson's Snipes are brown overall with buff stripes on the back with a distinctly striped head. The long straight bill and short legs are distinctive. They feed by probing their bills into the mud. They often are found sitting on wooden posts along wet hay meadows.

When flushed they have a zigzag flight pattern and a raspy call. This species is not known for its call as much as its "winnowing."

The winnowing flight display is performed day and night especially in the breeding season during late May and June. The snipe circles high in the air and then dives at high speed towards the ground. Air rushing past the spread outer tail feathers produces a low, pulsating whistling sound. This *"wa wa wa"* sound is reminiscent of a Boreal Owl call and is often heard before you see the bird as it performs high overhead. Flight displays are associated with courtship and are more frequent just prior to breeding.

Even though most migrate south of Montana, some stay year around in warm water springs and creeks in milder climates of the state. I have even observed them once in the ponds of Deer Lodge's Arrowstone Park in January when the water was open. We have recorded them on the last two Christmas Bird Counts west of Anaconda in a ditch that stays ice free most winters. Dutchman's Wetland area northeast of Anaconda has one of the highest densities of Wilson's snipes.

I have observed 29 species of shorebirds in the Upper Clark For Drainage. Once you found this one you only have 28 more to find and identify! ♦

LESSER YELLOWLEGS

Spring is an exciting time to be in the field. It is always fun to see birds that you have not seen since last summer. To add to the enjoyment of spring birding I keep track of the date that I first see a bird each spring and compare to previous years.

Some of the first migrants to show each spring are shorebirds. They usually show about mid-April in small numbers and then increase to fairly impressive numbers. You have to spend a lot of time in the field to catch them as they are only in our valley a few days "staging". Staging simply means they rest and feed, regain energy, and then continue their flight north to Canada, Alaska, and the Arctic Circle where they breed. The fall migration south is much more relaxed and an individual bird might "stage" for a week or more before moving south to wintering grounds.

LESSER YELLOWLEGS

Spring migration is short, only a couple of weeks, whereas fall migration can be spread out over a month or more. Spring migration is the easiest time to identify shorebirds as they are in breeding plumage and their feathers are fresh and crisp. In the Fall feathers are worn (non-breeding plumage) and much more difficult to identify. Shorebird is a general term for 62 species in North America. They are small to medium-size birds with thin bills and long legs. They typically forage on open shorelines and wet grasslands. Forty-one species have been found in Montana with thirteen species breeding in the state.

In the Upper Clark Fork Valley I have observed 29 species. Of these, seven breed locally and the remainder migrate further north.

The first migrant species that I observe most years is the Greater Yellowlegs. I occasionally see one or two Killdeer before the Greater Yellowlegs, but they occasionally overwinter and might not have migrated. My earliest observation of this species is April 1, 2015. The average date for spring arrival is April 16th. My earliest previous record was April 10, 2014 This observation was nine days earlier than previous years. The reason for this would be pure speculation, but it was probably tied to the warmer than usual weather in the spring of 2015. Northern migrants seem to sense the receding ice further north and time their migration accordingly. ♦

LESSER YELLOWLEGS BREEDING PLUMAGE

GREATER YELLOWLEGS

One of the first shorebirds to migrate into the valley most springs is the Greater Yellowlegs. You often see Killdeer before Greater Yellowlegs, but we always have Killdeer that overwinter, so you cannot tell if they are a spring migrant or an overwintering individual.

If the number of Killdeer suddenly increases that is often a clue that some individuals may be spring migrants. I started bird surveys at Warm Springs WMA this spring on March 17. I saw nine Killdeer on March 15, and assume that some might have been migrants. The next week, I only saw two, so who knows.

GREATER YELLOWLEGS

On April 13, I saw my first "official" spring shorebird migrant when I observed a single Greater Yellowlegs at Job Corps Pond 4 at Warm Springs Wildlife Management Area. In 2015 I saw my first Greater Yellowlegs on April 1, and in 2014 on April 10.

This year's observation had an interesting twist. As I was watching the yellowlegs I was debating about photographing the bird, when a Peregrine Falcon swooped down, grabbed him by the neck and back and carried him off. The bird made a few distress call, *"tew tew"* and went silent. I was left with the distinct sense that the Peregrine had killed the yellowlegs when it struck it.

Such is the way of nature, one species feeds on another. I was however struck with a feeling of sorrow. This bird had most likely come north after wintering in Texas or Mexico and had made it 1,500 miles or more on its way to Northern Canada to breed, only to be killed as it staged in Western Montana. It only stopped to take on more energy in the form of invertebrates and rest, probably for no more than one or two days. As these shorebirds migrate north in the spring they rest and feed very sparingly as they need to reach their destination, mate, raise young while food is readily available in the far north's short summer season.

Many of these Greater Yellowlegs as well as other shorebirds will be back to Montana by early to mid-August on their return south. Last year, one showed up a Warm Springs WMA on July 14. These early ones were probably unsuccessful breeders due to nest failure or predation and have simply migrated early. The majority of successful breeders return in August after the young of the year have fledged. I had high counts from August 11 through September 15. These birds tend to linger longer in staging areas as there is no urgency to their return to the coastal wintering grounds. Even later, the young of the year begin showing and continue through October. Last year my last observation of a juvenile Greater Yellowlegs was November 20th ! ♦

RED PHALAROPE

I wrote in the past about a rare sighting of a Long-tailed Jaeger that I had found in the Upper Clark Fork Valley in 2005. I mentioned that fall is a good time to find rare migrants that have strayed from their coastal migration routes. These "off migration path" species are typically the result of severe weather pushing birds inland.

In the fall of 2011 I observed four Fall migration rarities. They include Long-tailed Duck, Black Scoter, Sabine's Gull and Red Phalarope. The first three were at Warm Springs WMA, the last one at Silver Lake.

A Red Phalarope was reported at Silver Lake October 30 and I was able to relocate and photograph the bird on November 1. The sighting was the fifteenth for the state of Montana at that time. Eight more sightings have been added by 2021. Interestingly enough I previously observed a Red Phalarope at Silver Lake on October 29, 2009.

RED PHALAROPE, NON-BREEDING

Three Phalarope Species are found in Montana. The Wilson's Phalarope is the most common and breeds in the Upper Clark Fork. The Red-necked Phalarope migrates through our valley in groups of 30 to 300 in the Fall from the Arctic Circle to wintering grounds in South America. An increasing number of Red-necked Phalaropes are being seen in spring but still rare west of the divide. They are common in Northeast Montana in spring.

Red Phalaropes typically migrate off the west coast from Arctic coastal waters and winter from Southern California to Baja, Mexico in coastal seas. Like all phalaropes, females are larger and more colorful than the male. In fact, females do the courting and the males incubate and care for the chicks! Breeding plumage shows the female with black wings etched with golden edged feathers, black crown, white cheek patch, and chestnut red underparts and neck. The male is a duller version of the female without a black crown. The other distinguishing field mark is the thick, yellow, black tipped bill. The other two species have needle-thin bills.

After breeding Red Phalaropes molt to winter plumage quickly and the difference is dramatic. The picture I took at Silver Lake shows a winter plumage adult. They are pale gray above and white below. The head has a black eye patch with an all black bill. Sexes are not distinguishable in winter plumage.

Red Phalaropes swim buoyantly on the surface riding higher in the front than back. They feed by spinning in the water, creating a vortex that draws invertebrates to the surface.

Next fall take the time to see if you can find a rare migrant. ♦

Family Stercorariidae

Long-tailed Jaeger..76

Long-tailed Jaeger   *Stercorarius longicaudus*

LONG-TAILED JAEGER

Serious birders seek out rare migrant birds in the fall for their life lists. In 2005 I found my first Sabine's Gull. In Fall of 2014, during the third week of October, a Black Scoter, both at Warm Springs WMA. Both are high arctic species that migrate down the Pacific Coast to wintering grounds in Baja, Mexico and South America.

LONG-TAILED JAEGER

Occasionally juveniles lose their way, fly inland, particularly during stormy weather. Often these inland wanderers never find their way back and perish.

The rarest of these "lost juveniles" for me in the Upper Clark Fork Valley was in late August, 2005. My wife saw a strange gull-like bird at the Beck Hill Intersection north of Deer Lodge. I was out of town and immediately went looking for it when I returned. It was a juvenile Long-tailed Jaeger. Jaegers are a pelagic species usually far out in the Pacific Ocean.

Long-tailed Jaeger   *Stercorarius longicaudus*

Superficially, juvenile Long-tailed Jaegers look like a gull but adults are strikingly different. Adults have a very neat black cap, white face, neck and breast, with a pale black back and gray legs. The tail has long central feathers which can be broken or missing.

LONG-TAILED JAEGER

Juveniles appear in dark, intermediate and light phases. In all phases edges of the back feathers have crisp whitish edges giving a barred appearance. The bill is stubby and half black. Positive identification of the juvenile Jaeger was made with the photograph I took showing the beginnings of the long central tail feathers.

Jaegers are arctic breeders and migrate and feed well offshore. They forage by swooping to pluck prey from the ocean surface and on occasion plunge-dive. They also dive on gulls in flight forcing them to drop or regurgitate food to avoid continual harassment. Inland juveniles feed in plowed fields for insects and earthworms.

The juvenile I photographed was consuming grasshoppers along an asphalt road. The bird was relatively tame and allowed close views. It was reported by local residents to have been in the area for several weeks before I identified it. I immediately put out a *Rare Bird Alert*, and had a number of birders on site the next morning. Unfortunately the bird disappeared overnight and was never seen again.

There are two additional Jaeger species found in the US and Montana. The Parasitic and Pomarine. The Pomarine has been observed seven times, the Long-tailed 17 times and the Parasitic 24 times.

Please, if you see an odd or different looking bird contact myself or another experienced birder. You never know what rarity you might have found that others would enjoy seeing. ♦

Family Laridae

Sabine Gull	78
Bonaparte's Gull	80
Franklin's Gull	81
Heermann's Gull	82
Ring-billed Gull	84
California Gull	84
Herring Gull	85
Lesser Black-backed Gull	85

Sabine Gull   *Xema sabini*

SABINE GULL

The two most common gulls in the Upper Clark Fork Drainage are the Ring-billed Gull and the California Gull; both breed at the Warm Springs WMA. In addition to these two gulls you can often find small populations of Franklin and Bonaparte's Gulls. The Herring Gull is rare, but I see it several times a year. There has been one sighting of an Iceland (Thayer's) Gull. Our rarest regularly occurring gull in our area is the Sabine's Gull.

SABINE GULL

I have observed the Sabine's Gull eight times since 2005. All but one of these sightings was in the upper Clark Fork Drainage. My most recent sighting was September 29, 2020 at the Helena Holding Reservoir. My first sighting was of a juvenile reported at the sewage ponds at Warm Springs. As soon as I heard about the sighting I rushed out to the area and was unable to find the bird. I went back the following day and found it floating in the pond. The gull was very accommodating and I was able to get fairly close and obtain a decent picture which accompanies this article.

There have only been 60 observations in Montana according the *Montana Natural History Program*. That is not very many.

Out of the last 20 years there were no sightings in 10 of those years. The most sightings in a single year of different individuals was ten in 2007 and eight in 2018. Most sightings are of a single bird, rarely more than two. Most Montana birders have never seen this rarity. My grandson accumulated 333 species on his Montana life list before he saw one. It was also number 1,601 on his world life list.

Interestingly enough, the most common place to see this bird in Montana is the Warm Springs WMA with eight of the 60 observations. All of my observations have been at the Warm Springs WMA, with the exception of the Helena sighting. The majority of my sightings were in Pond One of the Sewage Lagoon Ponds including the juvenile pictured here. I have no idea why that is true.

Sabine's Gulls are a small tern like gull. The adult has a gray hood over the head with a yellow tipped black bill. Juveniles (August through December of their first year) have a brownish back and neck. When they fly the upper wing pattern forms a "W" or "M" both in the juvenile and adult. Sabine's nest on tundra ponds along coastal Alaska. Fall and spring migration is mostly off the Pacific Coast and they are rarely seen inland, making these Montana observations exceptional. They overwinter along the Southern Pacific Coast of Mexico and Central America. Juvenile birds are most often seen inland, suggesting they get lost or storm blown inland, as they move south for the first time. No one knows for sure how many of these inland gulls survive and make their winter grounds.

Fifty-nine of the sixty Montana observations have occurred in September and October, with the majority in September. That would suggest that most if not all are juveniles. If you hear of a Sabine's Gull in your area, you better make a priority of seeing it. They usually only stay a day or so and then they are gone. ♦

BIRDING IN BELIZE.

BONAPARTE'S GULL

Gull identification represents one of the most difficult challenges for birders. Adult gull plumages can take up to four years with as many as eight different plumage stages. You need a good gull book, a spotting scope, patience and a little luck to identify some individuals. There is some hybridization making for additional ID challenges.

Seventeen species of gulls have been identified in Montana. Six species have been found at the Warm Springs WMA. The two most common are the California and Ring-billed Gulls. The Herring and Sabine's Gulls are rare and the Franklins and Bonaparte's Gulls are seen yearly in the spring and occasionally in the fall at the WMA.

Franklin's and Bonaparte's are easily separated from the other four as they are small, black-headed gulls. The best field mark to distinguish adults apart in these two species is the

JUVENILE BONAPARTE'S GULL

red bill with a black ring near the tip on the Franklin's compared to an all black bill in the Bonaparte's. In flight the Franklin's wingtips show black. They have broad white eye-arcs and white primary feather tips that look like large white dots on the tail when the wings are folded. These traits are not present on the Bonaparte's. Franklin Gulls are also larger at ten ounces compared to seven for the Bonaparte's. Their wingspan is 36 inches with a length of 14.5 inches. Both sexes look alike in breeding adults.

ADULT BONAPARTE'S GULL

FRANKLIN'S GULL

Franklin's are transient to our area and mostly occur in early spring. I have seen from one to to 153 depending on the year at the Warm Springs WMA. Both species are occurring more often in the Upper Clark Fork compared to past years. Franklin's are listed as a species of concern in Montana and are known to only breed in five locations statewide.

FRANKLIN GULL

When this article was originally written the "go to" reference in Montana was the 12th edition of P.D. Skaar's, *2012 Montana Bird Distribution* (MBD) book. This was a valuable book for birding and was based on more than 800,000 records submitted by 2,700 Montana birders over the last decade. MBD gives you the distribution of all 427 Montana species in 2012 (442 species in 2022) their sighting frequency, breeding and overwintering status as well as special notes. Today that has been replaced with eBird, an online database by Cornell University. Montana data is then shared with the *Montana Natural Heritage Program* which is accessible to all. The frequencies I quote are from the MNHP. Please learn how to use eBird if you don't know how. Citizen scientists are a valuable resource to bird conservation. eBird is discussed in the front of the book on page 17. ♦

BIRDING ALONG THE CLARK FORK RIVER

HEERMANN'S GULL

Fall is a time that you often find rarities. Most of these rarities are juveniles that have not migrated before and get lost or storm driven off course and don't have the ability to get back where they belong.

That appears to be true of the juvenile bird that was found early on the morning of October 11, 2020. A local Polson birder found a juvenile Heermann's Gull on the dock in Sacajawea Park. If you are unfamiliar with Polson it is the park on the south end of Flathead Lake where Highway 93 crosses the Flathead River.

JUVENILE HERRMANN'S GULL

How rare was this species? It has only been seen once in Montana and that was in December of 2018. I was unable to find if the Heermann's Gull seen then was an adult or a juvenile.

This species is a year around breeder of coastal Baja California in Mexico. It is a summer resident of coastal California and post-breeding migrant along the Pacific Coast from Oregon to Washington.

Most likely this bird was migrating along the Pacific Ocean Coast and was swept inland with storms which had strong west to east winds.

The juvenile Heermann's sighting came across the internet around 11 AM. My wife Laura and I debated about going to see it and decided it wasn't that far for a state bird. I have seen the bird in the past along the Pacific Ocean in Washington. We left around 1:00 PM, arrived in Polson around 3:15, and found the bird on the dock within minutes of arriving. It was with eight Ring-billed Gulls and was not at all spooky. I was able to get reasonably close and got several good pictures. We left for home around 3:45 and made it back just before dark at 6:00 PM. I had gained a state bird in less than 5 hours which might be a record for me. That placed me at 377 species and tied for first place for number of birds seen in Montana on eBird.

Five people saw the gull the first day, no one saw it the next day and a party of three found it just at dusk on October 13. Then it was gone.

Moral of the story is that if a rarity shows up go as soon as you hear about it, they don't often stay long.

Heermann's Gull *Larus heermanni*

Once you reach 300 of the 442 species found in Montana it is difficult to find new species to add to your Montana life list. This was my third state bird in 2020 which is a lot considering the number of species I have on my Montana list. I almost had a fourth in January of 2020. An Ivory Gull was found on Flathead Lake. My Grandson and I went on a Saturday and no one saw the gull that day. The next day it was seen again and continued to be seen for several weeks after that. I only had the one day as I was scheduled to leave for a trip to Puerto Rico the day after I made my attempt. My grandson was fortunate enough to go back the next weekend and get it. He is now one up on me in Montana. Such is birding and that is what makes it such a great hobby.

I found two new species in 2019, two in 2018, nine in 2017, and 13 in 2016. Do you see the pattern? The more state birds you find the less likely you are to find the next state bird.

So what does this gull look like? Adults and juvenile are very different. Adults have a white head that is streaked brown in winter, a red bill with a black tip, dark gray body and a black tail with a white terminal band. The juvenile is overall light chocolate brown with white fringes on the feathers. The bill is whitish with a black tip. First winter birds are darker brown than juveniles. Second winter birds are not as dark brown, have a gray belly and buff tipped tail. Many gull species have a four year cycle to the adult plumage such as the Heermann's Gull.

HEERMANN'S GULL

My two photographs show the pale brown coloration, whitish edges to the feather and the black tipped bill of the juvenile.

The number of people who have seen 300 or more species in Montana is actually very small. Only 47 of the hundreds of birders in Montana have reached that goal as of 2021. It takes a lot of effort in time, finances and miles driven to accomplish 300 species. Even fewer birders have birded in every county in the state. There are only eight of us who have done that and I only reached that goal in the summer of 2020 adding Powder River and Carter counties. Not everyone wants to chase rarities, but I find it exciting, and rewarding.

They tell me a hole in one is exciting in golf as well. To each his own. ♦

RING-BILLED GULL

Gulls, not seagulls, are a rather recent phenomena in the Upper Clark Fork Valley and Georgetown Lake. The last ten years I have seen more and more gulls locally.

RING-BILLED GULL

In the Upper Clark Fork Valley there are breeding colonies of Ring-billed and California Gulls at the Warm Springs WMA. I am not aware of any other breeding colonies locally.

Some gulls have several plumage cycles from juvenile to adult. It can be difficult to distinguish between species. Adults are easy to tell apart. Adult Ringed-billed Gulls are rather light gray on the back, called the mantle, and have a broad ring on the outer portion of the bill. Ring-bills have five plumages as they age.

CALIFORNIA GULL

Adult California Gulls *(Larus californicus)* are larger, darker mantled and have red and black marks on the bill. California Gulls have seven plumages which includes breeding and non-breeding adults. The majority of gulls in Western Montana will be one of these two species.

Two black headed gulls, Franklin's and Bonaparte's, are increasing in the valley and a few are even breeding with limited success.

CALIFORNIA GULL

The adult Franklin's has broad white eye arcs and a red bill. The Bonaparte's has a black bill and white circle around the eye. You might also see a Herring Gull *(Larus argentatus)*, which is large gull, 2.5 pounds compared to the 1.3 pound California with a single red dot on the bill. These five species would make up 99 percent of the gulls found west of the Continental Divide with the exception of the Flathead Lake area.

East of the Continental Divide several other gull species are often seen. The two most frequented areas that birders find gulls are the Helena Landfill, Helena Holding Reservoir and in the Fort Peck area. Of the seventeen gull species observed in Montana seven have been observed in the Upper Clark Fork and eleven in the Helena Valley.

One of the recent rarities that I had the opportunity to observe was on November 13, 2020. A Lesser Black-backed Gull. As you can see by the picture the mantle is very dark, bright yellow legs, streaking on the head and the bill has a single red dot. It's size is between the Herring and California at 1.8 pounds.

RING-BILLED GULL

The Black-backed gull is rather rare in Montana. There have been 25 observation compared to 3,326 for the Ring-bill, 1,842 for the California, and 1,153 for the Franklin's Gull.

How does one find out about this rare species when they show in Montana? If you are familiar with eBird you can sign up for daily notifications of rare birds in Montana. If you are not familiar with eBird go to www.ebird.org and explore the site. It has a wealth of information and you can post your sightings if you are interested.

LESSER BLACK-BILLED GULL

Chasing rarities is a lot of fun and a great way to meet new birders. If there is a rarity somewhere chances are when you get there someone else will be watching it as well. Maybe you'll gain a new birding friend. ♦

Family Gaviidae

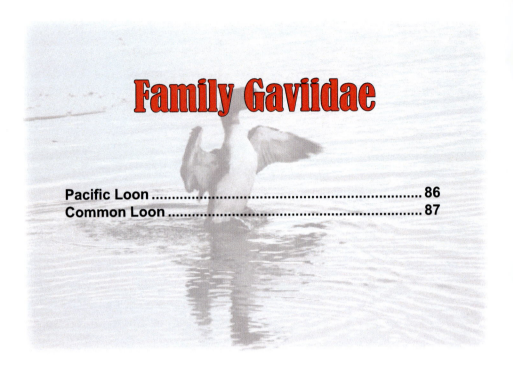

Pacific Loon 86
Common Loon 87

Pacific Loon   *Gavia pacifica*

PACIFIC LOON

Fall can be a wonderful time to see rarities that pass through our area in migration. I want to share with you a rarity that I encountered October 16, 2014, the Pacific Loon.

PACIFIC LOON IN NON-BREEDING PLUMAGE

On October 16, 2014 while doing a bird survey at Warm Springs WMA I saw a bird in the water that was too large to be a duck but too small for a Common Loon. The light was poor and the bird soon dove and I was not able to identify it. It was along one of the connecting channels between ponds. I drove quickly to the head of the channel, positioned my truck so I could look down the channel with my window mounted scope, and waited. When the bird came to the surface it was all the way

Pacific Loon   *Gavia pacifica*

at the other end of the channel but I could identify it as a Pacific Loon. I have never gotten a decent picture of this species as they are always several 100 yards from me and this one was no exception. The loon dove again but this time when it came to the surface it had split the distance between us in half. He kept doing this until he was within 20 feet of me! I couldn't believe it and snapped off a hundred frames or so. The picture with this article is the result.

Most are familiar with the Common Loon that is large, weighing nine pounds and is black and white. Even in non-breeding plumage they have that familiar large body and bill. They are browner with a white throat with only a remnant of the breeding plumage necklace. The Pacific Loon is much smaller at 3.7 pounds with a much smaller bill that is slightly upturned. Breeding plumage shows a gray head and neck with vertical stripes on the neck and a small patch of black and white stripes on the back. In this non-breeding adult picture the black and white patch on the back is barely visible and the neck stripes are absent.

This is the best picture I have ever gotten of this species. Although the day was heavily overcast and there is little contrast in the picture, I still managed to get a fairly good photo. I posted the sighting to Montana Outdoor Birders (MOB) on the Web as well as eBird and over the next few days a number of birders searched for the loon. It was never seen again, it was a one day rarity. Evidently the loon landed, rested, feed briefly and then moved on south for the winter.

So how do you get to see these rarities? Spend a lot of time in the field looking and occasionally you will run into one or it runs into you. Either way it makes for a great birding experience. ♦

Common Loon   *Gavia immer*

COMMON LOON

Fall is a great time to find migrant birds that are moving south to wintering grounds in Mexico, Central America, and South America. For some species migration takes them along the Pacific and Atlantic Coasts of North America.

One family of birds we get the opportunity to see during the fall migration are Loons. Loons are a mystical bird and a symbol of wilderness and all that is wild.

There are five species of Loons in the world: Arctic, Common, Pacific,

COMMON LOON IN BREEDING PLUMAGE

87

Red-throated and Yellow-billed. All but the Arctic have been seen in Montana. I have seen all four in Montana as well. When I was on the Pribilof Islands of Alaska birding in 2015 I had a chance to see the Arctic, but didn't. I was sick one day and did not go out and the group saw an Arctic Loon! The next day we went back to the site but couldn't locate the species again. Such is birding.

In Southwest Montana I've seen three of Montana's four Loon species. I've also seen the Yellow-billed Loon in the Missouri River near Great Falls.

Warm Springs WMA has Common Loons in spring and fall. They are not in large numbers with only four or five seen at a time with a high of 22 in 2018. They do not breed locally. They are transient only stopping to rest and feed (staging). They tend to stay 3-5 days then move to a new location. I've also seen Common Loons at Racetrack Pond, Silver Lake, East Fork Reservoir and Georgetown Lake.

In the fall I have seen Pacific Loons on both Silver Lake and Warm Springs WMA, but not every year. Seeing a Pacific Loon is a treat and a rarity.

To give you an idea of relative frequency of these four species the Montana Natural Heritage Program has recorded 9,000 sightings by birders for the Common Loon, 46 sightings for the Pacific Loon, 21 for the Red-throated, and 12 for the Yellow-billed Loon.

COMMON LOON NON-BREEDING PLUMAGE

The Common Loon is large at nine pounds, has a length of 32 inches, and wingspan of 46 inches. In breeding plumage the under-parts of the body are white, the back is checkered black and white. The bill is dagger like and black, eyes are blood red, and the head is glossy black. Below the head is a black and white neck band or collar. Winter plumage is dull brown overall with white neck and throat. The bill shows a lot of white especially on the lower mandible.

Common Loons are probably best known for their vocalizations of which they have three. The wail, a long almost mournful cry. The tremolo a high pitched, rapid, five-beat call and the best known is the yodel which is given only by males during territorial confrontations. These vocalizations are best heard on lakes where they breed. I have heard the yodel on birds staging at Warm Springs WMA.

The rarer Pacific Loon is only 3.7 pounds with a wingspan of 36 inches and a length of 25 inches. Because they are only seen locally in the fall they are in non-breeding plumage. In breeding plumage the nape is gray, neck has vertical black and white stripes and the back shows black and white barring. In non-breeding plumage backs are darker with just a hint of striping and the pale gray nape blends in with the back. The black throat of the breeding bird becomes white. Sexes are alike in plumage in both species.

Every fall you have the opportunity in September through November to look for both species at Warm Springs WMA, Silver Lake, East Fork Reservoir, Georgetown Lake, or Brown's Lake in northern Powell County. I have seen both species many times but it is always a thrill to see them again. ♦

Family Phalacrocoracidae

Double-crested Cormorant 89

Double-crested Cormorant   *Nannopterum auritum*

DOUBLE-CRESTED CORMORANT

Often, when I am out birding in wetlands I have someone ask me what the large black "duck" is that is sitting in the trees when it is not swimming in the water.

The mistake made by folks is that if it is in the water swimming around and it isn't a goose, it must be a duck. The fact is that there are a number of birds that are not ducks swimming in the water.

What people are asking about is the Double-crested Cormorant a common species in lakes in Southwest Montana. Since I originally wrote this article the Neotropic Cormorant has been seen once at Great Falls and once at Billings. Both were in the summer of 2021. There are seven species of Cormorants in North America in two families. Only two occur in Montana. Forty-one species occur in the world with some being called Shags, Anhinga and Darters. The Anhinga occurs in the southeast portion of United States. The Brandt's range is along the Pacific Coast. The Red-faced

DOUBLE-CRESTED CORMORANT

Double-crested Cormorant — *Nannopterum auritum*

along the Pacific Coast of Alaska, The Great along the Atlantic Coast, the Neotropic in the south central portion and Eastern Mexico, and the Double-crested Cormorant in all 48 continental states, Canada, Alaska and Mexico.

Double-crested can be difficult to distinguish from Neo-tropic and Great Cormorants where their ranges overlap. The Double-crested is the primary cormorant of inland locations and the only cormorant which prefers fresh water.

DOUBLE-CRESTED CORMORANT

It is a large bird weighing 3.7 pounds, wing span of 52 inches and a length of 33 inches. The female is larger than the male and the sexes look alike. The Double-crested is an all black reptilian looking bird. They spend most of their time sitting on piers or tree branches that will support their weight with heads drawn back, bill angled up, tail down, looking much like a snake ready to strike. The bill is thin yellowish orange at the base and hooked at the tip, giving an overall sinister look to the bird. Adults are iridescent black and immatures are gray-brown on the neck and upper body and black below. The name "double-crested" comes from shaggy feathered horns on the head that are difficult to see and are only present during breeding.

They are a colonial breeder and nest in groups of 100 or more. Their nest is a stick nest on the ground, usually close to the water. When you approach a nest site you can hear course bullfrog like grunts, otherwise they are silent. At Warm Springs WMA in the AR Pond 1 Complex there are about 65 breeding pairs most summers. They appear in Western Montana in late March and a few individuals linger into October before they all leave. I have seen them as late at September 25 in the Upper Clark Fork Valley. They winter on the Pacific Coast and Southeastern States. The peak number for the Upper Clark Valley is around 160 between adults and juveniles in early August.

DOUBLE-CRESTED CORMORANT

Double-crested do a lot of sitting on branches when not diving for fish. When in the water they sit low and often submerged with only the neck and head exposed with the head angled upward. When they emerge from the water they often spread their wings to dry as they have no waterproof oil in their feathers. They can hold this spread-winged appearance for a long time.

They are one of Montana's more unique water dependent species. ♦

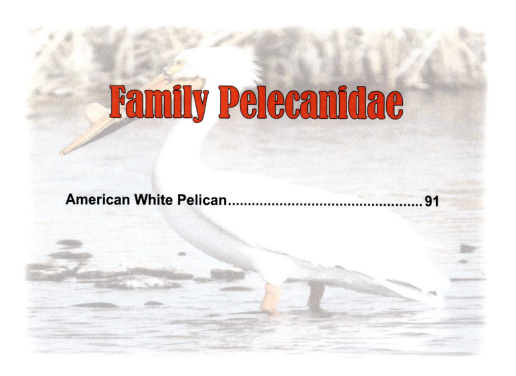

Family Pelecanidae

American White Pelican 91

American White Pelican *Pelecanus erythrorhynchos*

AMERICAN WHITE PELICAN

Everyone knows what pelicans look like. They are a large white bird with black trailing edges on the wings that are seen in flight with a large yellow orange bill that angles down when perched or swimming.

What else is there to know about them? Large is an understatement. They average 16.4 pounds. Wild Turkeys only average 9.2 pounds for females and 16.2 pounds for males. They have a 9½ foot wingspan. Golden Eagles are large, but their wingspan is only seven feet. You might think they would have trouble flying but a 9½ foot wingspan allows them to be agile in flight. Wing beats are slow, with several beats, followed by a long glide that seems to defy gravity. They typically fly in flocks often forming a 'V'. Breeding adults show a fibrous knob on the bill.

I can remember the first American White pelicans I saw in our valley. It was in August of 2006 along the Clark Fork River North of Deer Lodge. That year there was a dispersal of American

AMERICAN WHITE PELICAN

American White Pelican — *Pelecanus erythrorhynchos*

AMERICAN WHITE PELICAN

White Pelican populations in North Dakota and along the Missouri River. They have been present locally every year since. My records show from 15 to 50 individuals typically show in mid to late May and stay through late August to early September.

American White Pelicans are now distributed across much of the state. In most locations they are transient and breed in only four areas of Montana. These are Medicine Lake in Northeast Montana, Canyon Ferry Reservoir near Townsend, Arod Lake 15 miles northeast of Choteau, and Bowdoin National Wildlife Refuge at Malta. Fall migration finds the species along the Gulf States and southern Mexico.

American White Pelicans roost, feed and migrate in flocks. At Warm Springs WMA I see them roosting in crowded groups on islands with Double-crested Cormorants and gulls. Feeding birds sit high in the water and swim in a straight line to concentrate fish. When fish are concentrated they dip their bills, raise their heads and allow water to drain from their gular pouch then swallow their catch whole. In the Upper Clark Fork Drainage they typically feed either on the Clark Fork River or in the ponds at Warm Springs WMA.

BROWN PELICAN

A second pelican, the Brown, also occurs in North America along our coastal shores. Records exist for Brown Pelicans in Idaho, Wyoming, North and South Dakota. Perhaps in the future the Brown Pelican will be recorded in Montana. Browns are distinguished by smaller size, 8.2 pounds, and grayish brown color. The bill is dark rather than yellow. There is no knob in breeding adults.

Hopefully you will have the opportunity to see these graceful fliers soar overhead in the summer. ♦

Family Ardeidae

Great Blue Heron 93
Cattle Egret 95
Black-Crowned Night-Heron... 96

Great Blue Heron   *Ardea herodias*

GREAT BLUE HERON

The term shorebird is often used to describe the large group of moderately long legged birds that feed along pond edges and out into eight to ten inches of water.

There is another group of birds that occupy shorelines, lakes and rivers that have longer legs and necks than shorebirds and are collectively called waders. This group is made up of egrets, herons, bitterns, night-herons, storks, ibis, spoonbills and flamingos. Fortunately, this group is much easier to identify individuals to a species and there are only 20 species in North America in four families. Montana has 12 of these wader species. Worldwide there are 122 species in six families. Again, I have been fortunate to have seen 56 waders worldwide.

GREAT BLUE HERON

The two waders that are found consistently in the Upper Clark Fork Basin are the Black-crowned Night-Heron and the Great Blue Heron. Since 2003 the Great Egret has been seen four times in the Upper Clark Fork Basin with the latest on May 9, 2019. Total records in Montana are 101 observations. The White-faced Ibis is a yearly migrant in both spring and fall in the basin but sightings are uncommon. There is also a single record of an American Bittern sighting in the Upper Clark Fork Basin but I have not seen one locally. Least Bittern, Snowy Egret, Little Blue Heron, Green Heron, Yellow-crowned Night-Heron, Cattle Egret and Glossy Ibis have been seen in other parts of the state but the number of sightings range from three for the Yellow-crowned Night-Heron to 83 for Snowy Egret.

GREAT BLUE HERON

Great Blue Herons are familiar to most folks and are a 46 inch, large gray bird that is heavy bodied with a long lighter gray shaggy neck. In flight the neck is always curved back and appears to rest on the body. In flight the upper wing is two-toned gray. The bill is heavy and yellow. The upper thigh shows a rufous color near the body.

Adult sexes are similar with black plumes coming off the head that shows a white crown. Juveniles lack the plumes, have a dark crown and the neck is less shaggy and more the color of the body. Great Blues are found and breed statewide and there are numerous records of individuals overwintering in open water areas statewide.

Great Blues are colonial nesters and typically have a rookery high in cottonwood trees. However, the Great Blue Herons at the Warm Springs WMA nest in dead willows at water level in several of the smaller ponds which is unique for the species. In either location nests are safe from predators. They are a *Species of Concern* as the number of rookeries is slowly declining with an estimated 101 scattered across Montana. ♦

CATTLE EGRET

Fall is the time that you often get out-of-range and rare birds in Montana. One of the reasons for this is as bird migrate south out of Alaska, the Yukon and Northern Canada they can drift either east or west due to storms and prevailing winds. The second reason especially in late fall is that many of the migrants are juveniles and have not migrated south before. They are doing it by genetic instincts and can make mistakes in finding wintering grounds.

In the case of the two Cattle Egret seen in the Helena Valley for more than a week in October, 2018. I'm not sure where they flew in from. In Fall Cattle Egret are known to wander far north of their breeding grounds and this is apparently what happened. These two egrets were found in a pasture with cattle (of course) near Lake Helena on Merrit Lane. Spring and fall migration records have documented them along the Canadian border but only as accidental birds.

CATTLE EGRET

Cattle Egrets first migrated to South America from Africa then spread to Florida in the early 1950s and reached California by the mid-1960s. Today Cattle Egrets are year around residents of Mexico and the lower portions of Southern Tier States. They breed as far north as Southern Idaho, Utah and Colorado.

Cattle Egrets have only been observed in Montana 50 times. These sightings are from scattered sites across the state with no more than six sightings in any one year. Most sightings are from September through November.

CATTLE EGRET - BREEDING PLUMAGE

Cattle Egrets are easy to identify. They are obviously an egret, all white in their non-breeding plumage, a yellow bill and black legs and feet. One unique feature of this species is the white feathers that extend onto the lower mandible. My picture of the egret standing in the field shows this trait. The egret picture in flight shows the black feet and legs

Breeding adults, look somewhat different with reddish-buff on the head, back and breast, as well as a red rather than yellow bill.

As the name implies this egret associates closely with cattle. On birding trips I have taken to Africa I have seen them with herds of grazing ungulates and even

Cattle Egret *Bubulcus ibis*

zebra. They stand with their neck lowered and can quickly catch prey. It is thought that they co-exist with ungulates because their grazing stirs up insects and small rodents that egrets then feed on. While taking these photographs we watched one of the pair catch a field mouse and swallow it whole.

I would never have known this species was in the Helena Valley without the birding resource *(See page 17)* eBird. If you are really interested in seeing rare birds check out eBird.org on the web or download the free App for your smart phone. Be sure and click on the option "rare bird reports". eBird will then provide you with daily details about the sightings and a map indicating the exact location of the bird. ♦

CATTLE EGRET

Black-crowned Night-Heron *Nycticorax nycticorax*

BLACK-CROWED NIGHT-HERON

One of the main reasons people watch birds is that birds are watchable wildlife. If you get out into nature you are bound to see a bird or two. After awhile you realize that you need to keep a list of the birds you see so that you know when you see a "life bird" or a new bird in a specific area. In 2007 I had the privilege of documenting a new record for the Upper Clark Fork Valley.

There are 442 species of birds in Montana as of 2021. One hundred and one of these have been seen less than 20 times. Most serious birders have seen between 250 and 300 species in Montana. Currently according to eBird there are 49 birders who have seen more than 300 species in Montana. The most anyone has seen according to eBird is 378 species as of 2021. I am tied with one other birder for that position. I also hold the state record for the most species seen in a single year, 328 species in 2007. Birding takes on a new level of interest with friendly listing competitions and finding new state records.

BLACK-CROWNED NIGHT-HERON

The new record that I found was

a breeding pair of Black-crowned Night-Heron at the Warm Springs WMA in July of 2007. I found a single Black-crowned Night Heron at Warm Springs. I did not see another one until 2009. Then in 2010 I had numerous sightings and saw a juvenile in the fall but could not prove it was reared at Warm Springs.

Black-crowns are a 1.9 pound, stocky, hunched backed, large-headed, short-necked marsh wader. They also have a thick bill, red eye and short yellow legs. The back and cap are black

BLACK-CROWNED NIGHT-HERON

contrasting with whitish under-parts. They are a colonial roosting species and are inactive in the day time flying at dusk to feed. Their call is a loud quark or quok.

In 2012 I found a nesting pair. That nest was later abandoned and re-established about 100 yards away. Two chicks were successfully raised in the second nest. I continue to observe nest building and juvenile birds at Warm Springs WMA through 2021. These sightings represent the third record of

BLACK-CROWNED NIGHT-HERON

breeding Black-crowned Night-Herons in Western Montana. The others were in 1992 and 1994 at Lee Metcalf WMA near Corvallis. Black-crowns are more common in Eastern Montana and breed at Benton Lake, Bowdoin and Medicine Lake National Wildlife Refuges.

You can occasionally see this species from the Eastside Road with a spotting scope in the aquatic vegetation in WS WMA AR East Pond. If you find it you can add this species to your Deer Lodge County list. ♦

BLACK-CROWNED NIGHT-HERON

Family Threskiornithidae

White-faced Ibis 98

White-faced Ibis *Plegadis chihi*

WHITE-FACED IBIS

The White-faced Ibis has always been a fascinating bird to me. I remember the first time I saw one at Red Rocks Lake near Lima, Montana. The bird does not look like a species that you would find here in Montana, more like a species of the Everglades.

The species is a *Species of Concern* in Montana, meaning it is at risk due to declining populations because of threats to habitat or restricted distribution. The distribution of the White-faced Ibis is limited in Montana but has occurred over most of the state. Breeding records have been confirmed in only nine areas of the state with six of those areas being historic rather than recent. The remaining sightings are spring and fall migrants.

WHITE-FACED IBIS

In our valley I see them yearly in spring and fall in small groups of from two to twelve. My grandson documented 40 several times at Warm Springs WMA in recent years. They do not breed locally. They occur in a variety of places throughout the valley but mostly at Warm Springs WMA, Deer Lodge City Lagoon and various wet hay meadows.

The number of sightings recorded in Montana is not large. The *Montana Natural Heritage Program* only shows 502 records.

There are four species of Ibis in North America with two species the White-faced and Glossy occurring in Montana. The White and Scarlet are Eastern species with the Scarlet restricted to Southern Florida. The Glossy is rare in Montana with 10 recorded.

WHITE-FACED IBIS

Ibis are heron like birds, with long legs, and long slender down curved bills. The two Montana species are superficially alike and could be easily confused. Breeding adults of both species are chestnut colored with bronze tones. White-faced Ibis have long red legs, reddish eye and white-feathered border around red facial skin. Glossy Ibis have gray-green legs with red joints, dark eyes and less white on the face.

Juveniles of these two species are difficult to distinguish. Both have dark eyes and yellow-grey legs. White-faced Ibis juveniles have a paler chest but this would be hard to distinguish without both species together, which rarely happens.

Ibis forage in small groups walking slowly with heads down probing the mud with their bills. They roost and nest in trees close to their feeding mudflats.

Typically White-faced Ibis have left Montana for warm weather in Mexico by the end of September. In the Fall of 2013 I noticed two White-faced Ibis juveniles on October 11 at the West River Road Pond South of Deer Lodge and thought the date was late for fall departure. Upon doing some research I found that the latest departure date for this species was October 16. I continued watching daily and two days later a third juvenile showed!

WHITE-FACED IBIS

They continued to feed at the pond until October 26. It appears that they only departed on that day as a winter storm hit the next morning, bringing freezing temperatures and snow. Evidently they sensed the change in the weather and departed. The picture on this page was taken October 19, 2013.

Birds of Montana published in 2016 by Jeff Marks, Paul Hendricks and Dan Casey on the status, distribution and historical aspect of the then 429 Montana species had this to say about my October 26 observation, "The earliest recent sighting was by Sharon Browder of three migrants at Lee Metcalf NWR on 11 Apr 2000 and the latest was by Gary Swant of three juveniles at West River Pond near Racetrack on 26 Oct 2013. The latter birds were first seen on 11 Oct."

WHITE-FACED IBIS

This is the wonderful thing about birding. It's enjoyable, gets you outdoors, and provides opportunity for great photographs. More than most hobbies, it allows you to be citizen scientist providing important scientific data on the status, and distribution of birds. Much of what is known about birds comes from field notes from professional ornithologist and avid birders.

I can't think of another hobby with so many positives! Of course, I'm not looking either; I'm too busy watching birds. I hope you are as well. ♦

BIRDING IN THE PRIBILOF ISLANDS OF ALASKA

Family Cathartidae

Black Vulture... 101
Turkey Vulture... 104

Black Vulture *Coragyps atratus*

BLACK VULTURE

It's October and Halloween is coming. What do you think about at the mention of Halloween? Witches, goblins, big blackbirds, black cats? How about Vultures? That's what I think about when you mention Halloween. I must confess that almost anything you mention reminds me of a bird. I have even been accused of being a "bird brain" or at least birds are on my mind most of the time. You would love to ride with me to Spokane. I would tell you about all the birds I've seen along the way at this place and that place. And if that is not enough, I might even tell about all of the other birds in the genus of the bird I was just telling you about found in Montana.

So why does Halloween make me think of vultures and not cranes? First of all they have naked heads, no feath-

BLACK VULTURE

101

ers and that's pretty scary. Secondly, they thrust those naked heads into dead carcasses to extract large pieces of bloody and perhaps smelly rotten flesh. Most of the time there are several vultures on a carcass and they fight and peck at each other as well. I have seen vultures that are covered with ghoulish blood jumping excitedly as they tear flesh from bones. Sounds like a scary Halloween story to me!

There are 22 species of vultures in the world, seven in the New World (North, Central and South America), and 15 in the Old World (Europe and Africa). Some are huge and others are small. In North America there are only three: California Condor, Black and Turkey Vulture.

CALIFORNIA CONDOR

The condor is huge, weighing in at 23 pounds and has a length of 46 inches and wingspan of 109 inches. That's nine feet! The Black Vulture is next with a weight of 4.4 pounds, length 25 inches and a wingspan of 59 inches. The Turkey is the light weight at four pounds, length of 26 inches and a wingspan of 67 inches.

So how do you tell these three vultures apart in Montana. It's fairly easy. There are no California Condors in Montana but there may have been in the past. Lewis and Clark saw them in Washington and Idaho. If there was a good birder in Montana back then they might have found one along the Clark Fork Drainage. Of course there was no Montana then, and besides, a lot of Native Americans who knew their birds well never spoke of an orange-headed vulture.

Just in case a condor wanders into Montana here is what to look for in the adult. They're huge, in fact they are our largest North American raptor. They have a large naked orange head. The orange extends down the bill which ends in a yellow tip. The legs are grayish-white and in a side profile there is a white line separating the black body from the dark gray wings that extend to the end of the short tail. In flight there are large white patches on the underwing. In 1982 there were only 22 surviving in the wild. They were all captured and a captive breeding program began. The first releases were in 1991 and today there are 400 wild condors in California and the Grand Canyon area.

I could have said there were no Black Vultures in Montana as well, but two local birders in the Chouteau area found a single Black Vulture in a roost with ten Turkey Vultures. Black Vultures have an all-black body with a naked, wrinkled gray head and gray legs. The tail is short and barely extends beyond the wings when perched.

The Turkey Vulture has a red naked head with whitish legs and brownish-black body. The tail is long and extends beyond the wings when perched. Juveniles have gray heads so look to the tail for identification.

Turkey Vultures are common in Montana with over 2,313 observations with the *Montana Natural Heritage Program*. In fact, in the Upper Clark Fork Drainage they have become more common each year. There were several roost sites in Deer Lodge this past summer in which 10-12 individuals spent the night. They have been known to breed in the Philipsburg area on rocky cliffs.

So how do you find a vulture locally? The best way to find one is to go out in a short grass field and lay down and play dead. It even works better if you can find some rotten meat and rub it into your clothing. Vultures have the most sensitive "sense of smell" of any raptor in Montana. Just kidding! Look to the sky, they spend a lot of time soaring. Adult Turkey Vultures show silvery flight feathers and a black leading edge to the underwing. Black Vultures have silvery tips to the wings.

This Halloween don't worry about a Vulture circling you as a possible meal they migrate south by the end of September and early October.

BLACK VULTURE

Have a great Halloween and think about the birds, especially vultures, as you knock on doors looking for a handout. I guess that's acting a little like a vulture! ♦

BIRDING ON HARRISON LAKE

TURKEY VULTURE

It took me a long time to find a Turkey Vulture in the Upper Clark Fork Valley. Once I found one I saw them frequently and continue to do so. The fact is I was seeing them all along, I just wasn't identifying them. They look and act like other birds of prey until you know their field marks.

TURKEY VULTURE

I have seen up to 20 roosting in one tree along the Clark Fork River. Ranchers who calf late in the spring often have Turkey Vultures in competition with eagles for afterbirth in calving fields.

There is a second vulture in North America the Black, but it is only found in the southeast and as far west as central Texas and Mexico. Occasionally I get a call from someone in the valley claiming to have seen a Black Vulture. The confusion comes by not separating adults from juvenile Turkey Vultures. However in June of 2018 a Black Vulture was found in Choteau with a group of Turkey Vultures and I was fortunate to be able to see it. It is the only record for the state of Montana.

Adult Turkey Vultures are unmistakable with their all dark brown, not black, body and featherless red head. In flight the small bare head with yellow beak shows well. The upper body in flight is all brown, but beneath, silvery flight feathers contrast with the dark body and leading edge of the wings forming a two tone underwing. Their flight is diagnostic. When they soar wings are held in a pronounced dihedral. (Wings held in "V".) The wing beat is slow and the body moves up and down with each beat giving an unsteady rocking flight. The long tail shows the silver color of the flight feathers. Juveniles show a dark bare face rather than red, thus the confusion with an adult Black Vulture.

The Turkey Vultures are communal roosters and carrion-feeders. They find food by smell. They appear hump-backed and clumsy on the ground and often waddle, hop and run near carrion to scare away competition. The naked head appears to be an adaptation to feeding by sticking their heads into decaying tissue. A feathered head would be matted and stained with decaying flesh.

Turkey Vultures arrive in the Upper Clark Fork Valley in April/May and migrate south in August/September. The *Montana Natural Heritage Program* shows that all of Granite County and Southern Powell County are areas that have breeding records for this species. I have yet to find a nest for this species locally. I have found a nest in South Jefferson County on Milligan Canyon Road.

Next summer carefully look at soaring raptures for a Turkey Vulture. ♦

Family Pandionidae

Osprey 105

Osprey   *Pandion haliaetus*

OSPREY

The Osprey is a common bird along the Clark Fork River and most of Western Montana's major rivers. Many nests are found on man made platform stands of which there are a number from Missoula to Warm Springs and up the Bitterroot.

Ospreys are successful breeders along the Clark Fork River raising two to four chicks each year. The greatest threat to chick survival is Great Horned Owl predation. The other threat is plastic baling twine. Ospreys seem to have infinity for the stuff and nests are often lined with orange twine or have it hanging from the nest. I have observed Ospreys entangled in twine hanging upside down from the nest. Unless they are cut free quickly they die. Estimates are that annual deaths rate due to twine is ten percent of the population. Several studies have shown that bailing twine that is tan or natural colored is less attractive to Osprey. Ranchers using plastic twine in fields near nest and rivers should be more conscientious in not leaving twine

OSPREY

in fields. Both of these solutions are simple and doable and will go a long ways in increasing survival rates.

Ospreys arrive in Western Montana in early to mid-April after streams, lakes and ponds are ice free. They migrate south to coastal waters from Florida west to Texas and southern California by mid-October.

OSPREY

Osprey are a blackish-brown and white raptor with a 63 inch wingspan and weigh 3.5 lbs. They are most often seen perched on snags near water or sitting on their stick nest incubating eggs or feeding chicks. The smallish head appears white except for a brown mask from the neck through the yellow eyes. The bill is distinctly down turned. The belly and chest are bright white which is better seen in flight than when perched. In flight they seem headless with crooked wings that flap with slow, shallow, stiff beats. The contrast of the dark upper body and white below is distinctive.

When fishing they circle and hover over open water then plunge dive at an angle often submerging their entire body. Prey fish can be surprisingly large and are carried headfirst to a perch for feeding. This is in contrast to Bald Eagles that merely pluck fish from the surface of the water and do not orientate the fish's head forward. The pictured Osprey dove into a shallow pond and immediately perched on a fence post to feed. Unlike Bald Eagles, Ospreys rarely eat carrion.

Most Osprey nests are very accessible but one should avoid approaching too closely. They are wary when incubating and flush easily, circling the nest with loud *"pew pew pew"* calls. I have not heard of a nest being abandoned

OSPREY

because of the presence of humans but additional stress during incubation and chick rearing should be avoided

As you drive along rivers of Western Montana from April through September look for Osprey nests and observe their activities from a distance. Enjoy! ♦

Family Accipitridae

Sharp-shinned Hawk 107
Northern Goshawk 109
Bald Eagle 110
Red Tailed Hawk 113
Rough-legged Hawk 114
Harris's Hawk 115

Sharp-shinned Hawk   *Accipiter striatus*

SHARP-SHINNED HAWK

Winter is a productive time to feed birds in the Upper Clark Fork River Basin. Black oil sunflower seeds work the best. Scatter seed on the ground for ground feeding species increases the number of species that you will attract. Some species are hesitant to use a feeder. Avoid millet, it tends to draw House Sparrows which often drive other species away. Augment with a suet feeder to provide a high energy source.

Species you can expect to see in our area are House Finch, American Gold Finch, American Tree Sparrow, Northern Flicker, Downy Woodpecker, Eurasian-collared Dove, Black-billed Magpie, Black-capped and Mountain Chickadee. Of course there will always be that surprise species you did not expect.

ADULT SHARP-SHINNED HAWK

We have had another frequent species at our feeder recently, the Sharp-shinned Hawk. "Sharpies" are a specialist at eating small birds often frequenting backyard feeders in winter months. Sharpies are swift flyers and will aggressively attack feeder birds. The other day while we were enjoying lunch so was a Sharpie. A juvenile had caught a male House Sparrow and sat within 20 feet of our window plucking feathers and enjoying breast meat. We have given our feeder birds a fighting chance by providing a stick/brush pile about three feet tall close to the feeders which they can dive into and wait out the Sharpie. We have observed Sharpies work for many minutes trying to get a small bird from our brush pile, usually unsuccessfully. We have also set the feeders close to a dense hedge.

JUVENILE SHARP-SHINNED HAWK

Sharp-shinned Hawks are an accipiter which means they have rounded wings adapted for hunting among trees at fast speeds. The other two Montana acceptors are Cooper's Hawk and Northern Goshawk. Superficially Sharpies look similar to Cooper's Hawk but smaller. Sharpies are 10-14 inches in length and Cooper's are 14 -20. However, females are larger than males and female Sharpies can overlap in size with male Cooper's.

Sharpies are slim with a long square-tipped barred tail and small head. Adults have dark blue-gray backs, rusty-barred breast and red-orange eyes in females and red in males. Immatures are brown above with a thickly streaked rusty brown chest and belly. Juveniles have a yellow eye rather than a red eye.

If you feed birds in the winter you most likely will encounter a Sharpie in your yard. Don't despair over the loss of a feeder bird. You are feeding an accipiter and watching the energy pyramid at work in the avian world. ♦

NORTHERN GOSHAWK

I have been asked on occasion how I choose which bird to write about month to month. I do make an effort to write articles that are seasonal in nature. In the winter I tend to write about birds that overwinter in the Upper Clark Fork Valley, in the spring about migrants, in the summer about those that breed locally and in the fall migrants that are rare such as the Pacific Loon.

NORTHERN GOSHAWK

To be honest, it also depends on what quality photographs I have on hand. In this chapter I am writing about the Northern Goshawk because I was fortunate on December 4 , 2005 to find a very cooperative Northern Goshawk that I was able to photograph at about 20 yards. Not only are they typically not easy to find in our valley, but they are always out in a field somewhere on a branch of a tree 100 yards from the road. Most of the time when you stop to take a look through your binoculars or scope they lift off and fly out of sight. I hope that you enjoy this picture because I will probably never get the opportunity to photograph this outstanding raptor in all of the right conditions again. Even the sun was in the right position as well as clear skies in the background.

The Northern Goshawk is one of 22 "Birds of Prey" in Montana. This list includes: Turkey Vulture, Osprey, 2 Kites, 2 Eagles, 10 hawks and 5 falcons. In North America the list of "Birds of Prey" expands to 33 species.

The Northern Goshawk is rare in its Northern Tier Range. They are year around residents from Alaska south along the Pacific Coast to Northern California and south along the Continental Divide to Arizona and New Mexico. They are also year around residents east to the Atlantic Coast in Canada. In Montana they are year around residents and breed in Western Montana. Northern breeding residents winter in Eastern Montana and the Dakotas.

According to records with the *Montana Natural Heritage Program* the Northern Goshawk was observed 2,983 times in Montana. In the same period the common Red-tailed Hawk was reported being seen 92,993 times. The Northern Goshawk is listed as a *Species of Concern* (SOC) in Montana. SOC species are ones who are declining in number, declining habitat, or appear to be in need of concentrated conservation actions.

The Goshawk is one of three species in the genus Accipiter. Accipiters are characterized by relatively short rounded wings and long tails. They include the Sharp-shinned and Cooper's Hawks as well as the Northern Goshawk. All three are bird-eating predators of backyard feeders and woodlands.

The Northern Goshawk is large compared to the other two at 2.1 pounds compared to the five ounces for the Sharp-shinned and one pound for the Cooper's. The plumage is distinctive. The back and wings are gray with a black band through the red eye and a black cap. The supercilium or band above the eye is white. The bill is yellow with a black tip. The throat, chest and belly are white with fine gray barring. The female is larger than the male with courser barring on the belly.

The juvenile is brown with a speckled back and vertical buffy streaking on the chest and belly. The eye is yellow and the supercilium is white, but not as pronounced as in adults.

This may have been a "once in a lifetime" opportunity for a great photograph of this species. Amazingly, these rare opportunities do come along if you bird a lot. So get out there and see what you can find. ♦

Bald Eagle   *Haliaeetus leucocephalus*

BALD EAGLE

The other day while having coffee at one of our local restaurants it was suggested that I do an article on the Bald Eagle. This was an excellent suggestion as they are common locally and I know of several nest sites in the Upper Clark Fork Drainage.

The Bald Eagle is a recovery success story. In precolonial times it is estimated that the lower 48 state region contained 50,000 breeding pairs. By 1960 the population had plummeted to less than 400 pair nationwide! It is estimated there is about 4,000 breeding pair in the lower 48 states today, mostly in the Pacific Northwest.

In the early part of the twenty century much of the decline was due to habitat loss, shooting and trapping. Post World War II most of the decline was due to the use of pesticides, especially DDT. The DDT accumulated in fish, the major source of food for

ADULT BALD EAGLE

Bald Eagles, resulting in disruption of calcium metabolism producing thin eggshells. This thinning resulted in egg shells that broke or cracked during incubation. Shooting, trapping and poisoning is now illegal and DDT is banned in the United States. Good riparian habitat with mature cottonwood trees is still a concern as well as electrocution while perched on power lines.

Recovery in Montana has been astounding. In 1978 there were only 12 known breeding pairs. In 1994 the *Montana Bald Eagle Management Plan* was established and a goal was set of 345 breeding pairs by 2033. The goal was reached 25 years early in 2006. In 2007 the Bald Eagle was removed from the federal list of *Threatened and Endangered Species*, and the state ranking is currently vulnerable or special status species. Surveys in 2010 indicated there are nearly 550 breeding pairs statewide. The population appears to be growing at about ten percent per year. Montana is estimated to contain 15% of the total Bald Eagle pairs in the lower 48 states.

ADULT BALD EAGLE

The most densely populated area in the state for Bald Eagles is the Upper Columbia Basin. The Clark Fork River is the headwaters for the basin and includes the Flathead and Bitterroot Rivers. Two hundred and twenty-one pair were recorded in 2008 in the basin. That is 40% of the state's population.

There are three active breeding territories near my home on the Upper Clark Fork River. The most visible nest is four miles south of Deer Lodge where the Clark Fork River comes closest to the interstate. The nest is located in a mature cottonwood. The Bald Eagle photos with this article was taken at that location. The second nest is on the Eastside Road at AR Pond 2 in the Warm Springs Wildlife Management Area. That nest successfully fledges two and sometimes three offspring yearly. The third is found north of Deer Lodge at the cities' sewage treatment plant along the Clark Fork River.

JUVENILE BALD EAGLE

In the winter months Bald Eagles increase on all major rivers with overwintering birds from more northerly environments seeking rivers that remain open. Little Blackfoot River between Elliston and Garrison has a amazing number of overwinter eagles. I contribute this to fact that the Little Blackfoot does not have historical mining contaminates that have for so long plagued fish on the Clark Fork.

Bald Eagles reach maturity at five years of age and have a white head and tail contrasting with a dark brown body and wings. The bill, cere, legs and feet are yellow. Sexes are similar with females 25% larger than males. They are not easily confused with other raptures. Immature birds can be confused with Golden Eagles. Second and third year birds show more white in the underwing and belly than Golden Eagles. The legs of the Bald are featherless while those of the Golden Eagle are feathered. First year juveniles are very dark with little white. The pure white head develops in the fourth year of life.

ADULT BALD EAGLE

Bald Eagles should continue to flourish as long as proper protection and habitats are maintained. The greatest threat is loss of mature Cottonwood trees along rivers for nesting. Nest trees must be maintained and replaced with new trees over time. Current stream flow management does not encourage regrowth of cottonwoods. Rivers that minimize high spring run off fail to stimulate regeneration of cottonwoods. Nesting sites must have minimal human disturbance, thus we should avoid development near known nesting sites. Some researches also feel that wind turbine energy projects are a threat. Certainly these projects should not be located along streams, lakes or known migratory corridors. Lead poisoning is also a problem from fish that have ingested lead weights or from feeding on animals, especially gophers and bird carcasses killed with lead shot and bullets. Lead poisoning leads to nervous system problems, resulting in poor flight, increasing collisions with vehicles and power lines. Non-toxic fish weights, shot and bullets are available. We are privileged to live in the highest density area in the state of Montana for Bald Eagles. Take the time to view a nest next spring, at a distance, and enjoy our national symbol. ♦

ADULT BALD EAGLE

RED-TAILED HAWK

Raptors are birds of prey that soar for long distances in search of food. Similar body shaped raptors tend to hunt the same habitats for the same prey species. Most raptors prey on rodents but their diet can include snakes and birds. Large birds of prey, such as Golden Eagles, can take fawns and other new born ungulates.

The genus Buteos contains the hawks of North America with nine species. Buteos can be difficult to identify as there are extensive variations in plumage and body shape within each species.

Of the nine Buteos in North America six occur in Montana and five in the Upper Clark Fork Valley. These include the Broad-winged, Swainson's, Red-tailed, Rough-legged and Ferruginous Hawks.

This article is on our most common Montana raptor the Red-tailed Hawk. Red-tails are conspicuous perch-hunters that prefer to sit in the open on high sturdy perches such as power poles, billboards and fence posts.

RED-TAILED HAWK

They never perch on power lines or small trees that wave in the wind like Rough-legs do. Nor do they sit on the ground to observe prey like Ferruginous Hawks. Red-taileds can sit for long periods of time on the same perch day after day as long as prey species are abundant in an area.

In our valley Red-tails are easier to observe in winter months as they gather on power poles along alfalfa and hay fields in the valley floor where there are abundant rodents. Winter also brings migrants from Canada and Alaska. In summer months they are less visible and are dispersed throughout the valley and higher elevation forests containing meadows. A good place to observe Red-taileds in the winter where I live is along Eastside Road between Racetrack and Warm Springs or any of the roads west of Interstate 90 along roads near hay fields.

RED-TAILED HAWK

Red-taileds can be difficult to identify as juvenile plumages are different than adults and there are light, intermediate and dark plumages or morphs. In general, juveniles appear lankier and longer tailed than adults and do not show a red tail. Adults are stocky, short-tailed, dark-headed and rusty-tailed. The tail can vary from light rose to dark rust depending on the plumage. In light and intermediate plumages there is often a dark belly band on a white breast. The belly band is not visible on dark adults as the bird is entirely dark except for the rust-red tail. In flight a consistent field mark in all plumages are dark leading-edge wing feathers.

Vocalization is most often heard in the summer when you approach a nest site. Red-taileds are very protective of their nest and when you are as close as a half mile away they will fly over you with a loud shrill, raspy, descending two-noted "rEE-ehhhr". This is an extended call that will last until you leave the nest area.

Red-taileds also show regional variation in plumage and have been given names such as Krider's and Harlan's Red-taileds to denote regional subspecies.

I have seen light, intermediate and dark adults and juveniles in Western Montana. In my experience dark morphs make up ten to fifteen percent of our local population.

The pictured Red-tailed is a light-morph adult. Note the dark head and belly band. Unfortunately the rust tail is hidden behind the perch branch.

Get a good field guide like Sibley, Stokes or National Geographic that show all of the color morphs. Go out this winter and see how many morphs you can find. I will probably be out there somewhere watching as well. ♦

ROUGH-LEGGED HAWK

The Upper Clark Fork Valley affords the opportunity to view two birds of prey that are not found in the summer months. One is rare, the Gyrfalcon and only seen occasionally. I observed my first Gyrfalcon locally in 2002 and have observed the species 17 times since. My last sighting was January 1, 2020 during the Warm Springs Christmas Bird Count. From 2002 - 2007 a Gyrfalcon wintered in our southern valley. We suspect it was the same individual for five winters.

ROUGH-LEGGED HAWK

The more common winter resident is the Rough-legged Hawk. They typically appear in late October to early November and stay until late February into early March. They are numerous in Western Montana and it is not uncommon to observe 15 to 30 on a typical winter day. They are most often seen when snow is on the ground and they are forced out of the foothills to feed in hay meadows. I typically observe them on fences and power poles near hay and alfalfa fields between

Rough-legged Hawk   *Buteo lagopus*

Warm Springs and Racetrack. However, they can be perched anywhere along the interstate between Butte and Missoula.

Ten birds of prey breed in Montana, two breed in the arctic, and twelve live here year around. The Rough-legged Hawk is found here only in the winter. They feed in agricultural fields on abundant voles, mice and shrews. I have seen more than forty in a single outing along the Eastside Road from Deer Lodge to Warm Springs.

My earliest sighting of a "Rough-leg" is October 27 and the latest I have seen one is March 23. In the fall numbers continue to climb into late November and then level off. They typically sit on power poles and allow for close views or soar above meadows on wings held in a dihedral. Spring migration north begins in March. Males and juveniles tend to Winter further south than Montana so most birds you see locally will be females. This is explained by the fact that the female is 20 percent larger than the male and can withstand the colder temperatures.

Admittedly, hawks can be difficult to identify but with practice they are easily sorted out. In flight large black carpal patches at the "wrist" on the underside of the wing are a good field mark for Rough-legs. From above the white base of the tail is conspicuous. Males have 3-4 light bands on their dark tail and females have a single dark terminal band. From a distance they are identified by their long wings.

When perched Rough-legs show a whitish or pale head, variable chest streaking and a dark belly. Their legs are feathered and the bill and feet are small. Both light and dark morphs exist so it's a good idea to use a field guide. My picture shows a light morph adult female.

Take a drive along dirt roads in agriculture hay lands. The Big Hole Valley is famous for wintering Rough-legs. ♦

Harris's Hawk   *Parabuteo unicinctus*

HARRIS'S HAWK

In every state there is a great deal of effort made to keep track of bird species and their distribution. Montana's effort was originally spear-headed by Dr. David Skarr of Montana State University. He published the *1st edition of Montana Bird Distribution* (MBD) in 1975 with 357 species. By the time I started birding seriously in the mid 1980s the 3rd edition (1985) had 381 species. The 6th edition (2003) listed 411 species and the 7th edition (2012) listed 427 species. Currently, there are 442 species (2022)

HARRIS'S HAWK

Are bird species increasing in Montana or are there just more birders in the field making observations? I suspect both. As the climate warms southern species are migrating north and spring arrival for many species is earlier. I added seven species to my Montana list this year and five of the seven were southern species with few Montana records.

Observations are also increasing. The 3rd edition of MBD contained 4,000 more observations than the 2nd edition. By 1992 the MBD was based on 25,000 observations. By the 2003 an additional 39,000 observations were added. The 7th edition in 2012 contains 800,000 observations! The 7th edition included four birders (including myself) who had submitted more than 10,000 records each. Of the 442 current species 103 are rare and been seen less than 20 times.

In October, 2012 a Harris's Hawk was observed in Flathead County. This was a first for Montana. When the observation came across the Internet I immediately went to see it.

This hawk is fairly easy to identify. It is overall dark brown with rufous shoulders and white base and tail tip. Legs are long, yellow and the posture is erect.

Thus, we have a new Montana state species, or do we? Montana has a Montana Bird Records Committee (MRBC) made up of 13 birders who are responsible for the Montana state list. Each rare bird report is rigorously studied. To be included the bird must have come here on its own accord or be an established breeder after introduction. Most rare birds are blown in by a storm or are fall migrating juveniles who get off course.

The problem with including this adult Harris's Hawk is its home territory is Southern Texas, Arizona and Mexico and it tends to be a sedentary bird. Further complicating the issues is that it is a very popular bird for falconry and fairly easily obtained. The committee must determine if this bird came to Montana on its own or was a falconry bird that escaped. No one ever stepped forward and claimed the bird and there was no leg band or jesses (tether) on the leg. It also did not respond to a whistle or lure, again, suggesting wild origin. The problem is that this observation is far north of its expected range for a sedentary species. The bird stayed in the Elmo area for several weeks and was observed and photographed by a number of birders. On November 19 it was observed near Stevensville so it has survived for at least 4 weeks in our winter conditions.

Wyoming did accept an October record of an adult Harris's but Washington, Idaho and Oregon rejected inclusion of the species to their state lists when observed.

Will it be included in Montana's state list? Here is the entry with the Montana Rare Bird Committee (Harris's Hawk (Parabuteo unicinctus). QLL 14B, 2013. Unbanded adult seen and photographed by many observers. Wild origin questionable owing to the popularity of this species with falconers (MBRC 2013–002).

Quoting the chair of Montana's MRBC, Dan Casey, "I think it will be some time before the MBRC makes a decision regarding this bird. The conservative outcome would be to put the species on our "supplemental list" as being of questionable provenance."

Isn't birding fascinating! ♦

Family Strigidae

Western Screech-Owl 117
Great Horned Owl 119
Snowy Owl 121
Burrowing Owl 123
Barred Owl 125
Great Gray Owl 128
Short-Eared Owl 130
Boreal Owl 132

Western Screech-Owl   *Megascops kennicottii*

WESTERN SCREECH-OWL

Being nocturnal, Owls are hard to find and see. During the breeding season they can be heard calling, but that is mostly at night when the temperatures in February are often sub-freezing. There are 15 species of owls in Montana of which four are *Species of Concern* (SOC) and five are *Species of Interest*. *Species of Concern* are those species that are declining in population, range and/or habitat. *Species of Interest* are those species with unique breeding habits that warrant further study, or whose population status and distribution are poorly known in Montana. The owl with the greatest number of sightings according to the *Montana Natural History Program* (MTNHP) database is the Great Horned Owl at 3,652. Compare that to 18,028 for the Western Tanager. The lowest reported owl in the database is the Barn Owl (Family Tytonidae) with 83 sightings, followed by Northern Hawk Owl at

WESTERN SCREECH-OWL

97, Western Screech-Owl at 156 and Eastern Screech-Owl at 221.

I recently received an emailed photo from a local rancher wondering about a white bird in his hayfield last spring. The picture turned out to be the first record of a Cattle Egret in the Upper Clark Fork Drainage and only the 47th record in the Montana. I would have enjoyed seeing that egret and adding it to my Powell County list, but it was not to be. I emphasized to the rancher that it is important to let birders know if they or other outdoor enthusiasts find interesting birds. Recently, the same rancher, emailed me another photo of the bird with this article and said, "Is this bird of any interest to you?" I was in the field birding when I received the email and immediately called him. I asked, 'When did you see this one?" His reply, "Today, in fact I am still looking at it through the barn window." I spun my truck around and was at his house in 10 minutes.

I am aware that the Western Screech-Owl exist locally, but this was only the second one I have seen in the Upper Clark Fork Valley. They are illusive and hard to find, especially in the daytime. They are a *Species of Concern* in Montana due to so few sightings.

On January 2, 2016 the temperature was below zero, and the owl found a place in the corner of a coral where the sun was shining on a board fence and the temperature many degrees warmer. I must have taken 50 pictures or more at 15 feet or less and the owl never once considered moving. It was cold and survival was on its mind. It stayed at this location for several hours that day. The other time I saw this owl it was sitting on the limb of a tree on January 15, 2015. The temperature was 30 below zero. That bird just sat and tolerated me taking pictures for more than an hour. Both times the individuals appeared to be fairly tolerant of humans.

So how does the Western Screech-Owl differ from other owls? First of all, it's small. It only stands 8.5 inches and weighs 5 ounces. This is the same size and an ounce less than the Eastern Screech-Owl. These two screech-owls look much alike but can be distinguished by the chest pattern, bill and range. The bill is darker in the Western Screech-Owl and the vertical streaks on the chest have very weak cross bars. In the Eastern Screech-Owl the cross bars are nearly as thick as the vertical streaking. The range of these two species do not overlap in Montana. West of the Continental Divide you find the Western and East of divide you find the Eastern. The Western has two color morphs; gray and brown. The individuals that I photographed were the brown adult pacific form.

The vocalization of the Western can be likened to a "bouncing ball". It has 12 or so short, low, toots that began rather slowly and accelerate in frequency towards the end of the call. They vocalize most often at dusk. Vocalization begins in January and extends into February during the breeding season.

Owls are never easy to find but if you keep an eye out, especially in January through March, you can find them roosting in trees often close to the trunk. It is worth your while to walk along a riparian zone of a creek that contains cottonwood and junipers to find owls. Walk slowly, examining each tree, especially the junipers and you will most likely be rewarded with an owl sighting. You can also go out at night and listen for them. They often respond to recordings, but don't overdo it. ♦

GREAT HORNED OWL

Most of us are familiar with the "Who's awake? Me too" owl call. It's the call of our most common owl, the Great Horned Owl. You often hear this call in the background of movies and television shows. The call is reminiscent of a Mourning Dove call only much deeper in tone. Great Horned Owls are abundant in Alaska, Canada, United States and Mexico year around.

Of the fifteen owls found in Montana it is second only to the Snowy Owl in size. The Snowy weighs 4 pounds and the Great Horned is 3.1. Snowy Owls only winter in Montana and there are probably no more than 40 to 60 individuals a year in the state. (In 2012 a Snowy was photographed at Galen and is our first confirmed sighting for Deer Lodge County.) Great Horned Owls are abundant and number in the thousands.

GREAT HORNED OWL

Great Horned Owls prefer semi-secluded habitats of mixed juniper/cottonwood stands along streams and isolated cottonwood groves in grassland environments. The thicker the vegetation the more they prefer it. However, for years a few Great Horned Owls have nested along Cottonwood Creek in the 800 and 900 blocks of Missouri Avenue in Deer Lodge.

January through March you will often hear them calling as mating and nesting season begins. Continent wide however they can be found in almost any habitat including coniferous forests, deserts and along the sea coasts.

They are not strictly nocturnal; often feeding just before dark and into the sunrise hours. When young are in the nest adults hunt during the day. They often nest in an old Red-tailed Hawk or Black-billed Magpie nest. They feed on mice, voles, rats, birds including other

GREAT HORNED OWL CHICKS

Great Horned Owl — *Bubo virginianus*

owls, and occasionally domestic cats and small dogs.

A Great Horned Owl can be distinguished from other Montana owls by its very large size, bulky shape and prominent ear tufts which are spread far apart. Overall color is mottled brown, gray and black with under-parts being fine brown bars. Color can vary depending on location from warm browns in the east to blackish brown in the Northwest. In northern forests of Canada and Alaska they are pale silver and in desert environments they are gray. The facial disk is reddish-brown bordered by black with a lower border of white. The bill is dark, eyes are yellow, and there is a large white throat patch. Both sexes are similar in appearance.

GREAT HORNED OWL

The facial mask directs sound to the ears. Sensitive hearing is needed to hear mice and small rodents walking through grass. An interesting side note is that the Northern Harrier hunts the same environments for the same prey and also has a facial disk to direct sounds to its ears.

Great Horned, like most owls, will respond to electronic calls with hooting and fly byes.

Good areas to look for this species are in large cottonwood trees or juniper stands in Western Montana. ♦

GREAT HORNED OWL CHICKS

SNOWY OWL

There's something about white birds that connects them to humans. I'm not sure what it is, but I have noticed that folks are attracted to Snow Geese, Trumpeter Swans, Tundra Swans and of course Snowy Owls.

Of the fifteen species in Montana the Snowy Owl is unique in that it is the only owl that winters here and breeds in the Arctic Circle. All of the rest of them have winter records and ten are year around residents. Four are considered summer residents only.

SNOWY OWL

Snowy Owls tend to be erratic in their winter occurrence in Montana and are found mostly along the Highline area of Montana. In years of abundance they are common in the Polson/Kalispell area and I have even seen them in the Avon area. I have never seen one in the Upper Clark Valley but there are reports both from Deer Lodge and Warm Springs.

There have been a total of 1,216 observations of Snowy Owls in Montana. Since 1976 there have been observations every year but numbers vary significantly. As an example, in 2009 there was one observation as well as in 2010. In 2011 there were 81 observations, 123 in 2012 and back down to 8 in 2013 and five in 2020 and zero in 2021.

What contributes to these variations? The safest answer is that we really don't know. Many Snowy Owls appear to be regular migrants while others spend the winter near their arctic Winter grounds. It is well documented that breeding Snowy Owls feed almost exclusively on lemmings. We also know that lemmings have a 3-4 or 5-6 year population cycle. It was an easy answer to say that when lemming numbers were low Snowy Owls migrated south in search of food. However, after much study, scientists can only say that the link between Snow Owl irruptions and the lemming cycle is a convincing theory and at other times it is not.

I often say when teaching birding classes that birds don't read the same books we do and don't behave in predictable ways. Studies have determined that most, but not all, irruptive Snowy Owls are first year birds about five months old. This suggests that the preceding breeding season had abundant lemmings and the fledged owlet mortality was low. Certainly food availability and weather must play a major role in these southern winter migrations. Perhaps in time we will understand causing factors, but we are not there yet.

Snowy Owls differ from other owls largely by their color, they are mostly white

Snowy Owl   *Bubo scandiacus*

SNOWY OWL

as adults. First year birds show dense dark bars on a white background. Females show more dark bars than males and older males are nearly all white. It is often difficult to tell young Snowy Owls from adult females. In flight the underwing is all white. They are also large, weighing four pounds. Most folks are familiar with the Great Horned Owl, it only weighs 3.1 pounds. Their head is small compared to other owls and the eyes are yellow. There are no "ear" tufts.

If you want to see a Snowy, and many people have not, one reliable area is the Polson/Kalispell area. I remember in the winter of 2012 they wintered in a neighborhood of South Polson and I observed 12 in a single view of my binoculars. They begin to show in numbers in November in eruptive years and stay in Northern Montana through February and a few into March.

I took the roof picture with this article in Kalispell March 23, 2019. It is either a bird of the year or a female. I am not familiar enough with the species to distinguish the difference. The second photo was taken in January of 2006 near Avon when there were a number of Snowy Owls in Montana and they moved much further south than normal.

If Snowy Owls are present they are not hard to find. So as I did for this picture, find the general area they are in and then drive around until you find them. You may have to be persistent. I drove the general area three different times before I found one on the roof of a home.

So next winter, check with eBird to see if they are being observed, or call a birder such as myself who would know of their presence. Then jump in the car and make a day trip to Kalispell. The day I did this I was gone twelve hours, drove 462 miles, and not only did I see the Snowy Owl, but I also got an additional 11 year birds that were not on my 2019 bird List. ♦

BURROWING OWL

When I was in high school a friend and I were out gopher hunting. We weren't overly experienced and when a gopher popped its head up my friend shot and killed it. The problem was that it wasn't a gopher it was an owl! At that time neither of us even knew that there were owls that lived in the ground. In fact, the Burrowing Owl is the only owl species in the world that nests underground.

That innocent killing of a Burrowing Owl took place in the early 1960s. There were never many Burrowing Owls in the Upper Clark Fork Drainage. It was a shame that we killed one. I researched the Montana Natural Heritage Website and Northern Powell County has never had a burrowing owl record. Southern Powell County, where we killed one, has had a few records but none in the past 20 years. The range of this species is basically east of the Continental Divide to the North Dakota border.

In Montana, there have been 3,321 observations, mostly in well-established and protected prairie dog colonies.

BURROWING OWL

The highest densities of Burrowing Owls are found along the Highline between Havre and south to Lewistown in Hill, Blaine and Fergus Counties.

Burrowing Owls are dependent on abandoned burrows of prairie dogs, badgers, foxes and ground squirrels. The biome that contains most of these mammals is the extensive grasslands that dominate Eastern Montana. Most of my observations of this species are from Eastern Montana but in recent years I have been observing Burrowing Owls in small numbers 20 miles north of Dillon in native grasslands in abandoned badger holes.

Burrowing owls average 9.5 inches long with a wingspan of 21 inches and weigh 5 ounces. Compare that with the more familiar Great Horned Owl that averages 22 inches long with a wingspan of 44 inches and weigh 3.1 pounds.

Females Burrowing Owls are slightly larger than males. Males tend to be lighter in color than the darker brown of the female.

Burrowing Owls don't overwinter in Montana but migrate to coastal southern California and into much of Mexico. They migrate north into Montana in late April and May, breed in June and July and have mostly migrated south by the end of September.

Burrowing Owls have been decreasing in Montana and the nation for at least 30 years. The reasons vary from site to site but are related to two main factors.

BURROWING OWL

The eradication of prairie dogs colonies and other burrowing mammals and conversion of native grasslands into farmland. Grasslands have been altered more than other ecosystems as they tend to be at lower elevations, relatively flat, and have rich soils suitable for grain and other crops. It was a natural outgrowth of the expansion of the Homestead Act in the west.

Fortunately, if land is set aside and protected as historic sites like First Peoples Buffalo Jump near Great Falls; Burrowing Owls tend to recover fairly quickly. As an example, the Umatilla Chemical Depot on the south side of the Columbia River in North Central Oregon was decommissioned by the US Army in the mid-1970s. Because of its use, the area was restricted from development and some 6,000 acres of grassland was set aside as a natural area. At the time of decommissioning they estimated there were two pairs of Burrowing Owls on site. Due to the lack of burrowing mammals, artificial burrows were constructed from half of a 55 gallon barrel and 10 feet of corrugated plastic pipe tunnel connecting the nest camber barrel to the surface. In a period of five years the area went from two pairs to an estimated 60 pairs.

If you have never seen this little owl I hope you get the opportunity. One of the most reliable sites is First Peoples Buffalo Jump at Ulm. Ask at the visitor's center and they will direct you to the area where they nest.

I have observed Burrowing Owls north of Dillon on private ground. That particular colony seems to be growing in number, which is good news for the species, there aren't that many in Southwestern Montana. ♦

BARRED OWL

One of the enjoyable things about birdwatching is that the unexpected often happens. I have probably birded Warm Springs Wildlife Management Area more than anyone else in Montana. I average about 50 birding trips a year to Warm Springs and I bird areas others rarely bird. I have access to areas others don't because of my survey work for Atlantic Richfield and Montana Fish, Wildlife and Parks. During the last 20 years I have seen 229 of the 232 species that have been recorded for the area. I have also observed three rare species that no one else has seen on site; the Blackpoll Warbler, Whimbrel, and Black Scoter.

BARRED OWL

Others do bird the area and Don and Andrea Stierle of Missoula are two who do regularly. I was surprised when they called me October 19, 2013 and said they had seen and photographed a Barred Owl at Warm Springs WMA. I was surprised as I have only seen this species in three other locations in Montana, Columbia Falls, Orofino Campground in Deer Lodge County and McClean Creek near Helena. In all of these areas the owls were in proper habitat and breeding. There are no previous records of the Barred Owl on the WS WMA.

After their call I Immediately went to Warm Springs and could not find the bird in the area described, but found it a few hundred yards south in a Cottonwood Grove. Usually this species is rather docile and easy to approach. When located, it immediately lifted and flew west across AR Pond 2. When Don and Andrea saw the bird they were about 15 feet away. The picture with this article is theirs. It sat quietly while they took several photos from their vantage point. This individual was obviously transient to the area and was possibly a first year bird looking for suitable habitat which WS WMA is not. This sighting increased the number of known species to occur at WS WMA from 211 to 212 at that time. The Barred Owl is also

BARRED OWL *Photo by Iculizard*

the fifth species of Owl observed at WS WMA.

There are 15 species of owls in Montana and the Barred is one that is not often seen by birders with only 466 records. The reason is that proper habitat for this species is mostly restricted to Northwest Montana in wet bogs with mature coniferous trees not often birded.

It is one of the largest forest owls in Montana only exceeded in size by the Great Horned and Great Gray Owls. Snowy Owls are larger at four pounds, but not considered a forest owl. Barred Owls weigh 1.6 pounds compared to 3.1 for the Great Horned and 2.4 for the Great Gray. Some Montana owls are very small such as the Flammulated Owl at 2.1 ounces.

The Barred Owl is rather distinctive and easy to identify. The head is large and round with no ear tufts. The facial disk is prominent with dark eyes and an orange-yellow bill. The spots on the upper breast form a barred pattern across the neck and the lower breast and belly has vertical stripes. The brown back has white spots with white bars on the wings.

This species is very vocal, loud, and is often heard in the day time. It readily responds to it's call with a *"Who cooks for you? Who cooks for you-all"* response.

The Barred Owl is an aggressive and adaptable species and has invaded much of the Pacific Northwest in the last sixty years. The species is now common along the Pacific slopes of the Rocky Mountains. Currently they are beginning to occupy the territories of the Spotted Owl and Spotted Owl numbers are declining. Many former Spotted Owl territories are exclusively being used by Barred Owls. Evidence of hybridization of the two species has been documented which could genetically swamp the Spotted Owl out of existence. In response the US Fish and

Wildlife Service has announced (September, 2013) they will begin to kill as many as 3,600 Barred Owls over the next four years to protect the Spotted Owl.

One question that has not been answered is why the expansion of the Barred Owl's territory took place. Did mankind unknowingly change the environment that produced the invasion or is it just nature at work? Much research needs to be done.

Was the sighting at Warm Springs WMA the beginning of an invasion into our valley or just a chance sighting of a stray Barred Owl? Time and field observations will tell the story.

Since I wrote this article in 2013 the Barred Owl has been documented breeding in a spruce bog along the Continental Divide in Orofino Campground on the Deer Lodge to Boulder Road in Deer Lodge County.

In a straight line it is only about eight miles from the WMA so perhaps, as I stated earlier, the one seen at the WMA might have been a young of the year looking for suitable habitat.

If you hear of a Barred Owl being observed in your area you should make the effort to see it. Many birders never get the opportunity to see one. ♦

BIRDING IN THE CLOUD FOREST OF ECUADOR

GREAT GRAY OWL

There are 19 species of owls in North America with 15 species in Montana. The rarest in Montana are Barn, Snowy and Great Gray. A few Barn Owls breed in Montana, but difficult to find. Snowy Owls appear along the Highline each year during the winter in small numbers and occasionally we have an irruptive year when rodent populations are low in Canada. January of 2006 was such a year in which I observed 15 Snowy Owls in a field near Polson and two near Avon.

GREAT GRAY OWL

We are fortunate to have the Great Gray Owl year around in the Georgetown Lake area as well as the national forest of Southwest Montana. I have guided a number of out-of-state birders in their effort to put this one on their life list. In January of 2011, while leading a group of local birders, we observed two. I can find this species about half the time I look for it. The last time I found it was in June of 2020 sitting on a fence along a road.

The Great Gray is the largest North American Owl with a wingspan of 52 inches and a length of 27 inches and weighs 2.4 pounds. The Great Horned Owl familiar to most weighs more at 3.1 ponds, but only has a wingspan of 44 inches and length of 22 inches. The smallest owl in the Upper Clark Fork is the Northern Pygmy-Owl with a length of 6.75 inches, a wingspan of 12 inches and weighing only 2.5 ounces.

Great Gray Owls are flat-faced with small yellow eyes and bill, and a facial pattern of five concentric rings surrounding each eye in a large facial disk. The head is disproportionally large with a black and white "bow tie" between the neck and chest. The tail is long and the wings are broad. The overall coloration is sooty gray with combinations of whites, grays and browns. The breast pattern is vertical and contrasts with the wing pattern. The yellow legs and dark toes are heavily feathered.

The Great Gray is reasonably easy to observe in proper habitat because its

GREAT GRAY OWL

GREAT GRAY OWL

feeding habits are not strictly nocturnal. The bird is also rather tame and does not usually take flight when observed. The best way to see this owl is to travel roads in mature Lodge Pole Pine and Douglas Fir such as the area around Georgetown Lake and East Fork Reservoir in Granite County. They hunt from perches in trees and fence posts along the edge of meadows and grassy openings. They are a *Species of Concern* because they need mature stands of coniferous forest. They have been observed 638 times.

Take the time to observe the Great Grays at Georgetown Lake. Most folks do not have the opportunity to see such a rare bird often. ♦

ENJOYING A GREAT MEAL DURING A BIRDING TRIP TO ISRAEL

SHORT-EARED OWL

As I work on my "Year List" I'm always relived each time I observe another owl species. They seem hard for me to find, mostly because many of them are nocturnal and you have to go out at night to listen for them. There are 15 species of owls in Montana. Fourteen breed in Montana. The Snowy Owl only winters here, migrating south from Canada and Alaska. Most other owl species also winter here but several such as the Flammulated are in very small numbers.

The most owl species I ever saw in a single year was in 2007 during my big year attempt. I saw all but the Northern Hawk Owl that I saw in 2006 and again in 2008. In 2016 I saw six species and eight in 2020.

Two of the easiest to see are the Short-eared Owl and the Great Horned because they are both diurnal feeding in the day time as well as at night. Most people are familiar with the Great Horned Owl, our most common owl, because it dwells within cities as well as the countryside.

SHORT-EARED OWL

Short-eared Owls are found statewide as a transient species, and probably breed statewide as well, but lack of observations prohibit better understanding of the species. When I want to observe this species I make my annual trip to the Polson area. Around the Nine Pipes National Wildlife Refuge are hundreds of acres of waterfowl production grasslands which are ideal habitat for Short-eared Owls. I have driven the back roads of the area an hour before sunset and seen 10 to 12 individuals hunting the fields and sitting on fence posts. They nest on the ground in grass deep enough to conceal the nest. Typically three to eleven eggs are laid and incubation is 25 to 30 days.

So how do you identify Short-eared Owls from other owls? The facial disk, used for directing sound to the ears, is very prominent and there are two short ear-tufts at the top center of the head. Within the facial disk the eyes are surrounded by dark patches. The brownish females are spotted on the back and the breast is streaked being darker above and lighter below. Males are similar, but lighter in color especially on the breast. The picture with this article shows a male with the lighter breast. One might mix up this owl with the Northern Harrier which occupies the same niche in flight and also has a facial disk. The wing beat of the short-eared however, is rather slow and the wing tips nearly touch on the upswing.

During the last five summers we have been surveying birds on the Dutchman Wetlands west of the Warm Springs Ponds and the Opportunity Ponds Area South

SHORT-EARED OWL

of Montana Highway 48 east of Anaconda. Both areas have extensive undisturbed grasslands. The Dutchman has native grasses and the Opportunity Ponds Area has re-vegetated grasslands after the burial of heavy metal laden soils from the Clark Fork River Remediation Project and sediments from the removal of Bonner Dam near Missoula.

To my surprise I have documented Short-eared Owl pairs using both areas. At this point I don't know if it is a single pair using both areas or if it is two pair. It appears that they may have attempted to nest in the area but I have not found a nest or seen juvenile birds. To my knowledge this is the only Short-eared Owl sightings in the Upper Clark Fork.

There is an old saying that states "Build the right habitat and the birds will come." In this case the habitat is mature undisturbed grasslands with lots of cover for nesting and feeding. Nature abhors a vacuum and it will fill every niche with the right species, in this case Short-eared Owls.

I am always amazed at how efficient nature is in establishing new populations when the environmental conditions are right. This example should give us hope that all of the remediation work that is being done in the Upper Clark Fork River Riparian Zone will result in greater diversity and density of birds and other wildlife when the Clark Fork River and its tributaries are completely remediated.

In the Spring of 2020 I found a Short-eared Owl along the newly opened Old Yellowstone Trail North of Deer Lodge. This is my first record of the Short-eared in Powell County. Is this one of the Opportunity/Dutchman adults expanding its territory? Is it an offspring of the Deer Lodge County pair looking for it's own territory? These are questions we yet don't know the answer to but all of these scenarios are possible. We continue to monitor birds along the Clark Fork River Corridor and in time we will know the answer, that's what makes birding so interesting. ♦

BOREAL OWL

All owls can be a challenge to find, with the exception of the Great Horned Owl, which commonly lives among humans and has a familiar call. One of the most difficult owls to find is the Boreal Owl. That is why I was surprised in December 2013 when I looked out the window of a cabin we had rented near Phillipsburg for a family vacation and one was sitting in a tree not more than 20 feet from us.

BOREAL OWL

The easiest way to find a Boreal is to wait until dusk and play a recording in proper habitat in mid-March during the mating season. The rest of the year they tend to be silent. Their call is a distinctive *"hooo-too-too-too"* song over and over again. If they are in the area when you play their song they will typically respond. If you are fortunate they will even fly to a tree near you and call. You can then use a headlamp or flashlight to observe them.

What was so surprising about our Philipsburg Owl was that it was content to sit in the tree and let us approach to about ten feet and take photos. I had never gotten the chance to photograph this species in the daylight before and may never again. My grandson, who is also a birder, was especially excited for it was a "state bird" as well as "life bird" for him. I had only seen the bird once before and that was in February of 2007 in the Missoula Valley. They are indeed a rare sighting for most birders and many bird a lifetime and never see one.

Montana Natural Heritage Program records show that only four of Montana's fifteen owl species are seen less. The Boreal has been observed 426 times and the Barn Owl, the rarest, has been observed 83 times. In comparison the Great Horned was reported 3,655 times, the rare Northern Hawk Owl 97 times and the Great Gray Owl 638 times. Pete Dunn's *Field Guide Companion* book says this about the Boreal Owl, "Wide-ranging, but uncommon, nocturnal, rarely vocal (and damned difficult to find) northern resident."

Boreal Owls range across all of Canada into Alaska and down the west side of the Continental Divide in the US South into Utah. Their range also extends into Idaho and Eastern Washington.

They are 10 inches in length with a wingspan of 23 inches, weigh 4.7 ounces, making them one of Montana's smaller owls. Of the 15 owl species in Montana only the Northern Pygmy-Owl and Northern Saw-whet Owl are smaller. It is also one of ten year around resident owls.

They have a large, square, tuftless head, stocky body, and short tail. There is a dark "V" through the eyes extending from the top of the head to the pale

BOREAL OWL

bill. The whitish facial disk is bordered in black. The chest has brownish spots in vertical lines on a white background. The spots are more distinct below than above. The Boreal can be confused with the Northern Saw-whet and Northern Pygmy-Owls, but can be distinguished from them by the facial pattern of black "V" and black bordered whitish facial disk.

Owls are fascinating birds to see, I have found six species in the Upper Clark Fork Valley and all 15 in Montana. They are out there, but it takes a little work to find them. One way to see them is to find a stand of junipers and methodically search each tree. They like to hide among the thick needles of junipers. If you are really serious about seeing our local owls you might want to go out at dusk with a birder who is knowledgeable about playing their calls and songs. It is the easiest and most reliable way to find them. Good luck in seeing owls this year. ♦

Family Alcedinidae

Belted Kingfisher..134

Belted Kingfisher　　　　　　　　　　　　　　　　　　*Megaceryle alcyon*

BELTED KINGFISHER

    The Belted Kingfisher is a familiar bird to most Montanan's. It is a fairly common species in Western Montana and breeds and winters in the upper Clark Fork Valley. A reliable place to see the Belted Kingfisher year around is along the rivers with power lines crossing them. They often perch on the power lines above the river looking for a meal.

    The Belted Kingfisher has the widest distribution of the three species of common North American kingfishers. It is a year around resident of much of North America with the exception of Eastern Montana, North and South Dakota and the Great Lakes states. Those individuals migrate south and winter in Southern Nevada, Arizona, New Mexico, Western Texas and Mexico. The other two common species, the Ringed Kingfisher and Green Kingfisher, have very limited distributions in Southern

BELTED KINGFISHER

Belted Kingfisher — *Megaceryle alcyon*

BELTED KINGFISHER *Photo by konocti*

Texas, Southern Arizona and Mexico. There is only one place in the United States that you can reliably see all three species together and that is below Falcon Dam on the Rio Grande River in Texas. I was fortunate to see all three species at this location in February of 1996.

A fourth Kingfisher, the Amazon, is a species of Southern Mexico. It has been documented three times in Texas with photographs. All three sightings have been of females,

Belted Kingfishers are best described as a dagger-billed, shaggy-crested bird that typically perches over water. It is a medium sized bird and its oversized head with double peaked crest is distinctive. They are slate blue above and white below in all plumages. The head and back are separated by a white collar. Males have a single blue band across the chest and females have a second band below the blue which is rust in color. This is one of the few species where the female is more brightly colored than the male. They are solitary except during breeding and highly territorial and aggressive towards other Kingfishers that wander into their territory.

They plunge vertically from 10 to 40 feet above water for fish, reptiles and crustaceans. They are capable of hovering when searching for prey. If you approach a Belted Kingfisher they will often flush with a vocal response. The call is a loud, protracted, scratchy chattering rattle.

What I find fascinating about this bird is its nesting behavior. The nest consists of a slightly upward-sloping tunnel in a vertical bank of a stream or lake. Some nest sites can be a short distance from water in an appropriate cliff habitat. They prefer bank soils with high sand, low clay composition. Both males and females alternately dig and remove soil forming a tunnel ending in an enlarged nest chamber. Tunnels are usually 3 to 6 feet in length with some as long as 15 feet. The nest chamber is saucer shaped and lined with grass and leaves. Both sexes incubate six to eight white eggs which are an inch and half long. The young leave the nest after 34-35 days.

If you enjoy walking along rivers look for tunnel openings along the banks in sandy soils. You might just find a nest site and have an opportunity for some interesting observations of the Belted Kingfisher. ♦

Family Picidae

Lewis's Woodpecker 136
Red-Naped Sapsucker 138
Black-Backed Woodpecker 139

Lewis's Woodpecker   *Melanerpes lewis*

LEWIS'S WOODPECKER

BELTED KINGFISHER   *Photo By Ed Harper*

On May 27, 1806, the Lewis and Clark Expedition was camped on the Clearwater River in Idaho waiting for snow melt so they could cross the Bitterroot Mountains. Lewis describes a bird that was "new to science".

"The Black Woodpecker which I have frequently mentioned and which is found in most parts of the Rocky Mountains. I have never had an opportunity of examination until a few days since when we killed and preserved several of them." "The neck and as low as the crop in front is of an iron gray. The belly and breast is a curious mixture of white and blood red which has much the appearance of having been artificially painted - - - "

Lewis gave a specimen to a Philadelphia museum. Alexander Wilson, a pioneer American ornithologist made the first drawing and gave the bird its common name – Lewis's Woodpecker. In 1831 it was reclassified with a new scientific name Melanerpes lewis, which means Lewis's black creeper.

In my opinion, Lewis's Woodpecker is stunningly different in appearance than the other 12 woodpeckers found in Montana. Most, with the exception of the Northern Flicker, are a combination of contrasting black and white with red or yellow markings on the head. Northern Flickers are brown and black with gray heads with a spotted belly and a black crescent on the upper chest.

Lewis's Woodpecker's glossy black-green back, pink belly and pale gray collar is unique. Specifically, they are a rather large, dark, broad winged woodpecker that likes to sit high in a tree. They are rather odd shaped with a long tail and small head. The gray neck makes the head appear unattached to the body. Overall the bird is blackish above with an all dark head and red face. The collar is pale gray with gray above and rose below on the breast and belly. The undertail is dark.

Lewis's Woodpeckers are primarily restricted to Western Montana along riparian streams with mature cottonwoods stands. They seem to be dependent on mature cottonwood trees for nesting cavities. The lower Clark Fork River at Missoula and the Bitterroot River have abundant riparian Cottonwood stands and Lewis's Woodpeckers. The Upper Clark Fork River, probably due to heavy metal contamination, has few mature cottonwood riparian zones and thus this species is transient. There are no breeding records along the Clark Fork River above Garrison.

There are a few records of Lewis's in Montana in the winter. Winters are spent in Southern Utah and Colorado, South to Arizona and New Mexico.

I see the species annually but most often in the fall when juveniles are feeding in family groups. It is not uncommon to see these family groups along the Little Blackfoot River near Garrison.

If you see a woodpecker that is obviously different with a green sheen, and rose belly, check your field guide for Lewis's Woodpecker. ♦

CATCHING MY BREATH IN MADAGASCAR

RED-NAPED SAPSUCKER

There are twenty two species of woodpeckers in North America with thirteen species in Montana. Four species are in the genus *Sphyrapicus* or sapsuckers of which three are found in Montana. Williamson's Sapsucker is restricted to west of the continental divide and usually found at high elevations in coniferous forest. Yellow-bellied Sapsuckers are rare occurring mostly in northeast Montana with only 16 sightings with the *Montana Natural Heritage Program*. Red-naped is common and found in the western half of the state. Red-naped show up in the Upper Clark Fork Valley by late April and remain into September. Migration is mostly to Southern Arizona and Northern Mexico. A few have been known to winter in Northwest Montana.

RED-NAPED SAPSUCKER

All sapsuckers have a behavior of drilling evenly spaced holes in tree trunks which fill with sap. Sapsuckers not only drink the sap from these wells, but feed on the insects that get entrapped in the sap. Red-naped also glean trunks and branches for insects. In late summer when insects are abundant they will hawk insects out of the air.

Red-naped Sapsuckers spend much of their time drilling, maintaining and defending their sap-wells. I have a pine in my yard that has hundreds of holes evenly spaced around the trunk and are periodically inspected for sap and insects.

Red-naped males have a red crown, nape and throat. The head also shows a black and white pattern with a large black line through the eye. Females are similar, but the chin is white and the throat red. The back has extensive white markings in two rows.

Williamson's males are separated from Red-naped by an all black back. Female Williamson's are brown-headed with a black breast and a finely barred back. Williamson's are rarely found as a backyard bird. Yellow-bellied Sapsuckers have extensive white barring on the back and a yellowish cast to the belly. Their nape is white and the throat is red in males and white in females.

Our most common backyard woodpecker in the Upper Clark Fork Valley is the Northern Flicker. Other woodpeckers that are common locally are Downy and Hairy Woodpeckers. Take the time to examine each woodpecker you see as you might just have a Red-naped Sapsucker. Also look for sap wells in the trees in your yard as a sure sign of their presence.

I took this picture of a Red-naped Sapsucker in a cottonwood grove along the Clark Fork River in late June. Look carefully at the image for the traits that make this bird a female. She had young in a nest cavity and was making repeated trips to feed them such morsels as this dragonfly.

If you don't have a good guide which shows field marks consider *Sibley's Field Guide to Western North America, Peterson Field Guide to Birds,* or *National Geographic Field Guide to the Birds.* You also need the latest version as names change, splits and lumps occur and new species come to North America (ex. Eurasian-collared Dove). ♦

BLACK-BACKED WOODPECKER

Each year I try to find 300 or more species of birds in Montana. I don't make my goal most years. So why do I set it so high? I do it so that I get out and bird a lot. In 2020 I accomplished my goal with 303 species. I almost made it in 2019 with 298 species. The previous time I made my goal of 300 was in 2010 with 301 species.

Prior to 2007 no one had ever recorded 300 species in a year. The reason it had never been accomplished was the lack of availability of the internet, social media groups, and eBird to let people instantly know the location of birds. I was the first person to achieve 300 species in a single year in Montana and I found 328 species in 2007 in a marathon effort that is a story for another time. No one has ever broken my record, but someone will if they have the fire in their belly to do so. The effort will be huge to accomplish 329 species. I drove 24,000 miles and spent 150 nights away from home.

BLACK-BACKED WOODPECKER

Why do I mention all of this? I do so because there are a few birds that are difficult to get each year and without them you can't reach 300 species. One of these birds is the Black-backed Woodpecker. It has been a difficult bird for me to get every year. The reason is that their habitat need is so specific. Proper habitat is a coniferous forest burn that is less than three years old where trees are dead due to fire but the bark is still intact. Fires in a wilderness are usually a long ways from a road. Often fires are too hot and the bark is burned off or the tree is completely destroyed. I have had the most luck in finding these habitats in Glacier Park. Fires are allowed to burn in the park and are often close to roads and trails. The problem is that once you find such an area it's only good for two to three years and then you have to find a more recent burn.

So why is the habitat suitable for such a short time? Black-backed Woodpeckers feed exclusively on insect larva living under the bark next to the cambium layer. Apparently Black-backed Woodpeckers are not successful in removing bark in healthy unburned trees to get to the insects, but can remove the bark of trees damaged by fire. Note the picture with drill holes in a fire burned dead tree. I took it in the same area as I photographed the Black-backed Woodpecker. Black-backed Woodpeckers move up a tree in a spiral search pattern. They bore forcefully after larval insects throwing their whole body into the tapping action. Their purposeful drilled holes look like bullet impact sites with halos of blasted off bark.

Black-backed Woodpeckers colonize a burn as quickly as three months after a fire and remain in the area for two to four years until the bark sheds from the trees ending the opportunity to harvest larval insects.

I find Black-backed Woodpeckers by going to proper habitat and walk listening for their call or drumming. If you do your homework and spend time listening to audio recordings of their drumming you can easily distinguish their drum from other woodpeckers. The advantage of listening for their drumming is that the sound carries a long distance through the needleless forest, helping you to find them. On occasion I have been in proper habitat and have not heard calls or drums. I then play their drum using a bluetooth speaker and a field guide App on my notepad. If they are in hearing range of your drumming they often will respond with their own drumming or fly towards your drumming. It should be limited. It is illegal to use playback in a national park.

BARK REMOVAL

I usually don't get the opportunity to find this species until June or July when the snow has melted and I venture into Glacier Park. This year I found a Black-backed Woodpecker January 26, 2021! How did that happen?

My grandson and I went to a fire burn that occurred just north of Helena last fall. The burn was ideal for Black-backed Woodpeckers. The fire burned across the ground cooking the cambium layer just under the bark, killing the tree but not destroying the bark on 10 to 15 inch Ponderosa Pine. We really didn't know where to go in the burn and pulled off at the first wide spot we found. Upon exiting the car we immediately heard the drum of not only the Black-backed but another fire dependent woodpecker, the American Three-toed. I have never found a Black-backed this easily in my life! It just shows the old adage true, "You build the habitat and the birds will come." In this case nature built the habitat and the Black-backed Woodpeckers came. It will be interesting to see how long they will remain.

So how do you distinguish this woodpecker from others? They are the only woodpecker with an entirely black back, a mostly black face and heavily barred sides. All of these features can be seen in the accompanying photos. Males have a yellow cap and females have a solid black head. The Black-backed I photographed is a female.

The only woodpecker that you might confuse the Black-backed with is the American Three-toed Woodpecker which occupies the same habitat. The Three-toed is distinguished by a black and white barring down the center of the back.

BLACK-BACKED WOODPECKER

I feel fortunate to have seen this bird so early in the year and hope to revisit the area later, and perhaps get the opportunity to photograph a yellow capped male. ♦

GARY WHEN BIRDING IN AUSTRALIA

Family Falconidae

American Kestrel 142
Merlin 144
Gyrfalcon 145
Prairie Falcon 147

American Kestrel   *Falco sparverius*

AMERICAN KESTREL

AMERICAN KESTREL

There are more than 22 species of falcons in the world with nine species in North America, six in Montana, and I have seen five in the Upper Clark Fork Drainage. The rarest by far is the Crested Caracara with only one record of a juvenile in 2010. The bird landed in a pasture near Hot Springs, remained for 10 minutes, flew off and was not seen again. Its normal year around range is Southern Arizona, Texas and Mexico. The falcons in the Upper Clark Fork Basin in descending order of frequency from my observation are American Kestrel, Prairie Falcon, Merlin, Peregrine Falcon and Gyrfalcon. The Prairie is more common in the winter and the

Gyrfalcon is only found locally in the winter. This article is about the smallest and most common of the falcons, the American Kestrel. The *Montana Natural Heritage Program* website shows 20,607 observations for the Kestrel, 6,850 for the Prairie Falcon, 5,848 for the Merlin and 297 for the Gyrfalcon. Kestrels weigh in at 4.1 ounces compared to 3.1 pounds for the Gyrfalcon. The second smallest falcon, the Merlin, weighs 6.5 ounces.

The only falcon that you could misidentify as a Kestrel would be the Merlin. The Kestrel is slightly smaller with a length of nine inches and wing span of 22 inches compared to 10 inch length and 24 inch wingspan for the Merlin. A casual look at a Merlin shows a bulky bird that is dark backed with heavy breast streaking. The Kestrel on the other hand is slender with a boldly patterned head and rufous back and tail.

Specifically, the head has double black vertical stripes on a white face with a gray cap. As mentioned previously the back and tail are rufous. In flight the underwing is pale white. Males differ from females with blue-gray wing coverts (flight feathers), and the tail in the male has a single wide black band. The female has a series of narrow bands. This arrangement gives the male a brighter rufous tail than the female. Juveniles have heavier breast streaking than adults. The picture with this article is that of an adult male.

Kestrels typically hunt from a perch or power line. When perched the tail is often in motion to maintain balance. Merlins don't move the tail for balance. Kestrels often hunt by hovering over the ground for extended periods of time then landing on the ground to seize their prey. Due to their size, the main diet consists of insects and supplemented with small mammals. Kestrels rarely feed in flight as the Merlin does.

Because their main diet is insects, they leave the Upper Clark Fork Valley in the winter. My latest date for a Kestrel observation in the Upper Clark Fork is November 1 and they show in the spring in early April. They do overwinter in warmer areas of the state such at the Bitterroot Valley.

You probably won't see a Kestrel in the Upper Clark Fork Valley after November, I never have. You can find Merlins and Prairie Falcons all winter. If you're really fortunate you might even see a Gyrfalcon. Gyrfalcons are in the Upper Clark Fork Valley and Western Montana but only a few each Winter. Then next spring you can find the American Kestrel again, and if you're fortunate, a Peregrine Falcon. The best place to see a Peregrine is an area where shorebirds stage in migration such as the Warm Springs WMA mudflats. Peregrines prefer feeding on unsuspecting shorebirds which are staging (resting and feeding) from their long flight north on the mud flats. Gyrfalcons will also take ducks but shorebirds are easier.

One of the best ways to know where birds are year around is eBird. Be sure and subscribe to the email alerts, "Montana Rare Bird Alerts" and "Year Needs Alert for Montana". The rare bird alert gives you the location for any bird that is rare in a particular location. The Needs Alert compares your list for the year in eBird and alerts you when someone posts a bird species not on your list. There are several hundred Montana birders that post their findings. ♦

MERLIN

Falcons are easily distinguished from other birds of prey by their long narrow pointed wings that are bent at the wrist. Historically they have been placed genetically with hawks, but recent studies show they have a closer relationship to parrots and songbirds.

Older field guides have them grouped at the end of the hawks in the raptor section. In the new 7th edition of the *National Geographic Field Guide to the Birds of North America* they are after woodpeckers and before parrots. The official checklist for Montana (August, 2018) produced by Montana Audubon and the *Montana Natural Heritage Program*, falcons are found between woodpeckers and flycatchers as we have no parrots in our state.

MERLIN

There are nine falcon species in North America in two genera, Falco and Caracara. The Eurasian Hobby is a vagrant old world species that has been seen on the western Aleutians islands and Bering Sea region. The Old World Eurasian Kestrel has also been seen in the Western Aleutians and Bering Sea with a few sightings on the east coast from Maine to Florida. The Aplomado Falcon is found in Mexico although there are a few records from the 1940s and 50s in Arizona and New Mexico. The remaining six have all been seen in Montana.

The Crested Carcara has only been seen once and the remaining five are fairly common and all can be found in the Upper Clark Fork River Drainage. . The most common is the small, 4.1 ounce, American Kestrel. There have been 5,875 observations statewide. Few winter in our area but they do winter in warmer valleys such as the Bitterroot. Due to their small size much of their diet consist of insects such as grasshoppers and crickets. The rarest Montana falcon is the Gyrfalcon which breeds in the Arctic Circle and winters across Canada and the northern tier states. There have been 292 observations in Montana. Most winters this species is observed annually in the Upper Clark Fork Drainage. I have personally seen Gyrfalcons locally 17 times since 2005 with my most recent sighting in January 2020. Gyrfalcons are large weighing 3.1 pounds. Another rather rare falcon in our valley is the 1.6 pound Peregrine Falcon. It has been recorded in the state 1,932 times. I most often see them in spring and fall when they prey on shorebirds. Peregrines hunt from high in the sky, folding their wings in a fast stoop (dive) striking small birds in mid-air. I have seen them hit a shorebird in midair dropping the prey to the ground to feed. Some research suggests their horizontal flight can reach 60 mph

Merlin *Falco columbarius*

and more than 100 mph in a stoop after prey! A similar niche falcon is the similar sized (1.6 pound) Prairie Falcon which is more common with 2,882 observation in Montana. They increase in numbers in lower elevation valleys in the winter. You often see them sitting on power poles near alfalfa fields where they feed on mice and voles. Summer finds them at higher elevations and seen less often.

The bird featured in the photo is the Merlin which is slightly larger than the American Kestrel at 6.5 ounces. This species seems to be less familiar to people and has been recorded 1,758 times. Perhaps this is due because they are uniformly gray in color rather than the contrasting colors of the American Kestrel. Adult males are gray backed with vertical streaks on a orange white breast. Females are darker backed with vertical streaks on a white chest. Juveniles of both sexes resemble the adult female. In contrast, the American Kestrel is a combination of a rufous back, gray wings, dotted breast and two strong verticals lines on a white background on the face.

The Merlin photo is of an adult male which just caught what appears to be a Horned Lark although I am not completely sure of the identification of the prey. ♦

Gyrfalcon *Falco rusticolus*

GYRFALCON

The Gyrfalcon is one of the most sought after birds of prey in Montana as it is rather rare and only a winter visitor.

I have never seen more than one Gyrfalcon in the Upper Clark Fork Valley during any one winter season. The first one that I saw locally was in December of 2002. It was not until January of 2005 before I saw another one. Since then I have observed them in the Upper Clark Fork in 2006, 2007, 2011, 2013, 2016, 2018 and 2020. Total observations for me in this time period for the Upper Clark Fork Valley has been seventeen.

The 2016 Gyrfalcon was seen in late January and was observed for about two weeks, the longest period for any individual. A number of people visited the valley to see and photograph this specimen. This particular Gyrfalcon was a light phase adult probably a female because of its large size. Its appearance created a lot of excitement for

DARK ADULT GYRFALCON

local birders and generated reports on the Internet birding sites. The two photos with this article were taken in the Upper Clark Fork Valley.

One birder from Missoula called and said he had seen the bird on January 1 during our Warm Springs Christmas Bird Count, but did not have the confidence to call it a Gyrfalcon due to its rarity. After looking at the internet photos he was confident he saw the bird on the Warm Springs CBC. So perhaps the 2016 Gyrfalcon was in the valley from January 1 through February 9.

LIGHT ADULT GYRFALCON

Gyrfalcons are a year around Arctic species with a few migrating south to winter resulting in 292 total observations in Montana through 2020 according to the Montana Natural Heritage Program website.

There are nine species of falcons in two genera in North America with six species occurring in Montana. The Crested Caracara is the rarest with one record in 2010 and the American Kestrel is the most common with 20,607 observations through 2020. Within the genus Falco the Gyrfalcon is the largest species weighing 3.1 pounds with the next largest being the Peregrine and Prairie Falcons at 1.6 pounds. The smallest is the American Kestrel at 4.1 ounces.

Not only is the Gyrfalcon our largest falcon it is also the most powerful. It has been observed striking and killing Mallards in flight. It has a wingspan of 47 inches. In flight the wings have that typical pointed wingtip of falcons and flight is fast. The streamlined heavy breasted body, and pointed wing give the species a powerful appearance. The flight is unmistakable once you become accustomed to the flight patterns of raptorsl. The Buteo genus containing most of our local raptors such as Red-tailed and Rough-legged Hawks have rounded wings and slow flight.

Field marks for this species in an adult are a yellow-orange eye ring, cere (The area on the upper part of the beak that contains the nostrils.), and legs. Juveniles lack the yellow cere and eye ring and the legs are blue-gray. The tail is long and broad and extends far beyond the folded wings. In the somewhat similar Peregrine Falcon, the tail and wing tips are equal in length. The head appears small in proportion to the heavy body.

Gyrfalcon's plumages vary from white, gray or dark morph. The dark morph might be mis-identified as a Northern Goshawk but the Gyrfalcon is always in open areas and never in woods as is the Northern Goshawk. There is never a white eyebrow or supercilium on the Gyrfalcon.

Gyrfalcon feeds almost exclusively on birds up to the size of mallards with only an occasional small mammal. That is why you often see them in the Upper Clark

Fork Valley near the Warm Springs WMA. Most winters there are small pockets of open water with Mallards and Common Goldeneye present. The Clark Fork River is also open most of the winter except for the coldest of weather. When hunting they fly low along the ground and strike and stun their prey. I have often seen Gyrfalcons in our valley perched on a power pole with a full crop and a blood stained chest.

This is a rather rare species that does not migrate much further south than the upper half of Montana in the Winter. Consider yourself fortunate if you see a Gyrfalcon. The only other place I have seen Gyrfalcons is along the Rocky Mountain front west of Augusta.

Don't be hesitant to bird January through March, there are many birding opportunities in the winter months to see interesting birds and their behaviors. In 2020 I saw 102 species from January 1st to March 30th. ♦

PRAIRIE FALCON

I have been asked more than once, "How much time do you spend birding?" If the person asking the question really understood serious birders, they would know that's the wrong question.

You see, serious birders are always birding. That is to say regardless of what else we might be doing we are always scanning the sky, hedges, road sides, grasslands, forest, trees and lawns for birds. You can be deep in conversation with a person, trying to maintain eye contact, but the slightest movement in the background and we instantly zero in with both our eyes and ears for an identification. It's just what happens after years of studying field guides, reading articles and listening to sound tracts of bird songs.

PRAIRIE FALCON

We become as aware of our environment as a solider does in war time looking for the enemy. Only we are looking for that next life, yard or year bird.

It happened to me and my grandson a while back. My wife and I had decided to downsize as we are getting older and moved from 15 acres in the country to a corner lot in town. We are sort of kitty-corner from the old St Joseph's Hospital property in Deer Lodge. On that property is a brick chimney from the steam plant that heated the facility. While working in the yard on many occasions I have observed Rock Pigeons, (formerly Rock Dove) roosting on that chimney.

My grandson is as trained as I am, only with better ears and vision, to watch for birds. As you get older you can't hear or see as well. As he left the house the other day I said bye and walked back into the house. Seconds later he came running back in the house asking for binoculars. He had spotted a bird that was not a pigeon on the top of the chimney but it was too far away to identify. He grabbed my binos, I grabbed my camera and we ran across the street. As he worked on the identification I snapped off two dozen pictures. My camera takes six frames per second.

PRAIRIE FALCON

It was an unexpected, but an easily identified Prairie Falcon. Note the white eyebrow and dark vertical mustachio line. This was the first time I have ever seen one in the city limits. I always find them, mostly in the winter, in fields south of town on power poles and trees looking for a meal of rodents or birds.

This individual definitely gave you a clue as to what he was doing. There wasn't a pigeon in sight, instead just a single falcon. If you look closely at his chest and belly you will see a reddish wash. That's not the color of his feathers, that's blood. He had obviously just made a kill. The falcon remained perched the rest of the afternoon and no pigeons returned.

The next day the falcon was gone, pigeons were back, and I haven't seen a falcon since. I wish I had witnessed the kill, it would have been something to see.

Every time I go out the door now I glance over at the brick chimney perch. I may never observe a falcon on that chimney again but if I keep my eyes and ears attuned to nature as I putter around my yard who knows what I might see next time Maybe a Northern Pygmy-Owl stalking a house sparrow?

Most people never notice a bird all day long. I see birds all day long, every day. What's the difference? I have trained myself to clue in on birds. I hope you do as well. Far too many beginning birders stay that way the rest of their lives. They don't take the time and effort to get better or become aware of their surroundings.

Nature is full of interesting observations, many are never seen. What's lurking near your back yard? ♦

Family Tyrannidae

Western Kingbird 149
Eastern Kingbird 150

Western Kingbird   *Tyrannus verticalis*

WESTERN KINGBIRD

There are a number of species of flycatchers in Montana. In all, the Montana checklist shows 20 species. Most have the word flycatcher in their name such as Willow Flycatcher but others are wood-pewees, phoebes, and kingbirds.

I want to discuss two flycatchers that are found across Montana; the Eastern and Western Kingbird. Unlike many flycatchers in the genus Empidonax, which are nearly indistinguishable except by song, the kingbirds in the genus Tyrannus are fairly easy to distinguish. There is a third kingbird species, Cassin's Kingbird in Montana, but it is only found in Southeast Montana.

WESTERN KINGBIRD

Western Kingbird *Tyrannus verticalis*

Both the Western and Eastern Kingbird are found and breed statewide. The Eastern is far more abundant in the state with 7,578 observations compared to 4,033 for the Western Kingbird in the *Montana Natural Heritage Program* database. That is a three to two ratio in favor of the Eastern Kingbird. I have also found that ratio to be true with my own observations. On a typical outing I might observe as many as 20 Eastern Flycatchers and would be surprised to see more than seven Western Kingbirds.

Eastern Kingbird *Tyrannus tyrannus*

EASTERN KINGBIRD

EASTERN KINGBIRD

I really don't have an explanation for the difference in distribution. The range map for Eastern Kingbirds covers most of the 48 contagious states except for the Pacific Coast states, Nevada, Arizona, New Mexico and Western Texas. The Western Kingbird range rarely extends further east than a line drawn down the edge of Eastern North Dakota to Texas.

What I really like about these two species is they are relatively tame and perch on fence lines and posts and are easily photographed. Both weigh 1.4 ounces and are approximately the same size. The Western Kingbird has a length of 8.75 inches and a wingspan of 15.5 inches. The Eastern is slightly smaller by less that a half inch of the same measurements. Looking at them in the field the Western seems bigger and bulker in its stance.

There is no mistaking the difference in plumage in these two species. The Eastern Kingbird has a plain grayish-black back and clean white belly. The black cap is in stark contrast to the white throat. Sexes look alike and if you look closely there is an orange-red crown stripe within the black cap. I rarely see this in the field but in the hand the red feathers are obvious. Another good field mark is the white tip of the tail. In contrast, the Western Kingbird has a pale gray cap, whitish-gray throat and breast and yellow belly. The back is gray-green and the wings are dark. In flight you can see outer white tail feathers.

Like all flycatchers, if you watch them for a few minutes, they will sortie up into the air, take an insect, and then fly back to the same perch. This is repeated time after time as long as insects are flying near them.

If you have thought about bird photography, this is a good species to practice taking photographs of in the wild. Drive back roads of your area and watch for these two species on hedgerows, wire fences and on posts. If you see one drive slowly to within photographic range. Stay in your car as it makes the best blind. If the bird flies up for an insect you can move a little closer to its perch as they most often return to the same "insect outpost". When photographing with a long lens such as a 400 or 500 mm or 40X zoom or more, the higher the shutter speed the sharper the picture. It's been my experience that if you set your shutter speed to 1/2000 of a second or more you get good results. You can also rest your camera on the window using a bean bag to increase steadiness.

Most of the time you have to crop bird images as birds can be amazingly small in an image. If the image has any distortion (noise) at all it becomes blurry quickly. I often shoot at 1/4000 of a second but I increase the ASA/ISO from 200 to 400 or Auto ISO to allow for depth of field.

Go find a Kingbird one of these weekends and see what kind of image you can capture. If you like your picture consider posting it on *Montana Birders Facebook Page*. It is a closed group but it is easy to join. Several hundred birders have done just that and it is a delight to look at what others have seen and photographed. It is also a good way to learn your Montana birds. Grab your camera, binos, and go birding! ♦

BIRDING IN THE GALAPAGOS ISLANDS

Family Vireonidae

Cassin's Vireo 152
Red-Eyed Vireo 153

Cassin's Vireo *Vireo cassinii*

CASSIN'S VIREO

CASSIN'S VIREO

The challenge in writing these articles is not in getting the facts right, it's getting the picture right. Most of the time I use pictures I have taken, but occasionally I just don't have a good photo in my files. When that happens I seek assistance from other Montana Birders. I am connected to over 9,000 Facebook Page birders at Montana Birding. Many in that group photograph birds and when I asked for photos of a Common Nighthawk eight folks sent pictures.

This article features the Cassin's Vireo and Red-eyed Vireo. I took pictures associated with this story in July 2018 near Beavertail Hill in Missoula County. When I have a bird in mind, but not a good picture, I go to proper habitat. In this case it was a riparian stream with thick willow growth and I played their territorial song. Almost immediately I got a response from a Red-eyed Vireo perched in the willows and began singing.

Now all I need to do is get the picture. I use a Nikon D750 which produces a 24 megapixel image. I set the camera to shoot seven frames per second with a 1/3 F-stop bracket difference between each picture. In order to make this work you need a memory card that is fast and has a minimum of 32 GB of storage. I shoot in RAW and convert to JPEG. I get about 1000 pictures on an extreme compact flash card. I have both a 350 and 500 mm telephoto lens and use the 500 mm most of the time. It is amazing how small the bird is on the image even with a 500 mm lens. A 500 mm lens really needs to be on a tripod to reduce vibration, but that is not possible with the action shots that are taken following a bird through the brush. Therefore, I use a shutter speed of 1/2000 of a second and let the camera set the F-stop. I also use "auto ISO" so if the light is insufficient, which is often the case in dense brush, the camera can readjust the ISO. I set the upper limit on the ISO at 800 so the image is not too grainy with a minimum shutter speed at 1/1000. I then take a lot of pictures.

RED-EYED VIREO

RED-EYED VIREO

I took 240 pictures of the Red-eyed Vireo, in bright light, low light, perched, flying, singing and catching bugs over a two hour period. Once I have the pictures I select those I think are good using the camera's monitor. Then I use the internal retouch menu and crop if necessary. Only then do I use Photoshop and Capture One to adjust brightness, color, sharpness and a whole host of other tweaks. Of the 250 pictures taken I ended up with 5 photos that I liked.

Vireos are represented by 14 species in North America and nine species in Montana. Of those nine, two have been seen less than 20 times in Montana. The three that are common in Western Montana are Cassin's, Warbling and Red-eyed Vireo. Warbling is the most common with nearly 15,000 sightings in the last decade. Warbling can be distinguished by a rather drab appearance, washed yellow underparts, small bill and weak eye line. It is best identified by its song which is a rapid warble without pause that goes on and on. The Cassin's Vireo has a uniform greenish back and side, pale yellowish breast and a distinct white spectacle which is a bold ring around the eye and a white line extending to the small beak.

The Red-eyed is larger than the other two Western Montana vireos and has a green back, white breast and pale yellow undertail. The most distinctive mark is the gray crown with a dark border. Above and below the eye is a white line with a black streak through the red eye. The bill is large.

In summer see if you can find all three of these Vireos in Western Montana. ♦

Family Laniidae

Northern Shrike 154

Northern Shrike *Lanius borealis*

NORTHERN SHRIKE

NORTHERN SHIRKE

The Northern Shrike is a unique passerine or perching bird. This species is a songbird but its feeding habitats are not what we typically think of with songbirds.

Shrikes are found most often singularly, in open brushy fields, hedgerows and along the edges of forest. I often see them on fence posts and wires along country roads. I also see them in the riparian zone of rivers and streams.

What makes this bird unique is that they are predators. I suppose you could say an American Robin is a predator on earth worms but the Northern Shrike takes it much further. Their adaptation for feeding is a strong hooked bill reminisce of the much larger raptors such as the American Kestrel and Merlin. This hooked bill is used to kill and dismember prey.

Once they catch a prey, they often hang the corpse on thorns for later consumption, therefore the nickname Butcher Bird. I have on several occasions seen chickadees and shrews impaled on barb wire. There is much speculation as to the cause of this impaling of prey. Some ornithologists feel it is a way to age or tenderize the meat. Others feel it is just an efficient way to store food for later consumption. Recent research has indicated they may be marking a winter feeding territory, much like canines do with urine.

NORTHERN SHIRKE

Northern Shrikes are uncommon northern breeders in Alaska and the Northwest Territories. They are mostly an insect eater in the summer. Winter migration brings them to Southern Canada and the northern tier states South to Nevada, Utah and Colorado. Their winter diet changes to vertebrates including small reptiles, mammals and birds. When foraging they perch out in the open on fence posts, power poles and treetops. They are capable of hovering and floating to the ground while hunting.

At a distance Northern Shrikes are light gray birds with black wings and tail. With closer inspection you will note the breast is lightly barred. The rump is whitish. In flight large white wing patches are obvious both above and below. There is a black mask or band from the beak through, but not above the eye. The bill is dark, large and distinctly hooked.

Juveniles look much different. The barring on the breast is much more prominent and the head and back are brownish in color. The mask of the adult is barely visible or on the one that I photographed in my yard not present.

JUVINILE NORTHERN SHIRKE

There is a southern counterpart to the Northern Shrike called the Loggerhead Shrike. This species is darker gray on the back, broader masked with a shorter less hooked beak. They winter in the southern tier states and summer east of the Continual Divide in Montana, Wyoming, Dakotas and Missouri River drainage states. They are common south of Dillon in the Bannack area and I have increasingly seen them in the Clark Fork River Drainage. As of 2021 there is no evidence of breeding. ♦

Family Corvidae

Canada Jay	156
Stellers Jay	158
Blue Jay	159
Clark's Nutcracker	160
Black-Billed Magpie	162
American Crow	164
Common Raven	165

Canada Jay   *Perisoreus canadensis*

CANADA JAY

CANADA JAY

The Canada Jay (Gray Jay) is a member of the Corvid family of which there are nine species in Montana and 19 in North America. Here in Montana other familiar species in this family include the magpie, crow, raven, nutcracker and two jays; Steller's and blue.

When I was growing up here in the Upper Clark Fork Drainage, I knew this bird as the camp robber. We spent a lot of time camping in the woods and Canada Jays would come and steal food that we left uncovered. In fact, after a day or two and with a little patience, you could get them to come and feed out of your hand. They are the tamest and least afraid of all of the Jays. The other thing about them is that they are always in small groups of three to five birds. If one came to your camp so did others.

In the past the Gray Jay (now the Canada Jay) was known as the Canada Jay, but it has been known as the Gray Jay for the last 70 some years. In 1957 the Nomenclature and Classification Committee of the American Ornithologist Society (AOS) changed the name to be officially Gray Jay. They didn't even use the old world spelling of 'grey' (used in Canada) rather than the American version, gray. The species had been called Canada Jay for at least 185 years before 1957. There doesn't seem to be any reason in AOS notes of the time as to why the species name was changed. After all, the species lives in boreal/taiga forest of which much of Canada consists.

Canada, like many countries has a national tree, national animal but had no national bird species. There was an effort when Canada celebrated its 150 anniversary in 2017 to make the Gray Jay the official national bird of Canada but there was little enthusiasm for a bird with the name Gray Jay even though the vast majority of the bird's range is in Canada.

Therefore, Canada went through its 150 year celebration without a national bird. It did however spark a campaign to change the name back to Canada Jay. A committee was formed and a proposal was submitted to the North American Classification Committee of the AOS in December 2017. The committee approved the change back to Canada Jay in June 2018 as part of the 59th Supplement to the *Checklist of North American Birds*.

CLARK'S NUTCRACKER

One-hundred and ninety-five countries have official national birds. Canada is not one of them yet but I suspect that it won't be long before Canada's parliament votes and there will be 196 countries with national birds. (Since writing this article Canada's parliament approved the Canada Jay as their national bird.)

There is another bird that looks somewhat like a Canada Jay and occupies the same niche as the Canada Jay; Clark's Nutcracker. They are easy to tell apart. The bill on the Clark's is much larger, the wings are black and the vent is bright white. The Canada Jay has a small beak, light gray body with no black wings and mostly white head. Pacific and Taiga subspecies show extensive black on the head.

At times I'm frustrated with name changes but I think this is a good one. Canada needed a national bird and there isn't a better bird to reflect much of Canada's Taiga forest ecosystem. True, the bird is gray, I mean grey, but hey, what could be better for Canada than finally having a Canadian national bird. ♦

STELLER'S JAY

Montana has nine species of Jays all of which are rather common except for the California Scrub-Jay that used to be called the Western Scrub-Jay and has only been seen four times in Montana. The remaining Corvids in Montana are; Pinyon Jay, Steller's Jay, Blue Jay, Clark's Nutcracker, Black-billed Magpie, American Crow and Common Raven.

Most of these species are familiar to all of us but I am surprised at the number of people who confuse Steller's and Blue Jays. I think the confusion comes from the fact that everyone has heard of a Blue Jay so when they see a Steller's they simply say Blue Jay.

Blue Jays are rather irruptive and not often seen in the Upper Clark Fork Drainage so I am always suspicious when someone tells me they have a Blue Jay in their yard. They are more common in the Flathead and Eastern Montana.

STELLER'S JAY

Blue Jays are pale sky blue with a dark necklace extending up to the blue crest on the head. The breast is gray and there are white wing markings. I often hear them before I see them. Their *queedle-queedle-queedle* call is distinctive and carries a long distance. They co-exist with humans and are often found at feeders. In the winter of 2017 we had three to five individuals that stayed in our neighborhood for a month and they were quite tame. I would set peanuts in the shell on my deck railing and they would readily come and take them. The Blue Jay picture with this article is from my deck.

Steller's Jay on the other hand is dark blue overall with a blackish head, back and neck. The crest is larger than that of the Blue Jay and is more upright. The Pacific Coast Steller's Jay lacks the white forehead markings found on the Interior West Steller's Jay. The photo I took of a local Steller's Jay shows the white markings.

Steller's Jays are confined to the western half of the state in coniferous forest more than in residential areas, like the Blue Jays. Reliable areas to find Steller's Jay are Georgetown Lake, Discovery Ski Run and Sunnyside Road in Anaconda. Blue Jays are found statewide in small numbers. There are more than three times as many observations recorded with the *Montana Natural Heritage Program* for Steller's Jays (2,602) than Blue Jays (932). Blue Jays are more abundant in eastern states than in Montana.

Blue Jay *Cyanocitta cristata*

Blue Jays have been slowly colonizing Montana for more than a decade. During the winter of 2020 they were recorded in all of Montana. It remains to be seen if they continue in this expansion across the state.

So, the next time you see an obvious "Blue" Jay check to see if it is dark or light blue and call it by its correct name. It'll make me happy and I know Jays will appreciate it as well. Who wants to be called Bob when your name is Joe! ♦

BLUE JAY

BLUE JAY INVASION

This is a second article on the Blue Jay because of its appearance in the Deer Lodge Valley.

One of the great things about writing these articles that were published in various newspapers is that I have met many people through emails and phone calls about their bird sightings. I encourage you to keep those communications coming.

In mid-October 2017 I began getting emails from folks in Butte that were seeing Blue Jays at their feeders. One person even wrote they were getting "real Blue Jays" at their feeders. This is a reference to the fact that many inexperienced birders often refer to the Steller's Jay as a Blue Jay. More on the identification differences later.

At first I thought that it was an isolated case but throughout the latter half of October and November 2017 I received many phone calls from throughout the Butte area of Blue Jay sightings. My last communications on Butte Blue Jays was in early December.

The Blue Jay is a member of the Corvidae family which includes Jays, Crows, Ravens and Magpies. There are 19 members of this family represented in North America and 117 worldwide. In Montana there are nine species and in the Upper Clark Fork Valley there are seven. Blue Jays are found scattered throughout the state but the only breeding records are in Northwest Montana. Blue Jays have been documented 932 times and Steller's Jays 2,602 times. I am seeing Blue Jays in our valley with increas-

BLUE JAY

159

Blue Jay   *Cyanocitta cristata*

ing frequency. In fact in the Fall of 2020 I had four at my feeders nearly every day. Their occurrence and number continue to increase into 2021. Blue Jays have come to my peanut feeder for more than 120 consecutive days. Most amazing is that on some days I have as many as eight individuals. It will be interesting to see if they stay the summer of 2021 and breed. If they do that is an expansion that was unexpected. Unlike statewide wanderings of the Blue Jay, Steller's Jay is found only West of the Continental Divide.

Blue Jays are a year around species and if you consult a field guide you will see they are very abundant from the Dakota's south to Texas to the East Coast and uncommon West of that line.

Blue Jays are easily recognized with pale blue head, back and tail. The breast is gray, with white wing bars and obvious white tail spots and wing edges in flight. The crest is blue with a dark necklace extending from the crest to the breast. In contrast Steller's head, upper breast and back are blue-black, the head has a long crest. The lower back, tail and breast are dull blue. Steller's are not found in Eastern United States.

In your local travels when you see a jay remember there are three species of jays with some shade of blue in Southwest Montana if you count the Pinyon Jay. The Pinyon is easy to separate as it is dull blue over its entire body. Corvidae is a diverse and interesting family locally and worldwide! ♦

Clark's Nutcracker   *Nucifraga columbiana*

CLARK'S NUTCRACKER

CLARK'S NUTCRACKER

On August 22, 1805, William Clark, while floating the Salmon River in what is now Idaho, noticed a bird that had not yet been described in North America. He wrote in his journal, "I saw today [a] Bird of the woodpecker kind which feeds on Pine Purs, its tale white, the wings black every other part." On May 28, 1806 he further describes the bird and corrects his first report. "I have killed several birds of the corvus genus of a kind found only in the Rocky

Mountains and neighborhood. [it] has a loud squawling note, -- the beak of this bird is 1 ½ inches long."

By his second entry he realizes that the bird is not a woodpecker but is of the Corvidae or crow family. His May 28th entry goes on to describe the bird in detail. He names it Clark's Crow.

In the past it was common to name a bird after the person who discovered it or to honor someone who had made significant contributions to ornithology. Audubon's Warbler is good example. The problem with such names is that though they honor a person, they do not describe the bird. Audubon's Warbler has since been renamed Yellow-rumped Warbler and Clark's Crow is now Clark's Nutcracker. Both new names describe a field mark or trait of the bird.

CLARK'S NUTCRACKER

Clark's Nutcracker is a member of the crow family of which there are 19 species in North America and nine species in Montana. I have seen seven of those nine species in the Upper Clark Fork Drainage and all nine in Montana. The two I have not seen locally are the Pinyon Jay and California Scrub-Jay. The Pinyon Jay is mostly found in Southeastern Montana but can be found in the Helena and Lewis & Clark State Park areas as well. The California Scrub Jay has been seen only four times in Montana. The other corvids are common and include Canada Jay, Steller's Jay, Blue Jay, Black-billed Magpie, American Crow and Common Raven. Of the seven seen in our valley all breed locally except the Blue Jay which is infrequent and transient.

The habitat requirements of the Clark's Nutcracker are coniferous forests, especially where there are lodge pole, ponderosa, pinyon and white-bark pines. This habitat is also occupied by the Canada Jay and Steller's Jay and they co-habit without undue competition for food.

All Corvids are noisy songsters but I hear the Clark's more often than Canada or Steller's. Their call is a long ascending harsh trilled snarl – *"rrrrrah"*. Once you hear the call and see the bird it is one of those calls that is not forgotten. This jay is crestless and has a bold black, white and gray pattern. Specifically the body is pale gray with a white face. Wings are black with small white patches.

The tail is black with white outer tail feathers. The vent area is also white. The large bill is black as well as the legs and feet. It is a *Species of Concern* and is declining in numbers across the west. This decline is probably due to the decreasing pine densities caused by fire, disease and pine bark beetles.

Clark's Nutcracker   *Nucifraga columbiana*

Although Clark's Nutcrackers eat a lot of pine seeds they also store seeds in the ground in caches of 5-15 seeds. Research shows that a single bird can cache up to a 100,000 seeds in a good seed crop year. Even though they have excellent long term memory not all seeds cached are eaten. Through this caching and over-storing of pine seeds, seedlings are distributed across most mountain habitats. In turn, the plants the nutcrackers are dependent upon are perpetuated into the future.

Whitebark Pine is totally dependent on the nutcracker for seed dispersal. These two species are dependent enough on each other for survival that the behavior is called Whitebark Pine/Clark's Nutcracker Mutualism.

Many novice birders confuse the Canada Jay with the Clark's. They are easily separated as the Canada Jay, though gray bodied, lacks the black wings. Canada Jay's white on the head is more extensive and the beak is short in comparison. Canada Jays are much tamer and will approach humans while the Clark's keeps their distance.

Both species are year around Montana residents. On your next trip to a coniferous forest see if you can find both species and distinguish the difference. ♦

Black-billed Magpie   *Pica hudsonia*

BLACK-BILLED MAGPIE

The featured bird for this article was requested by one of my readers. He mentioned that he was fascinated by Magpies. I also have a lot of admiration for the Magpie; they are smart, resourceful and quite beautiful. The only problem is that they are very common, a little bit of a pest (love to steal dog food), and either ignored or despised by most of us. When I was in college working in a truck stop drivers would come in off the highway and ask about the beautiful black and white bird with the really long tail! If Magpies were rare they would be a sought after species by many a birder.

Prior to 2001 there were only two Magpies (genus Pica) in the world. One was the Yellow-billed Magpie found only in West-Central California and the Black-billed Magpie. Black-billed Mag-

BLACK-BILLED MAGPIE

pies were further split in to 13 sub-species worldwide. In 2001 the subspecies Pica pica pica of Western Europe was elevated to species level and named Eurasian or Common Magpie. The Black-billed subspecies in North America is Pica pica hudsonia. I had seen the European Magpie prior to the split in both England and Holland and after the split I gained a species on my life list without ever leaving home. That is the advantage of keeping accurate records.

Magpies are very common in Western Montana and less common the further east you go but are found and breed statewide. They are however a bird of the west and are not found further east than a line drawn down the eastern edge of North Dakota south. They range north to the southern portions of Alaska and south to Northern Arizona and New Mexico as year around residents. They are not found on the Pacific Coast. Lewis and Clark were the first to scientifically describe this species and it was the only species of birds that survived the trip back to the East Coast after the expedition ended.

Black-billed Magpies are rather large with a length of 19 inches and a wingspan of 25 inches and weigh six ounces. They are pied in color with a black head, chest, back, contrasting with the white scapulars (upper wing) and belly. The wings and tail are iridescent blue/green. Sexes are similar. Their call is loud, nasal and harsh. Their *"mag mag mag"* or *"yak yak yak"* vocalization is very familiar.

They are prolific breeders with seven to thirteen eggs in a stick nest usually found in low bushes. By mid June to early July you will often see very short to almost tailless young of the year.

Yes, they are common, **BLACK-BILLED MAGPIE** but also an important scavenger cleaning up road kills and other carrion. They are known to eat eggs and nestlings of other species, but not to an extent that endangers those species. In the past, counties in Montana had bounties on magpies as an agricultural pest but that is no longer the case.

So enjoy looking at the Black-billed Magpie. Birders in the Eastern United States would relish the idea of looking at this pied, long tailed beauty. ♦

AMERICAN CROW

During the winter months you will see a lot of "black birds" along our highways making a meal out of road killed animals. There is often a lot of confusion about the identification of these "black birds" by inexperienced birders. Was that bird a Crow or a Raven? Hopefully this article will show you how to distinguish between them in the future.

Both Common Ravens and American Crows are members of the family Corvidae of which there are 19 members in North America. Two of the nineteen are raven species and four are crow species. In June 2020 the Northwestern Crow was merged with the American Crow, due to genetic swamping or hybridization of their genes, until the two species were no longer recognizable. We now only have three crow species. In Montana there are nine Corvidae species of which there is only one raven and one crow. The differences in the American Crow and the Common Raven are obvious when seen together. The raven weighs on average 2.6 pounds and has a wingspan of 53 inches. The average American Crow weighs one pound with a wingspan of 39 inches. The raven is more than twice the size of the crow. However, when they are not together, crows can look deceivingly large, especially through binoculars.

AMERICAN CROW

You need to look for other field marks to distinguish them from each other when they are not in the same field of view. The raven's most obvious field mark, other than size, is the extremely large bill which has a massive base attachment to the head. The crow's bill is petite in comparison. In flight the raven's tail is long and wedged-shaped or longer in the middle than on the sides verses a more rounded shorter tail in the crow. Ravens often soar in flight, crows never soar.

If the light is right the throat appears very shaggy in an adult Common Ra-

COMMON RAVEN

American Crow *Corvus brachyrhynchos*

ven. This is due to long, thin, neck feathers. Their voices are also distinctly different. Ravens have deep, course, resonant calls and crows have drawn out *"caws"* calls which are higher pitched than that of the Raven.

COMMON RAVEN HOLDING A FROG

Common Raven *Corvis corax*

COMMON RAVEN

Common Ravens are more abundant in the Upper Clark Fork Valley than American Crows. In winter, ravens are much more abundant as most crows migrate to warmer parts of the state or to more southern states. The 2019 Grant-Kohrs Christmas Bird Count yielded 267 Common Ravens and two American Crows.

Both species are gregarious and provide an important role in nature as they are ground feeding predators and scavengers; meaning they will eat practically anything. Their diet consists of various road kills, insects, frogs, snakes, mice, grain, fast food wastes, bird eggs and nestlings. Both species show high intelligence and can open garbage bags, use their bills to pry lids off cans and raid dog dishes.

Hopefully, the next time you see a "murder" (large group) of crows or ravens you will be able to instantly separate the two species. Good birding along our highways in the winter. ♦

Family Paridae

Black-Capped Chickadee... 166
Mountain Chickadee.. 167
Chestnut-Backed Chickadee... 168
Boreal Chicadee 169

Black-capped Chickadee   *Poecile atricapillus*

BLACK-CAPPED CHICKADEE

In the fall with cooler weather just around the corner it is time to put out feeders for the birds. Using black sunflower seed, not millet or millet/sunflower mixes, gives the best chance for a variety of bird species. Millet draws House Sparrows which discourages other species from using the feeders. Adding a thistle feeder, suet and water, especially a water drip, greatly enhances the number of species possible.

Placing the feeders near shrubs, such as juniper, provides protection and increases the number of species that use feeders.

The most common species using feeders in our area are chickadees and House Finches. Let's concentrate on knowing our Montana chickadees. Did you know there are four species of chickadees in Western Montana and seven in North America?

BLACK-CAPPED CHICKADEE

MOUNTAIN CHICKADEE

The most common in our valley is the Black-capped. The second most common is the Mountain Chickadee which primarily lives in Western Montana and east of the divide in higher elevation coniferous forests. These are the only two we will get at feeders locally, unless you live in Northwest Montana.

MOUNTAIN CHICKADEE

The remaining two chickadees you may not be familiar with are first the Chestnut-backed Chickadee. It is a West Coast moist coniferous forest species that occurs in similar habitat in Northwest Montana, especially Glacier Park. Small numbers are also found in the moist Rattlesnake and Grant Creek drainages in Missoula and similar habitats in the Bitterroot. This species has obvious chestnut back and flanks. The rarest of Montana's chickadees is the Boreal primarily found in Canada, the Northwest Territories and Alaska in spruce and sub-alpine fir forests. We only find this species in a few drainages of extreme Northwest Montana and Glacier Park where there is similar spruce/fir habitat. This species is black-capped, short tailed and brownish gray overall.

The three remaining North American chickadees are the Carolina of Southeast US, the Mexican found in very limited habitats in Southeast Arizona and Southwest New Mexico and the Gray-headed in extreme Northern Alaska.

The Black-capped is found in all Canadian providences, Alaska and the northern half of the US. They are identified by a black cap and bib, with a white check patch below the eye extending to the nape. The back is gray and the sides are buffy. They are common in residential areas and extend their range to mid elevations in deciduous woods and willows bottoms. They are named after their call - *chick-a-dee-dee dee* .

The Mountain Chickadee is found at higher elevations in coniferous forests. In the winter they often migrate to lower elevations and co-exist with Black-capped, especially at yard feeders. Mountain is distinguished from Black-capped by the black cap being divided by a white line over the eye. The call is a more rapid *sick-a-see-see*.

Chickadees by nature are tame but nervous birds that will perch in trees near feeders, but spend very little time at the feeder itself. They come to the feeder, quickly grab a seed, then fly to protection in a hedge or juniper to consume the seed. Typically they will do this many times before they leave your feeder.

They respond well to their call and are easily observed. ♦

CHESTNUT-BACKED CHICKADEE

The Chestnut Chickadee is mainly in Northwest Montana with only a few records in Missoula and the Hamilton Valley. There are no records in the Upper Clark Fork Drainage from Garrison to Butte in more than 20 years. There are only 1,173 observations with the *Montana Natural Heritage Database* for the Chestnut-backed Chickadee. The species is however, common along the West Coast from California to Alaska.

CHESTNUT-BACKED CHICKADEE   *Photo by alukich*

The fourth chickadee is the Boreal Chickadee and is even rarer with 251 observations. This species is found across much of Canada and Alaska extending down into the United States in the border areas of Northwest Montana, Idaho and Washington. I have observed them a number of times but never outside of Glacier National Park. In comparison to these rarer chickadees the Black-capped Chickadee has been recorded 11,151 times and the Mountain Chickadee 17,451.

In my yard the Black-capped Chickadee is more common at my feeders but I do get Mountain Chickadee as well. The ratio is probably six to one. In the mountains of Western Montana the ratio is reversed in favor of the Mountain Chickadee.

Black-capped can be found statewide, the Mountain in the western two-thirds of the state and Chestnut-backed and Boreal in Northwest Montana.

So how do you tell one species from the other? First

BLACK-CAPPED CHICKADEE

BOREAL CHICKADEE

each has a distinct call, but that is beyond the scope of this article. They can also be told apart on physical traits as well.

BOREAL CHICKADEE *Photo by mirceax*

The Black-capped has a black cap that extend over the eye and has a black bib and white chest. The Mountain has a small black cap with a white eyebrow below the cap and a second black line through the eye and a black bib. The Chestnut-sided has a brown sooty cap and chestnut colored back and sides. The Boreal has a grayish brown cap and back with pinkish brown sides.

MOUNTAIN CHICKADEE

There are three additional chickadees in North America that have never been seen in Montana. The Carolina is very similar to the Black-capped but is only found in the southeast portion of the lower 48 states. Mexican Chickadees have an extensive black bib and are confined to Mexico with sightings in extreme Southeast Arizona and Southwest New Mexico. The final chickadee, the Gray-headed, has a gray-brown cap and white cheeks and is found in Northern Alaska and the Northwest Territories. ♦

Family Alaudidae

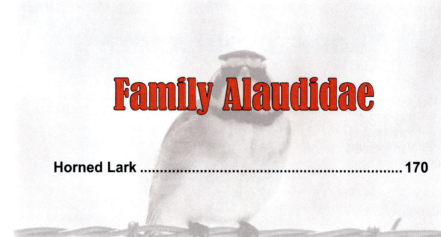

Horned Lark 170

Horned Lark   *Eremophilia alpestris*

HORNED LARK

INTERIOR WEST HORNED LARK

Horned Larks are a species that is easiest seen in the winter. They are in the Upper Clark Fork Valley in the summer but are scattered in small flocks. In the winter when snow is on the ground they concentrate in fields that have blown free of snow and feed on grass and hay seeds.

These large flocks, sometimes over a thousand individuals, often attract other species to feed with them. The most common of those species in the Upper Clark Fork Drainage are Snow Buntings and Lapland Longspurs.

Snow Buntings are easily separated from the larks by their breeding plumage of a white body, black back and wing tips or the non-breeding whitish plumage with brownish

Horned Lark — *Eremophilia alpestris*

back, shoulders and face. In flight all Snow Bunting show a white wing with black tips.

I have never seen an adult breeding Lapland Long-spur with its black chest, and chestnut nape locally. By the time they are in breeding plumage they are back on their breeding grounds in the Arctic Circle in Northern Canada and Alaska. Wintering males and females are similar and show a dark breast band, whitish throat, with reddish or chestnut wing bars. Look for the chestnut wing bar as the most obvious field mark.

The best way to find Horned Larks is to drive the dirt roads along fields when snow is covering the ground looking for a few individuals on the road or perched on fence lines. Once you see them stop and search the adjoining fields. Rarely will you find only a few individuals. Search bare spots around cow dung. Seeds are often concentrated in the dung and the birds will be feeding on the "cow pie" for seeds.

There are six recognized races or sub-species that are geographic in distribution. The most abundant in our area is the Interior West race. This race is grayish backed with a clear white breast and belly. The throat is light yellow and the black "collar" extends to the nape. I have also seen the Western Arctic Race in the Upper Clark Fork Drainage in the winter. The Western Arctic is easily distinguished from the Interior West by a white throat rather than a yellow throat. The name "horned lark" comes from feathers that protrude from the head.

Field guide distribution maps show Horned Larks as breeding in the Arctic, migrating through Northern Canada and year around in most of the continental Unites States. In the summer I observe mostly Interior West Horned Larks. In the winter the number of Western Arctic Horned Larks greatly increases. In our valley, even though we have Horned Larks year around, they may not necessarily be the same individuals winter and summer. I suspect that most of the Horned Larks that summer locally move south in the fall and are replaced by Western Arctic Horned Larks that breed in the arctic and Interior West Horned Larks that breed in Southern Canada.

SHOWING THE FEATHER HORNS

When you are observing flocks of Horned Larks have patience and remain with the flock for an hour or more. You will probably be rewarded with a Prairie Falcon (Gyrfalcon in the winter) or Peregrine Falcon making a dive into the flock looking for a quick meal. They often miss and then a hot pursuit follows with the falcon close behind the flock or even in among the flock. I have observed this a number of times and it is always a thrill to see the predator/prey behavior in action.

Winter can be slow bird wise, but the opportunity to see these large flocks of Longspurs is a winter treat. ♦

Family Hirundinidae

Tree Swallow.. 172
Purple Martin... 173

Tree Swallow　　　　　　　　　　　　　　　　*Tachycineta bicolor*

TREE SWALLOW

TREE SWALLOW

There are eight species of swallows in North America with seven species in Montana. The Cave Swallow is mostly found in Texas and Mexico. Tree, Violet-green, Northern Rough-winged, Bank, Barn and Cliff are found and breed statewide. Each spring the first to arrive are the Tree and Violet-green Swallows followed by Bank, Cliff and then a few weeks later Northern Rough-winged. The last to appear in the Upper Clark Fork Drainage are the Barn Swallows. Tree Swallows can begin showing in early March and the Barn Swallow does not typically show until mid-April.

The most famous and well known of these swallows is the Purple Martin with

Purple Martin   *Progne subis*

PURPLE MARTIN

many home owners putting up elaborate multi-dwelling houses for them to nest. Homeowners do this not only to enjoy the species, but they are very efficient in reducing flying insects entering your yard.

Occasionally, someone will report finding a Purple Martin in their yard in Western Montana but it is most often a misidentification. I did that once in my early years of birding. I saw what I believed to be a Purple Martin along the Clark Fork River and submitted a rare bird report. The species turned out to be a Tree Swallow. My mistake was I was new to birding and my inexperience did not look at the fine details of the bird. Basically, the Purple Martin occurrence is limited to Northeast Montana in the Plentywood and Westby areas where they breed. In the lower 48 states they are a bird of the east and extend into Eastern North and South Dakota then south to Eastern Texas.

The *Montana Natural Heritage's Database* shows 60 observations for Purple Martins in Montana compared to 6,470 observations for the Tree Sparrow.

Of all of the swallows the Purple Martin could only be confused with the Tree Swallow. So what are the main differences? The Purple Martin is large weighing two ounces, compared to .7 ounces for the Tree Swallow. The Purple Martin has a wingspan of 18 inches and a length of 8 inches. The Tree Swallow has a wingspan of 14.5 inches and a length just under six inches. Size can be deceptive, especially looking through binoculars, so look at the field marks. The adult male Purple Martin is uniformly bluish-black over the entire body with the wings more black than blue. Females have a bluish cap and upper back. Their wings are black but the belly is smudgy gray-brown with a gray collar and throat. The juveniles are a lighter version of the female. The head is large for a swallow and the chest is broad giving them an impressive stance unlike the dainty appearance of other swallows.

In the east, Purple Martins are very dependent on multi-chambered houses placed in yards. Most are found in cities and suburban areas inhabited by humans. Martins are a cavity nester and in some areas are found in natural cavities such as saguaro cactus in the southwest and woodpecker cavities in coastal forest.

Purple Martin   *Progne subis*

PURPLE MARTIN

The Purple Martins I have seen in Montana have all been in man made structures in both Westby and Plentywood. The picture with the multi-chambered "martin house" with the male and female on the roof was taken in Westby in the spring of 2016. The other picture is of a Tree Swallow for comparison.

So the next time you are in Westby or Plentywood, you've probably never been there, look around for a "martin house" and add this species to your Montana bird list.

The best place in Westby is up the hill from the south end of the city park and in Plentywood, east of the Dairy Queen in the alley. In both cases look for multi-dwelling structures. ♦

JUNGLE CANOPY BRIDGE IN CENTRAL PANAMA

Family Bombycillidae

Bohemian Waxwing 175
Cedar Waxwing 176

Bohemian Waxwing   *Bombycilla garrulus*

BOHEMIAN WAXWING

There are three North American species that were once called "silky-flycatchers" because their body plumage has a silky appearance. That term is no longer used but it is still descriptive of the two waxwing species that can be found in Montana. The other "silky" species is the Phainopepla of the Southwestern US. The waxwing family, Bombycillidae is small with only three waxwing species worldwide; Bohemian, Cedar and Japanese. The Japenese is restricted to Korea. In comparison, there are nine Wren species in the United States and 79 species worldwide.

BOHEMIAN WAXWING

The Bohemian Waxwing is the less common of the two North American waxwings and breeds in sub-arctic coniferous forest throughout most northern parts of Europe, Asia and Western North America. In fact, the Bohemian circumnavigates all the continents just below the sub-Arctic latitudes. It's closely related species, the Cedar Waxwing, only inhabits North and Central America.

Superficially, Bohemians and Cedar Waxwings look alike but are easily told apart both physically and by season.

Seasonally, Bohemians are only in Western Montana in the winter months and breed in Northern Canada and Alaska. Cedar Waxwings breed locally, a few winter locally, but most migrate to the southern tier states and Mexico. ♦

CEDAR WAXWING

CEDAR WAXWING

Waxwings are unique with sleek plumage, crest, black eye strip, pointed wings and short yellow tipped tails.

Bohemians, about the size of an American Robin, are the larger of the two species at two ounces compared to 1.1 ounces and a wingspan of 14.5 compared to 12 inches. The heavier biomass allows the Bohemian to breed further north than the Cedar.

The Bohemian has a gray belly and throat verses a pale yellowish belly and warm brown breast and neck in the Cedar. The Cedar shows only red on the wingtips, whereas the Bohemian has white, red and yellow edges to the wing feathers. The under tail area is whitish in the Cedar and rufous in the Bohemian.

Except when nesting Waxwings are in flocks, sometimes up to several hundred, and are constantly making high-pitched calls. They are often found in yards in the winter where apple trees with fruit or shrubs with berries are available. A large flock can quickly clean a yard of available food and then move to another yard. Cedars feed on flying insects in the summer and will readily use backyard water fountains for bathing. Juveniles of both species are less colorful and can be distinguished by streaky breast rather than the uniform color of the adult.

CEDAR WAXWING

Winter Waxwing flocks will be predominately Bohemian but it is fun to see if you can sort through them and find a few Cedars. When not feeding they are often found roosting high in deciduous trees such as cottonwoods along riparian stream areas.

Waxwings are a common winter birds in the Upper Clark Fork Drainage and enjoyable to watch and photograph. I hope you will take the time to go look for them in winter. ♦

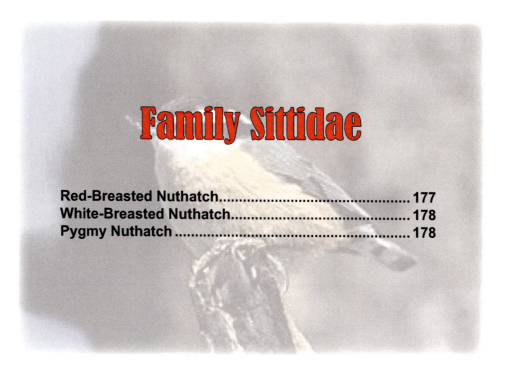

Family Sittidae

Red-Breasted Nuthatch 177
White-Breasted Nuthatch 178
Pygmy Nuthatch 178

Red-breasted Nuthatch   *Sitta canadensis*

RED-BREASTED NUTHATCH

    Nuthatches are distinctive with short tails, long bills and bulky bodies. They are also unique in their tree climbing abilities. They most often feed on insects gleaned from bark crevices by climbing head down around a tree.
    Worldwide there are 25 species of nuthatches with four species in North America. The Brown-headed Nuthatch, range is East Texas to Florida and north to Virginia along the Atlantic Coast and is the only one not found in Montana.
    The most common and widespread of the Nuthatches in Montana is the Red-breasted and it occurs statewide. There are 23,399 reported sightings of this species in Montana with the *Montana Natural Heritage Program* (MNHP). This 4 ½ inch species is abundant in the Upper Clark Fork Valley. It's field marks are a broad black line through the eye,

RED-BREASTED NUTHATCH

a white line above the black eye strip and a black cap. The back is gray and underparts are rusty. If you feed birds in a coniferous habitat this species is a frequent visitor and associates with chickadees.

The White-breasted Nuthatch is our largest nuthatch at 5 ½ inches and has the widest distribution in the United States, but not Montana. The extensive grasslands of Eastern Montana do not contain this species except along the major rivers like the Yellowstone and Missouri. Field marks are a white-breast, black cap, gray back, white face and chest. The under tail feathers are chestnut. There are historic records for this species in the Upper Clark Fork, but not many recent records. It prefers Cottonwood stands which have been mostly eliminated by the contamination of the 1908 flood. MNHP shows 2,244 observations in Montana.

WHITE-BREASTED NUTHATCH

Our smallest nuthatch is the Pygmy Nuthatch *(Sitta pygmaea)* and is only 4 ¼ inches long. It's distribution is restricted to West Central and Northwest Montana. MNHP shows 744 observations in Montana. This species is found exclusively in coniferous pine and most often in Ponderosa Pine. The Upper Clark Fork Drainage has very little Ponderosa Pine. Ponderosa increases downstream in the Drummond area and is the dominate species in lower elevation valleys such as the Missoula and Bitterroot drainages. There is some speculation that Ponderosa is very sensitive to air pollutants and may have been present in the Upper Clark Fork prior to heavy metal smelting in the Butte/Anaconda region. There are isolated stands of Ponderosa in ravines that were protected from the airborne pollutants like arsenic.

It will be interesting to see if the Pygmy returns to the Upper Clark Fork Drainage after the soil within the alluvial flood plain is rehabilitated. I suspect it will be dependent on the return of Ponderosa Pine to our valley through successful plantings. Pygmy Nuthatches are abundant in Helena and Missoula in mature stands of Ponderosa, but there are no records in the Upper Clark Fork Drainage.

Field marks for this species are a gray-brownish cap coming down to the eye with a whitish spot on the nape. The breast has a blush of rust. This species is found in small flocks more than the others two species.

PYGMY NUTHATCH

The accompanying photo is of one individual in a flock of Pygmy Nuthatch I coaxed in by playing their call. I was in a mature stand of Ponderosa Pine at Council Grove State Park west of Missoula along the Bitterroot River.

See if you can see all three species this year in your birding excursions. ♦

Family Certhiidae

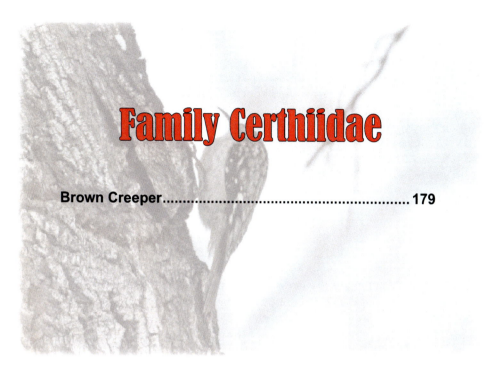

Brown Creeper 179

Brown Creeper *Certhia americana*

BROWN CREEPER

Some birds I rarely see and it's not because they aren't around. I can't hear them so I don't realize I need to look for them. The Brown Creeper is such a bird. Their call is a very high pitched, soft *"see see see titi see"*.

In proper habitat of large coniferous and deciduous trees I sometimes try to coax a view by playing their call. I have trouble even hearing its song through my Bluetooth speaker it is so soft and high pitched. Loss of hearing is one of the downfalls of birding as you get older. When you have the time you can't see or hear anymore! Just kidding about the seeing part for me, but it is an issue for many older birders.

I have offset my hearing loss with quality hearing aids that can be adjusted through my iPhone. When birding I set the mid and high frequency settings to the maximum. It helps, but it's not like

BROWN CREEPER

the hearing of my youth. When I bird with my grandson I am amazed at the birds that he hears. He birds by ear and I bird by sight. Life has its stages and you must embrace each with enthusiasm otherwise you get a little cranky as you age.

Recently I was sitting at my computer working on a bird article when I looked up and saw a movement on the large ash tree just outside my office window. I thought it was probably a Northern Flicker as I have a suet feeder on the tree. I focused and yelled to my wife, "BROWN CREEPER". Why the excitement? Well for one, it was a new yard bird, number 79. We moved from the country where we had lived for 48 years into town and had a country yard list of 145 yard birds. Here in town, just two miles from where we used to live, we have seen 79 species in four years. Secondly, I have never been able to photograph a Brown Creeper.

Fortunately my camera was in my office which is usually not true. I bird a lot and my camera is typically in my truck so I don't forget to take it with me. I quickly snuck out my office door and began taking photos of the Brown Creeper as it moved up the trunk of my ash tree.

One could not confuse the Brown Creeper with any other species. No other bark creeping bird looks like it. I suppose the novice who knows nothing of birds might think it is a Nuthatch or a Chickadee.

So let's separate the three species. Brown Creepers overall coloration matches the bark of many trees so well they really are camouflaged. They are blackish above with whitish spots and sooty tinged underparts making them hard to see even when one hears them. To me the most distinguishing field mark is the thin, long slightly decurved bill. Their behavior is also a clue to identification. When feeding on insects, especially spiders in the winter, they start low on the tree and spirally work their way up until they encounter branches. They then fly to the base of another tree and begin their search again. When feeding they are very active with a constant jerky climb upward. They use their tail as a prop much like a woodpecker and probe deep into the bark's cracks with their long needle like bill. When disturbed they freeze and hug the bark nearly becoming indistinguishable.

The Red-breasted nuthatch typically moves down the tree when it feeds. Their bill is thin, but not curved. They have a black cap, white eye line, bluish back and pale orange belly. They also have a loud rather than soft call which sounds much like a toy tin horn. In the Upper Clark Fork Valley we have few White-breasted Nuthatches due to the lack of cottonwood riparian areas. In the Bitterroot Valley where cottonwood stands are numerous and extensive you'll encounter White-breasted Nuthatches. Field marks are a black cap and nape, white face, grayish back and white belly. The bill is thin, but not curved. They are robust in stature at .74 ounces compared to .29 ounces for the Brown Creeper.

The two chickadees that associate with creepers are the Mountain and Black-capped. Black-capped indeed have a black cap extending to the eye, black throat, a white cheek and buffy flanks. The bill is tiny. They are a noisy feeder with their familiar *"chickadee dee dee dee"* call. Mountain Chickadees have a black cap with a white line through the cap above the eye. The flank and wings are plain gray. They are much drabber in appearance than the Black-capped.

Enjoy my photograph. I sure am, as it may be a long time before I get the opportunity to take a Creeper's picture again. ♦

Family Polioptilidae

Blue-Gray Gnatcatcher 181

Blue-gray Gnatcatcher   *Polioptila caerulea*

BLUE-GRAY GNATCATCHER

    Gnatcatchers belong to the family Polioptilidae of which there are 15 species. All are found in the Western Hemisphere. Only four species are found in North America. Three of these; the California, Black-tailed and Black-capped are found along the border states with Mexico. The exception is the Black-tailed which extends into Southern Nevada. All three inhabit dry pinyon-juniper chaparral environments. Only the Blue-gray Gnatcatcher has a wide distribution across the Eastern United States and southern tier states. They winter in Florida, coastal states, along the Gulf of Mexico and Mexico. In Montana there have been 61 sightings. Until recently all of these sightings were coming from the Pryor Mountains at the mouth of Bear Canyon in the Warren area south of Billings. Bear Canyon has similar habitat to Southwest Arizona being hot, dry and a

BLUE-GRAY GNATCATCHER

mix of Juniper and Giant Sage. Beginning in 2014 there have been sightings in Lewis & Clark State Park area that has similar habitat. Isn't it interesting that these birds can travel the country either purposely or by storm and accidentally find suitable habitat. The Gnatcatchers have established themselves at Bear Canyon as a breeding population and it appears the same has happened at Lewis and Clark State Park. Once established they migrate north in the spring from southern tier states and find these same small breeding areas.

The unanswerable question is were these 2014 Gnatcatchers vagrants from the Bear Canyon population or were they new birds that had flown north and found suitable habitat? The dry juniper/chaparral of Lewis and Clark Caverns State Park is remarkably similar to that of Bear Canyon. The only way the question could be answered is if Bear Canyon birds had been banded and then observed at Lewis & Clark Caverns State Park. Incidental, but not observable evidence, is that they are breeding at the caverns is the fact that they have been seen for several years since 2014.

To add to the intrigue I have observed higher than normal numbers of the Gnatcatchers at Bear Canyon compared to past observations. Perhaps there have been a number of years with good brood success and thus the young expanded into other parts of Montana.

The Blue-gray is very small with a weight of .21 ounces and a wingspan of six inches with a length of 4.5 inches. Overall they are bluish-gray with the underparts whitish blue. They have an obvious eye ring and small bill. The breeding males have a black forehead and the black extends just beyond the eye. Both males and females have outer white tail feathers on a dark tail. The white outer tail feathers are very obvious in flight. In behavior they are always in motion and difficult to photograph. Their erratic behavior coupled with jerky tail movements and small size are another field mark to their identification.

The picture with this article is a male I photographed in Bear Canyon in June of 2015. I was able to photograph it because I played its territorial song and it jumped up on a juniper to see who the competition was for its breeding territory. Almost immediately it dove back into the brush and was gone. This is by far the best picture I have of this species. The song is a thin, scratchy warble with a distinct nasal quality.

In Montana the Blue-gray is listed as a *Species of Concern* (SOC) which means the population is either threatened or endangered. The Blue-gray is probably listed because of the small population in a single area. However, with the recent sightings in the Lewis & Clark Caverns area this species appears to be expanding into other suitable habitat in Montana.

This is why it is so important to report bird findings to the eBird system on the internet so trends can be noticed and studied. If you are not familiar with the eBird reporting system, review page 17 of this book.

Enjoy birding this summer and into fall. Again, if you have a rare or unusual sighting, please post it to eBird or notify someone like myself to do it for you. ♦

Family Troglodytidae

Rock Wren 183
Marsh Wren 185
Carolina Wren 187

Rock Wren   *Salpinctes obsoletus*

ROCK WREN

Wrens are a fascinating family of birds. All of them are energetic, darting here and there with quick movements as they seek out insects. In addition, most have songs that are rapid, loud and match the energy of their movements.

In North America eleven species have been recognized but worldwide there are 79 species of which I have seen 20. In Montana there are nine species. The Carolina Wren's status is accidental having only been observed once. That observation was near Arlee on March 31, 2010 and I was fortunate to see it. Three species are *Species of Concern*, the Pacific, Winter and Sedge Wrens. A *Species of Concern* is one in which numbers are declining, habitat is declining, or both. In 2010 Winter Wren was split into Pacific and Winter Wren. The Pacific is found in the western half of Montana to the Pacific Coast and South

ROCK WREN

into California. Winter Wren is found in the extreme northeast corner of Montana and all lands east of that in the United States with the exception of Florida.

Sedge Wren is also an Eastern US Species with a small presence in Northeast Montana having been recorded 36 times. Pacific Wren has been recorded 3,593 times and the Winter Wren only four times.

Bewick's Wren is rather rare with only 22 sightings, most coming from the Bitterroot Valley north to Kalispell.

Canyon Wrens overwinter in small numbers in Montana and have been observed 281 times. One Canyon Wren was observed on the Christmas Bird Count on January 1, 2007 on Dry Cottonwood Creek and was observed for over a week. I believe it is the only sighting of this species in Southern Powell County.

ROCK WREN

House Wrens are common backyard birds in all of Montana as well in riparian areas of the state. There have been 9,338 observations reported. Marsh Wrens are also very abundant in the riparian areas of lakes, ponds and rivers. Marsh Wrens have been observed 1,692 times, far less than the House Wren, only because House Wrens live among humans and are observed more often.

The last Wren in Montana is the Rock Wren that has been observed 3,593 times across the entire state.

In summary the House, Marsh and Rock Wrens can be seen statewide. Canyon Wrens can be found in all of the state except for the northeast quarter of the state. Canyon Wren distribution is limited to proper habitats of canyons with steep walls and large rocks. Sedge and Winter Wrens have only been observed in Sheridan County in Northeast Montana. Pacific is generally in the western half of the state, Bewick's along the riparian of the Bitterroot and Flathead Rivers and Carolina was accidental at Arlee with one sighting.

Canyon and Pacific overwinter in most of their habitats. Marsh Wren is known to overwinter in warmer climes in the state where marshes typically do not freeze in the winter.

It is easy to identify a wren to the family Troglodytidae as they all are rather chunky with slender decurved bills and tails that are typically up tilted. After recognizing a species is a Wren, check the habitat as most Wrens are habitat specific. In the case of the Rock Wren, pictured with this article you find them in rock out-croppings. Rock Wrens are rather common in Southwestern Montana in rock outcrops. Observing one may be more difficult and playing their call with loud and vigorous territorial defense calls usually gets them to jump up on a rock to see who in singing. If you choose to play their call use discretion and cease the moment you have identified them.

Rock Wrens are dull gray overall with a cinnamon rump, buffy tipped tail with black bars across the tail. The breast has fine streaks. Canyon Wrens, can be misidentified as Rock Wrens because they sometimes use the same habitat, but they have a distinct white throat and breast, chestnut belly, long tail with widely separated black bars and a long decurved bill.

If you're a ticker, (bird lister) with a little effort you can find most of Montana's wrens with the exception of the Winter and Sedge Wrens. If you want to get them all you will have to visit Sheridan County and Westby in Northeast Montana.

In Summer make a habit of visiting areas known for wrens and see how many species you can find. ♦

MARSH WREN

Each spring I look forward to birding wetlands at Warm Springs WMA as they contain the first easily observable migrants. The first migrating ducks to show are Northern Pintails and Northern Shovelers in early March and the last are the Ruddy Ducks and Blue-winged Teal in mid to late April. One of the first passerines (perching birds) to arrive is the Marsh Wren. They are often overshadowed by the more showy marsh species such as the Yellow-headed and Red-winged Blackbirds.

MARSH WREN

Most years I hear this tiny bird singing from the cattails long before I see it. Its call is quite loud for its size and unmistakable. They sing day and night. Their song is varied, complicated, fast and bubbly. There is really no other song quite like it in the marsh and can be described as "*cheh –ch – ch- cheh*". It most resembles the clicking of a rotary phone or rapidly ticking Geiger counter.

There are nine wren species in North America. All but the Cactus Wren have been seen in Montana. In the Upper Clark Fork Valley the House and Marsh Wrens are common. There is one record of a Canyon Wren in the Dry Cottonwood drainage, and a few records of Pacific (formerly Winter) Wren in some of the wet-

MARSH WREN

ter mountain riparian areas draining into the valley. Sedge Wren is limited to the Northeast corner of the state. Bewick's Wren has been seen less than 22 times and there is a single record of a Carolina Wren which occurred in March of 2010 near Arlee.

Marsh Wrens are found in marshes and sedge beds statewide. In the Upper Clark Fork Valley wherever there are cattail beds you will find Marsh Wrens. Sit quietly, and within minutes you will hear their distinctive chatter-like song. Given a little patience you will soon see them darting in and out of the cattail stems and occasionally sitting atop a cattail head singing. You often see them in a comical stance with each leg on a different cattail stem – spread eagle.

Marsh wrens are small, five inches in length and weighing .4 ounces. They appear stocky with a long slightly curved bill. The head is large without a neck and the tail is fairly long, narrow, barred and nearly always up-cocked. The back is mostly brown with a blackish-brown crown. The wings and tail show ruddy highlights with a grayish brown wash on the sides. The underparts are pale. There is a distinct white eyebrow and white streaking on the back.

MARSH WREN

Take time to visit a cattail marsh the first chance you get. Even though this is a sulky species more often heard than seen, a little patience will produce views of a common bird in our area that you might not have seen before or overlooked in the past. ♦

CAROLINA WREN

At the end of July 2021 the official bird list for Montana was 442 species. As of March, 2010 the list was at 425 species. Obviously these additions are rare birds. What makes a bird rare? The official definition is a bird which has been documented less than 20 times. There are 103 birds in that category or about one-fourth of our species.

The challenge in adding a rare bird to your state list is to be willing to drop everything and travel immediately. Many times these birds are seen for a few days at the most. In 2006 a Tufted Duck was observed north of Thompson Falls and the notice went out on Saturday. I planned to go on Sunday but woke sick and didn't go until Monday. We drove 500 miles and were the first to confirm the bird was no longer there! It was in the area for a short time and only a few birders were able to see it.

CAROLINA WREN *Photo by matthew2000*

If a rarity shows in the fall it most likely dies with the approaching cold weather. If one shows in the spring it has a chance of surviving. It can stay the summer and migrate south in the fall if it has the proper food sources. One rarity, a Curved-billed Thrasher, a species of Southern Arizona, New Mexico and Texas showed up in the fall of 2007 in Libby. The home owner bought and feed it meal worms and it survived the winter. Strangely enough another Curved-billed showed up in Roundup the same year. This species has only been seen twice since then in Montana for a total of four times.

What causes a species to show up a thousand or more miles out-of-range? Most rarities are fall juveniles that are in migration and simply get lost. At other times severe weather may force a species off course. Most rarities are spring and fall migrants.

I have been fortunate to see many of the additions to Montana's bird list. In July of 2009 two students from the University of Montana were doing breeding bird surveys on private ground near Ennis. They were hearing many Western Meadowlarks when they heard one sing that didn't sound right. Eastern and Western Meadowlarks look much the same but their songs are distinctive. This was Montana's first documented Eastern Meadowlark. The landowner was only interested in a few birders on his property and I was one of about thirty birders who had the privilege of seeing it.

Another species was a Lesser Black-backed Gull in mid-summer of 2009 at Harrison Lake. This species has never been seen in the Northwest states of Montana, Idaho, Washington and Oregon. The news of this find spread quickly. Within hours several birders were there but the bird could not be relocated. I arrived the next morning, but the species was never seen again. Unbelievably, another one was seen in Great Falls in September, 2009 on the Missouri River. It stayed for several days and was observed by all who wanted to see it, including me. Since then it has been seen 25 times and no longer considered rare.

On March 29, 2010 there was a report of a Carolina Wren at Arlee. I was skeptical as the Bewick's Wren, another rare species, and a species of southwest and west coast states had been observed ten miles South of Arlee on December 2009. Observers were able to record the suspected Carolina Wren's call notes and posted them on the Internet. It was definitely a Carolina, not a Bewick's Wren! I was in Arlee before 8:00 am the next morning. We heard the bird immediately and had good views and fair photographs. It was observed through April 12.

One of the reasons I bird is to chase rarities. I am willing to chase to build my Montana list. My list stands at 352 species and counting. There are only six people (14 at the end of 2021) who have exceeded 350 species in Montana. I have set a goal of reaching 375 species. I probably won't reach 375, it is an ambitious goal, but it sure is fun trying. In the summer of 2020 I reached my goal of 375 species with the addition of a Yellow Rail near Bozeman. Currently, as of November 2021, my Montana list is 352.

You can see by the picture that in addition to its call that is different it is a much richer brown color than the Bewick's Wren. ♦

TAKING A CAMEL RIDE WHILE BIRDING IN ISRAEL.

Family Mimidae

Gray Catbird 189
Curved-Bill Thrasher 191
Sage Thrasher 192

Gray Catbird   *Dumetella carolinensis*

GRAY CATBIRD

One of the most interesting and unique birds is the Gray Catbird. If you look at the image with this article it is obviously gray but why catbird? The name comes from the cat like mewing song of the bird. You don't even have to use a lot of imagination, they can actually sound like a domestic cat. They are common in Montana with 4,097 observations in the Natural Heritage Database. They come to our valley by mid-May with most migrating south by the end of August. There are a few overwinter records in lower elevations across the state. They winter in Florida, all along the Gulf of Mexico and south into Central America.

This species is known to mimic bird songs of other species but not to the extent of the Northern Mocking Bird. In addition to the mewing call there is a long succession of musical babble consisting of whistles, squeaks and whines with a few stolen notes from other species.

GRAY CATBIRD

Their plumage is distinctive. They are an all gray bird with a black cap, long tail and a rufous undertail or vent that is unique among songbirds. Sexes are alike. We had a breeding pair in our yard this past summer and they were a delight to observe in our lilac hedge where they nested. They were frequent users of our water drip for drinks and bathing. In general this species is a skulker, spending most of its time in thick brush. They tend to prefer moist understories. They hold their tail slightly cocked above the horizon but not as much as a wren.

One of the delights of this species is that they are fairly tolerant of humans. Even though they prefer bushy undergrowth you can see them often on the ground as they use their long beak to probe leaf litter for insects.

GRAY CATBIRD IN WATER DRIP

Males when singing typically perch on fairly high exposed perches. At the breakfast table we often observe the male of the pair singing from the top of a metal fence post in our garden. Our pair, this past summer, was one of the most reliably observed bird species in our yard. Many hours were spent observing them feeding on the ground and carrying insects to their offspring.

So how do you attract such a special bird to your yard? The key is to provide plenty of dense cover. We do this by not over trimming our lilac hedge. Another key is providing a consistent supply of water. Also avoid the over use of insecticides. Birds need three things to use your yard; cover for protection (thick vegetation), a food source (insects or seed feeders) and water, (preferably dripping water so they can hear and find it). If you keep these three things in mind as you develop your yard for birds they will come. We also scare off domestic cats to the point they know they are not welcome in our yard. If you do all this, who knows, you might get a pair of Gray Catbirds nesting in your yard providing many hours of enjoyment for you as well.

I encourage you to provide feeders with black sunflower seeds, thistle seeds and suet in winter for overwintering birds. Providing water is a little more work. We have a flat plastic pan that will not break when the water freezes, suspended about three feet above the ground, and replace the water daily.

The rewards for your efforts will far exceed the time you spend in keeping the feeders full and the water fresh. Plan on seeing chickadees, finches, creepers, nuthatches and siskins, as well as a few surprise species, you never planned to see.

I'm look forward to my winter birds with anticipation hoping to see a new winter yard bird. ♦

CURVE-BILLED THRASHER

"*10 year old finds rare bird!*" That is the kind of headline that will catch my eye, I hope it did yours.

The Inman family in the Ennis area is trying to teach their children the wonders of nature. Their son Will is 10 years old and I am sure he is a normal kid. He probably likes all of the electronic gadgets and has one or two like most kids. I also know that these parents want their children to have more than an indoor experience with friends on these devices. They want them to appreciate the wonder and beauty of nature. They have decided that birding is an easy and natural way for their children to enjoy nature. After all, birds are the most watchable wildlife in nature. There are 442 (2021) species in Montana with at least 200 or more of those species available to watch in most areas of the state. In addition, birds typically are in flocks and easy to watch.

In my yard I have provided water, cover, black sunflower seed, Niger seed and suet in winter. I have an average of 15 – 20 different species and about 150 individual birds daily to watch. It can be a little messy on the deck and in the yard, and runs me about $20.00 a month for feed, but it is well worth it for the enjoyment my wife and I receive. So far we have tallied 104 species on our yard list.

My friends in Ennis have the same attitude. Birds are watchable wildlife that brings great enjoyment to them and their children.

CURVED-BILLED THRASHER *Photo by Kris Inman*

Will has been provided with binoculars and knows most of the birds in their yard. On August 10 I received this email from Will's father, Bob, "Will, our 10 year old, has begun birding this summer. He came inside three days ago saying that he saw a "mystery bird," but I never saw what he had seen. Today he came running inside and said the mystery bird was back. It was a thrasher. It is still here now and has probably been here for a few days."

They assumed that the bird was a Sage Thrasher as that species is common in the area. However, after referring to the field guides they were unsure. That is when they emailed me an excellent picture and asked my opinion. Bob's email said, "We just watched and photographed what we assumed at first was a Sage Thrasher. But the bill of the bird we watched was far larger than either of the field guides we have show. (Sibley's 2000, National Geographic 1987) We see one record from Idaho of a Curve-billed. From the descriptions in our books a Curve-billed Thrasher looks most similar. Attached photos. What do you think?"

SAGE THRASHER

Indeed, the bird was a Curve-billed Thrasher. It was far from it's normal range of Arizona, New Mexico part of Texas and Mexico. Turns out that their sighting was the fourth Montana record. The other three records were in 2007 with one in Libby and two birds in Roundup. (That is two) A word of caution, field guides are not specific enough to show rare sightings within a state. Distribution maps in field guides though useful are general in nature. If the Inmans had referred to P.D.

SAGE THRASHER

Skarr's Montana Bird Distribution - 7th Edition, or the Montana Natural Heritage Program's "Montana Field Guide" on their website, they would have found the 2007 sightings.

So how are these two thrasher species distinguished from each other. The Curved-billed has a heavy, strongly decurved bill and a mottled breast. The Sage has a straight bill, yellow eye, streaked breast and white cornered tail. The Curved-bill is larger with a length of 11 inches compared to 8 1/2 in the Sage.

Look at the photos of the Sage and Curved-billed Thrashers. The Sage is my photo, and the Curved-billed is Kris Inman's photo. Would you have noticed the difference in these two species? Will did, even when the field guide said it wasn't in Montana. Great birding Will!

If you see a rare bird, please contact me. Birding is so much fun. I hope you think so too! ♦

BIRDING IN PUERTO RICO

Family Sturnidae

European Starling 193

European Starling   *Sturnus vulgaris*

EUROPEAN STARLING

    I almost didn't write about the European Starling, as I dislike this species so much, but you might find the facts about this bird interesting.

    This species is a native of Europe and is a member of a rather large showy family of birds. Worldwide there are 76 species of starlings with the majority of them found in Africa, Asia, India and China. I have seen 15 species of starlings and some are very beautiful birds. The European Starling is no beauty in either the breeding or non-breeding plumage.

    In 1890 sixty European Starlings were released into New York's Central Park. The idea behind this introduction was to have all of the bird species in Shakespeare's plays breeding in New

EUROPEAN STARLING

York. Those 60 original individuals had spread to the west coast in less than 60 years. Unfortunately, in the process they usurped the habitat of many native species and forever changed avian populations in America. Starlings prefer the company of humans and do well in urban environments. Typically perches are power lines and roof edges. As the country side turned into urban environments starlings flourished and generally became a pest species. In a little more than a century this species grew from sixty individuals to more than an estimated 200,000,000 birds. They are aggressive cavity nesters and out compete native species for nesting sites. Bluebird and woodpecker populations have been especially hard hit . Starlings are a colonial rooster and as many as a million birds have been known to occupy a roost site creating health issues that are hard to manage.

In Montana they breed statewide and overwinter in much of the state. In the Upper Clark Fork Valley winter numbers are not large but by April you begin to see flocks of several hundred. In the fall migrating flocks can reach a thousand or more. Fall flocks often contain several species of blackbirds as well.

European Starlings are about the size of a meadowlark with an obvious short tail and sharply pointed large bill that is yellow in breeding and black in non-breeding birds. The breeding plumage is iridescent with faint white spots. Winter plumage shows a heavy speckling of white dots. The difference is enough that novice birders think the two plumages are separate species. Their song is a combination of harsh whistle, clicks and chuckles. They often mimic other birds and do an amazing imitation of a Red-tailed Hawk.

Eradication programs have killed millions of starlings by trapping and poisoning but it has had little effect on the total population. I am not aware of any major eradication programs being conducted in Montana.

The next time you see a European Starling realize that taking a species from one habitat and transplanting into another habitat has its risks. Without the natural predators that have developed with a species over time the population can explode. An out-of-balance population can be a threat to native species. Fortunately, we have learned from our mistakes and rarely are species moved from one part of the world to another any longer. ♦

Family Cinclidae

American Dipper 195

American Dipper　　　　　　　　　　　　　　　　*Cinclus mexicanus*

AMERICAN DIPPER

The American Dipper is a year around resident of Western Montana streams and is the only songbird in North America that regularly swims. This song bird is totally dependent on fast, clear mountain and valley streams that have sand and rocky bottoms with exposed rocks, fallen logs and overhangs.

Once you see this songbird you will never forget it. It's a plumb, fist-shaped, no necked, seven and half inch bird with a short tail and straight bill. They first appear to be all slate gray in color, but if the light is right, the head is somewhat browner than the body. The legs and feet are pale white.

Dippers are unique in their behavior. They are usually standing in or at the edge of water or flying over the surface of a stream just a few inches above the water. If you watch for a time you will see them foraging and realize this song-

AMERICAN DIPPER

bird is very different. Dippers are dependent on aquatic insects which are found in streams beds with clear, clean water. Dippers typically stand on a rock and "dip" or "bob" up and down, then dive under water and reappear several seconds later. They can also walk in the water with their head submerged or plunge-dive from rocks and stream banks. When they reappear at the surface they are never wet because special oil glands keep the feathers waterproof. Their feeding seems a little hurried and frenzied as does their flights up and down the stream. They spend hours "dipping" their entire bodies with a quick jerking motion and blinking white eyelids.

American Dipper distribution in Montana is basically west of the Continental Divide where mountain streams are found. If you want to see one go to a fast moving stream and search for them. They often nest under bridges. If streams stay ice free all winter dippers do not migrate. If they do migrate it is a short distance to portions of the stream that remain ice free or another drainage that is ice free. When a stream remains ice free individual birds can complete their entire life cycle in a three to five-hundred foot section of a stream.

The Dipper's nest is an extraordinary piece of bird architecture. It is typically large, made of moss and ferns, and usually found under a waterfall or upon a slick rock face where it is almost impossible for anything to reach it. They also seem to have an attraction to building nests under bridges.

Dippers in Montana are not endangered and will not be so as long as we have mountain streams with healthy riparian zones.

Historically, this bird was called the Water Ouzel but you rarely hear that name today. If you have never seen one make the effort to explore a stream and have a delightful adventure with one of nature's most unique songbirds, the America Dipper. ♦

BIRDING ALONG THE CLARK FORK RIVER

Family Turdidae

Eastern Bluebird 197
Mountain Bluebird 199
Townsend's Solitaire 200
American Robin 202

Eastern Bluebird *Sialia sialis*

EASTERN BLUEBIRD

One of the things that is enjoyable about birding is the unexpected birds that are observed that are rare, out-of-season, or out-of-range.

That happened in Anaconda on December 14, 2018. Steve Wickliffe, a local birder from Anaconda, while looking for an out of season White-crowned Sparrow found an out-of-range and out-of-season male Eastern Bluebird at Washoe Park.

There are three bluebird species in Montana: the Western, Eastern and Mountain. The most common of the three by far is the Mountain with 22,153 sightings statewide in the *Montana Natural Heritage Program* (MNHS) database.

The other two species have fewer records with 379 for the Western Bluebird and 267 sightings for the Eastern Bluebird on MNHS.

EASTERN BLUEBIRD
Photo by unknown Anaconda Birder.

Eastern Bluebird — *Sialia sialis*

As the name implies, Western Bluebirds are found in most western states at lower elevations. In Montana they are predominately west of the divide, but there have been sightings in Helena and Bozeman. Western Bluebirds winter in Utah, Nevada, Arizona and Texas. They look superficially like an Eastern Bluebird but we will get to the field marks later. There is evidence that the Western Bluebird is out competing Mountain Bluebirds where they co-exist for nesting cavities in Montana.

EASTERN BLUEBIRD
Photo by unknown Anaconda Birder.

Mountain Bluebirds are found state-wide and in all western states including the western half of North and South Dakota, south to Texas where they winter along the southern border states.

Eastern Bluebirds are found along the eastern edge of Montana and most eastern states including Texas. They winter in the southeastern states.

The Mountain Bluebird, familiar to most folks, is the easiest of the three to separate from the other two. It is sky blue above, paler below with a white belly. Females are gray-blue with bluish wings and a gray-white belly. Bluebirds are members of the thrush family, Turdidae, therefore juveniles of all three species show a spotted breast. You may be familiar with the spotted breast of a juvenile American Robin which is also a thrush.

Western and Eastern Bluebirds both have rusty-red breasts. The Eastern shows a bright white belly and the Western shows a blue belly. Females of both species show a subdued rusty chest unlike the gray breast of the Mountain Bluebird. Female Eastern show the bright white belly like the male and the Western female has a grayish belly.

The male Eastern Bluebird's rusty-red chest extends up the throat all the way to the lower mandible and extends to the sides of the throat. In the Western Bluebird the head and throat are blue. The reddish color of the chest in the Eastern extends down the back above the blue wing and can be more of a chestnut color. All bluebirds are insect and grub feeders so they all arrive in fair numbers starting in late March and April when insects are abundant. Mountain Bluebirds have been reported year around in lower valleys in small numbers. Western Bluebirds have not been recorded in December and January. Eastern Bluebirds have had single observations in January and February but no observations in March, April, November or December.

It's unlikely we will ever see another Eastern Bluebird in the Upper Clark Fork Valley, but who knows. It is also unlikely that this Eastern Bluebird survived. Being an insect and grub eater it is doubtful this male could find enough food source to survive the temperature and short days of a Montana December.

As you are out and about keep looking for that rare one; it's fun to speculate on how they got here. ♦

MOUNTAIN BLUEBIRD

On March 8th I saw the first species that indicated that spring is here, never mind the calendar. There were a few snowflakes in the air, but a Mountain Blue Bird is a sure sign of spring. The next day the same area had six inches of fresh snow and the bluebirds were nowhere to be found.

On the day that I found the Mountain Bluebird I had 91 species of birds of my 2017 year list, so why the conclusion? I had seen other birds in February and March that don't winter locally so why is this bird the harbinger of spring?

As an example, the same week I saw the bluebird I also found Northern Pintails. Pintails don't winter here but the vast majority of them don't summer here either. They are just moving through so not much to get excited about. I also saw a Great Blue Heron that same week. They stay the summer and breed locally but I saw one on January 17. There are always a few herons that overwinter.

MALE MOUNTAIN BLUEBIRD

Lots of folks think that when you see an American Robin surely spring is not far behind. The problem with robins is that I saw my first one here in the valley on January 14. I looked up the American Robin in the *Montana Natural Heritage Program* and there are wintering records for robins in 37 of Montana's 56 counties including my county of Powell.

I looked through my 91 species and not one qualifies except for the Mountain Bluebird as an indicator of spring. So what are its qualifications? It's a true migrant. Most winter in Southern Utah, Nevada and South into Arizona, New Mexico and Western Texas. There are no documented sightings of a Mountain Bluebird overwintering in the state. There are 15 counties where a Mountain Bluebird was seen during the winter but not regular records. It takes repeated records between December 15 and February 15 to qualify as overwintering. Secondly, they breed in Montana and the Upper Clark Fork Basin. All nine of the bluebirds I saw on March 8th were

FEMALE MOUNTAIN BLUEBIRD

males. They were here to set up breeding territories. The females won't be here for another 2-3 weeks. By then the males will have staked out breeding territories and will be singing up a storm in an attempt to get a female interested enough to breed, nest and rear young together.

MOUNTAIN BLUEBIRD

Did you notice I said singing? That's the real key to their being the harbinger of spring. Mountain Bluebirds are songbirds, they're here to set up shop, sing and raise a family. We all know that spring is the time that birds breed, nest and raise their young. Spring is here despite the fact that on March 9th, one day after my spring sighting, I woke up to six inches of fresh snow. It's still snowing 12 hours later and more snow is predicted.

Am I an optimist? Absolutely, you have to be one to be a birder. I am always thinking that today is the day that I will find that rare bird. It seldom happens. I go out anyway with great enthusiasm knowing that it will happen if I just go out often enough and sure enough it does once in a while.

Keep the faith, winters over! ♦

Townsend's Solitaire   *Myadestes townsendi*

TOWNSEND'S SOLITAIRE

TOWNSEND'S SOLITAIRE

The total number of species that I have seen in the Upper Clark Fork Valley is 256. Overwintering (December 15 to February 15) species drops to 98 with 51 confirmed and 48 "most-likely" overwintering. This is a decrease of a 157 species yet we still have some truly remarkable winter birds to see and enjoy. I want to introduce you to one of the most vocal of our winter species, the Townsend's Solitaire.

The Townsend's Solitaire is a member of the familiar Thrush family that contains the American Robin, Eastern, Western and Mountain Bluebirds. There are many less familiar thrushes of which the Veery, Swainson's and Hermit Thrush are found in the Upper Clark Fork Valley.

One of the common traits of thrushes is the spotted breast in adult plumage on some species or a spotted breast in juveniles. The American Robin is an example. The juvenile has a spotted breast and the adult has an unspotted red breast.

The Townsend's Solitaire is common and abundant year around locally. They are often associated with Juniper shrubs both for cover and food. They have the habit of perching at the top of these shrubs while singing and they sing year around. It is assumed they sing in the winter, not for a breeding territory, but for a feeding territory.

TOWNSEND'S SOLITAIRE

Townsend's are slightly smaller than the American Robin at 8½ inches compared to 10 inches in the American Robin and are slender in appearance. They are gray-brown overall with a bold white eye ring. The buffy wing patches are a good field mark when perched. The tail is dark and the white outer tail feathers are conspicuous in flight. The call note is a high-pitched *"eek"* and their melodious warbling song is fairly loud. This species is rather tame, curious and will often fly in close to inspect you. The juveniles have boldly spotted plumage on the breast, head and back. They have the same buffy wing patches as adults and dark tails with outer white tail feathers. The first time you see a juvenile Townsend's you might not recognize it because of the spots, but it quickly becomes apparent that this juvenile is showing the familiar spots of the Thrush family.

A good place to look for Solitaires is in the lower timberline areas along creeks and foothills with a mixture of Douglas fir and Juniper. Dry Cottonwood Gulch near Galen and lands west of Butte along Interstate 90 are excellent areas.

Several years ago after Christmas we placed juniper branches we had used for decorations on our deck. Within a few days we had a Townsend's Solitaire feeding on the Juniper berries. The picture of the Townsend's feeding on berries was that occasion.

Take a drive during winter along the foothills of our valley and search and listen for this species. As you bird you will most likely see other winter species such as Red-breasted Nuthatch, Mountain and Black-capped Chickadee and Red-tailed Hawk. If you are fortunate you may see a Prairie Falcon, Gyrfalcon or a Rough-legged Hawk which winter in our valley and summer in Canada.

Don't be mistaken in thinking that winter has few birds to see. There are 40 species that can easily be seen with more than 90 possibilities. ♦

AMERICAN ROBIN

The American Robin or Robin is familiar to nearly all of us but Europeans birders are often confused when they first visit the United States and see this species. They also have a bird called Robin and it looks similar with a red breast and throat, but is in an entirely different family; Old World Flycatchers. I have seen both and understand why both are called Robins as the word means red breast.

Many consider the American Robin the most abundant bird in North America estimating the population to be in excess of forty million nationwide. The domestic chicken is the most abundant bird in North America but that hardly counts being a domesticated bird.

These common yard birds are one of the first birds to return to Montana in large numbers and I have personal records of seeing them locally each month of the year. Fall migration of local robins is only a short distance to warmer areas of Utah and Arizona.

American Robins are members of the Thrush family. There are eleven thrush species statewide. I have seen seven species of this family in our valley. Some are common such as the Townsend's Solitaire and Mountain Bluebird. Western Bluebirds can be seen in migration in early spring but do not nest locally. Several local thrushes are very melodious and are heard but not often seen that include the Veery, Hermit and Swainson's Thrush. The Varied Thrush is common in Northwest Montana, especially Glacier Park, and can be seen in spruce forests in the Missoula and Bitterroot valleys. The final two species are rare in Montana. The Wood Thrush has been seen 11 times. The Gray-cheeked Thrush is only found in extreme Eastern Montana in the Plentywood/Westby area with 43 observations.

AMERICAN ROBIN

American Robins are a chesty thrush with slate gray upper parts and a red/orange breast. At first glance sexes look alike but the female breast is paler, even

American Robin
Turdus migratorius

AMERICAN ROBIN

looking orange on some individuals. The duller or paler head of the female is also distinguishing when looked at carefully. Both sexes have white striping on the throat and white eye arcs. The juveniles of mid to late summer have a washed orange breast with dark spots. The accompanying photographs are of males.

Their familiar behavior is one of short runs across a lawn, cocking their head as if listening for earth earthworms, followed by a comical tug-a-war for consumption. Actually, they are only looking for evidence of an earthworm, and if they see a burrow, stab at the hole hoping to get a worm. Being omnivorous they also utilize fruits and berries. American Robins have adapted well to urban life though they nest in almost every conceivable habitat from the Bering Sea to Southern Mexico. Each spring I have a pair build a nest on top of our outdoor light directly above our back door! I suspect they enjoy the warmth of the light but make a terrible mess on our doorstep. Each time we step out the door they fly away but quickly return. I question the wisdom of a nest which requires flights away from the nest many times a day but they have successfully raised 2-3 young for several years.

The next time you see an American Robin stop and think of the variety of birds represented by the thrush family here in our valley and across Montana. ♦

Family Fringillidae

Evening Grosbeak	204
Gray-Crowned Rosy Finch	206
House Finch	208
Common Redpoll	209
Red Crossbill	211
White-Winged Crossbill	212
Lesser Goldfinch	213
American Goldfinch	214

Evening Grosbeak   *Coccothraustes vespertinus*

EVENING GROSBEAK

In my opinion the Evening Grosbeak is one of the most strikingly beautiful feeder birds that can visit your yard. Unfortunately, each year they seem to be less and less abundant. Twenty years ago they were very common in our yard both spring and fall with a few throughout the summer and winter. Now I don't get them every year and when I do I just get a few, rather than 20-30 at a time as in the past. Longterm studies show the decline to be 33% per decade across the west. The cause is not well defined but maybe due to loss of habitat or cyclic with spruce budworm outbreaks or lack thereof. The male featured with this article was photographed in my yard on May 5, 2012. There were two males and a female at my feeder for four hours that day.

I have moved into town and have had 10-15 adults all summer in 2020. In the Fall I got large numbers of juveniles.

MALE EVENING GROSBEAK

Evening Grosbeak　　　　　　　　　　　　　　　　　　　*Coccothraustes vespertinus*

I found they will come to a platform feeder but not a tube feeder. It will be interesting to see if we get large numbers in our yard in 2021.

Evening Grosbeaks are in the Finch family of which there are fifteen species in seven geniuses in Montana. Evening Grosbeaks are most closely related to Pine Grosbeak and the rare Brambling. However, the three species do not look alike.

Evening Grosbeaks are distinctive with a massive head and beak. In flight the wings are relatively short for the size of the body and show white wing-patches. They are sexually-dimorphic with the male showing a bright mustard-yellow belly, large white wing patch on black wings and a black tail. The head is dark with a yellow to olive gray bill. A yellow supercilium or eyebrow is conspicuous. Females are slate gray with a black bar through the eye. The white on the wing is less solid than on the male giving the female an overall drab appearance. Both sexes are bulky in general appearance.

FEMALE EVENING GROSBEAK

Vocalizations are a loud shrill, explosive, whistled *"Peeer"* that allows them to often be heard before they are seen.

Evening Grosbeaks are found year around west of the Continental Divide and Canadian populations winter in Eastern Montana. They thrive in mature, open canopy mixed coniferous forest of spruce, fir and pine. Their occurrence is irruptive and irregular and based on food supplies. A yard platform feeder with straight black sunflower seed is the best way to attract them. They occur at feeders most often during spring and fall migration, but can occur all year long

If you find them at your feeder you are fortunate and you should make sure other members of your household see them as they are an uncommon treat. Good luck and good birding on this beautiful feeder bird in our area. ♦

GRAY-CROWNED ROSY-FINCH

The Grey-crowned Rosy-Finch is a year around bird in the Flint Creek and Pintler Mountain ranges of Southwest Montana. It is however a difficult bird to find. The reason is that its niche is very restricted. They breed at or above tree line. Getting to their habitat at tree line can be challenging in some areas. Their nests are built in holes and cracks of cliff faces or talus slopes above alpine-tundra meadows. Alpine-tundra is not extensive in our area and occurs in limited areas of the Flint Creek Range, Deer Lodge Peak, Mount Powell, and more extensively above Alpine Lake and below East and West Goat Peaks. Alpine-Tundra is also found in the Pintlar Range around Goat Flats, but I am less familiar with that area.

GRAY-CROWNED ROSY-FINCH

Tundra is defined as a vast flat, treeless Arctic region of Europe, Asia, and North America in which the sub-soils are permanently frozen. Tundra is caused by a lack of direct sunlight in latitudes of 55 to 75 degrees north. Alpine-tundra has similar plant and animal characteristics but is caused by elevation rather than latitude. For every 1,000 feet of rise, the temperature on average is three degrees cooler. This phenomenon is known as the environmental lapse rate. This temperature change is why it rains in the valleys and often snows in the mountains in the spring and fall. In our local valleys, these Alpine-tundra environments occur at around 9,000 feet.

The most extensive Alpine-tundra areas in Montana are in the Beartooth Mountain Range south of Red Lodge. Gray-crowned Rosy-finch don't live in the Beartooths, Black and Gray-crowned Rosy-finch are mutually exclusive breeders. Mountains in this area extend to 12,000 feet with Montana's highest peak, Granite Peak at 12,807 feet.

The lowest elevation Alpine Tundra occurs in Glacier National Park around 7,500 feet. The latitude of Glacier Park is 48 Degrees north, compared to a latitude of 45 degrees north in the Beartooth range.

There are three rosy-finch species in North America. The Gray-crowned which is the most widely distributed, the Black, and the Brown-capped Rosy-Finch. There are no sightings of the Brown-capped in Montana. Brown-capped are restricted to Southern Wyoming, Colorado, and Northern New Mexico. The Black-crowned is most easily seen in the Beartooth range, but there are a few records from all the higher elevation mountain ranges of Southwest Montana. The Montana Natural Heritage Program has 618 records for the Gray-crowned and 146 for the Black

Rosy-finch.

Gray-crowned are a rather large finch, with a gray cap, and russet brown colored body. The head is obviously round with a short conical shaped bill. The legs are short and they appear to crouch as they feed.

Males have a dark bill. The female is a drabber version of the brighter plumaged male with a yellow bill compared to the dark bill of the male. Gray-crowned are a *Species of Concern* in Montana due to the limited habitat necessary for their survival.

You occasionally see Gray-crowned Rosy-finch in the spring and fall after heavy snowstorms which push them out of the mountains to feed. This happened in the spring of 2020 on April 11 after a particularly heavy snowstorm. I observed six of them on the Eastside Road feeding with a flock of Dark-eyed Juncos. Other Gray-crowned Rosy-finches were reported in several locations in Southwestern Montana at the same time.

How did I find them? I thought maybe the late snowstorm might have

GRAY-CROWNED ROSY-FINCH

pushed something new into the valley and I should go look. I am glad I did. I was rewarded with my second observation of this species in the Upper Clark Fork Valley floor.

Even more amazingly, were two Gray-crowned Rosy-finch in late November of 2020, after a snow storm in my yard. They were mixed in with House Finches and only stayed a few hours and were gone. I suspect they moved back up to higher elevations when the storm subsided.

Why do some birders see good birds consistently? They are watching the weather patterns and are out in the field looking for that unusual or rare bird.

I purposely bird at least 200 days a year. I know that it seems over the top to some, but others golf, fish, snowmobile, and ski as often as they can. As I get older I realize that to "keep moving, you have to keep moving". For me that means go birding again and again and again.

Good fall and winter birding to all of you. Look for scoters, they're only here in the fall. ♦

GRAY-CROWNED ROSY-FINCH

HOUSE FINCH

There are several common native winter birds in Western Montana including Black-capped Chickadees, American Goldfinch, American Tree Sparrow, Pine Siskin and House Finch that you can expect at your feeders. Of course you will also have House Sparrows, but they are a non-native European species. I am amazed

HOUSE FINCH

at how many folks who feed birds cannot identify the most common of these species, the House Finch.

The House Finch is a year around species in the continental United States and Mexico. They extend into Canada only in the lowest elevations along the US Border.

House Finches are fairly small, slender, small-headed birds with short, stubby, conical bills. They are sexually dimorphic, so we need to describe both sexes. The first thing that is noticed about the adult male is the overall red look. The front of the head, chest, and rump are red, but on occasion can be orange or occasionally yellow. The chest or bib is distinctly set off from the streaked underparts or belly. The belly has distinct streaks on a white background. The cap is brown and there is a brown streak through the eye. The tail lacks a notch and is noticeably square.

The female and all juveniles are brown overall and finely streaked on the head, back chest and belly. In contrast to the male the belly is dirty buff in color. The overall look of the bird is nondescript.

House Finch   *Haemorhous mexicanus*

House Finches are social and forage in flocks. If you have them at your feeder they will usually number between ten and thirty. They are noisy feeders with an excitable descending rapid song.

The only species they can be confused with are Purple and Cassin's Finch. Purple Finches are rosy red in color over most of the adult male's body with less streaking. Females and juveniles are more heavily streaked than House Finches. Purple Finches most often occur in extreme Eastern Montana migrating north into Canada during the breeding season. I have never seen one west of the continental divide, although there are a few records. This species is easily confused with House Finch by novice birders.

Cassin's Finches have more of a red cap, and show little color on the nape, throat and chest. The tail is strongly notched. Females are heavily streaked on a whitish background. Cassin's Finches are summer residents in the Upper Clark Fork Valley, but do winter in low elevation winter valleys in Northeast and Southwest Montana.

The *Montana Natural Heritage Program* shows 3,124 observations for the House Finch, 132 for the Purple Finch, and 2,920 for the Cassin's Finch. The Cassin's finch is a *Species of Concern* in Montana due to declining numbers.

Watch in the spring for both Cassin's and House Finches at your feeders in Western Montana and all three if you live in Eastern Montana. Remember, straight black sunflower seed, Niger seed and a suet feeder is the best combination to attract birds to your yard in the winter. In the summer add a water drip. Always place your feeders near shrubs and other vegetation for protection of yard birds from weather and predators such as Sharp-shinned Hawks. ♦

Common Redpoll   *Acanthis flammea*

COMMON REDPOLL

There are a number of familiar birds that you can count on being at your feeder every winter here in Southwestern Montana.

What you have at your feeders depends somewhat on what you are feeding. If you feed millet, which I don't recommend, you will get mostly House Sparrows. If you spread the millet on the ground or use a platform feeder that birds can spill the millet on the ground you will probably get an abundance of Eurasian-collared Doves.

I recommend using black sunflower seed, which you can purchase in 40

COMMON REDPOLL

pound bags. Use a feeder that can hold a three to four day supply of seed. Preferably this should be a tube feeder with a cage around the tube that allows small birds to feed, but keeps out larger birds that pull out the seed and waste it. Unfortunately, House Sparrows can enter most cages and waste seed. A neat trick is to tie fishing line about three inches apart to the top of the feeder and let the line dangle below the feeder. For some reason that I don't understand, House Sparrows won't cross through the fish line but other species are not bothered by the line and continue to feed. Black sunflower seeds will attract House Finches, Black-capped and Mountain Chickadees.

Placing a suet feeder in the general area of the tube feeder will bring in Red-breasted Nuthatch, Hairy and Downy Woodpeckers, Northern Flickers, and Black-billed Magpies.

A thistle feeder should be your third feeder and will attract American Goldfinch, and Pine Siskin. This winter we have added peanuts on our railing and are getting 2-4 Blue Jays feeding in the early morning.

To top all of this off, you should add a water pan. The water should be no deeper than an inch and have a flat rock or two in the water for birds to perch. You can obtain a heated pan for the winter, but that is not really necessary. Birds seem to get enough water in the winter from snow and snow melt on vegetation and on the ground.

You will have more birds and more variety if you place your feeders in or near brushy or woody vegetation. Birds in general avoid feeders out in the open. I have mine placed so they can be seen and enjoyed from the house in a lilac hedge. The hedge provides protection from cats and that occasional Sharp-tailed Hawk or Pygmy Owl which specialize in meals from backyard feeders. Shy birds like Chickadees do best if they can be protected in a thicket of twigs. They dart out for a sunflower seed, then dart back in and consume it at their leisure.

This year we have an irruptive species from Canada feeding at our home and I suspect most other feeders in the area as well. If you see a finch like bird with a small red cap, yellow bill, and black chin you're seeing a Common Redpoll. These birds summer and breed in Alaska and the Yukon Territories and migrate south during winter months. They rarely migrate further south than Montana and some years stay north of the Montana/Canadian border.

This irruptive behavior is probably linked to food availability to the north of us. They seem to be in abundance in Montana on a two to three year cycle

The other day I had more than 50 of these little red capped beauties feeding with the House Finches. I am going through a lot of seed, but I'm well aware that next year I might not see any of these streaky little finches so enjoy them while there here.

Good birding as always and report those rare findings. ♦

RED CROSSBILL

One of things that keeps a person interested in birding is finding new birds for your state or country lists. Birding is always giving you the unexpected, whether it is a new bird, or a familiar bird in an unexpected place. That happened to us the first week of April, 2018 at our home.

There are many birds that typically are only found in flocks such as blackbirds, starling, and crossbills.

Whenever I see crossbill, most often in the mountains, there are always a flock of 10-12 with a mix of juveniles and adults. Crossbills are one of those species where the females, juveniles and immatures are distinctly different than the red males.

On April 5th a single White-winged Crossbill showed up at our feeders and stayed through April 9, 2018. I thought it was odd that only a single bird showed as crossbills are an irruptive species feeding on coniferous cones. They travel in small to large groups and are here today and gone tomorrow. In my mind that makes this visit to our feeders unique. We don't have a coniferous tree in our yard but he seemed content to forage for black sunflower seeds on the ground and at our feeders. Some days we only saw him a few times and on other days he spent the entire day in the shrubbery near the feeders making sorties to the feeders. ♦

RED CROSSBILL

White-winged Crossbill   *Loxia leucoptera*

WHITE WINGED CROSSBILL

There are actually two crossbill species in Montana; Red and White-winged. The later being much rarer than the former. The database at the *Montana Natural Heritage Program* shows how rare sightings for the White-wing are. There have been 9,793 sighting records turned in for the Red Cross-bill and only 435 for the White-wing Crossbill!

Both crossbill species are identified by bill tips that overlap or cross.. You can see that in the photo of our visitor. This unique characteristic allows them the leverage needed to pry open cones and extract the seeds.

The two species are separated by both the male and the female White-wing having two bold white bars on a black wing. Red Crossbill wings are not as black and lack the white bars. In addition, Red Crossbills are brighter red than White-wings. Many White-wings are almost pink in color, but not the one that visited our feeders. Another distinguishing feature is that the bill is stouter with greater overlap of the tips in the Red Crossbill. In both species juveniles are brownish with heavily streak breast and the females are yellow overall. Immatures, or first year, White-winged males are also yellow, but show patches of red or pink.

There are many sub-species within the Red Crossbills which are distinguished by size, vocalization and "home range". There is a growing consensus that there may be several species within what we currently call the Red Crossbill. The first of these sub-species to be given full species status is the Cassis Crossbill whose home range is south of Twin Falls Idaho in the Sawtooth National forest above 7,000 feet. I traveled to the Sawtooth National Forest in Idaho in August of 2018 and was able to see several Cassis Crossbills and add the species to my world life list.

WHITE-WINGED CROSSBILL

In summary, you never know what bird will show in your yard, especially spring and fall as bird migrate from one latitude to another and from one elevation to another. So keep your feeders full, take time to watch them, and make a yard list so that you know when you get a new arrival.

Enjoy birding this year and be sure to email me if you think you have found a unique or unusual bird. If you can, include a digital image, it's hard to identify birds from written descriptions. ♦

BIRDING IN GREECE

LESSER GOLDFINCH

I often get calls in the spring or summer that someone has a "yellow canary" in their yard. In actuality, they are seeing an American Goldfinch or Yellow Warbler. There are three goldfinch species in North America; the Laurence's, Lesser, and American. Only the American and Lesser have been found in Montana. The Laurence's is confined to the southwest portion of the United States in California and Southern Arizona.

The American Goldfinch is very common in Montana and occurs both east and west of the continental divide. The Lesser, on the other hand, is uncommon and has been seen only 454 times. I suspect this number is low. Lesser Goldfinches are being seen in the Bitterroot and Missoula Valleys on a

LESSER GOLDFINCH

regular basis. Most sightings the last few years have been in Billings and Missoula, but I have had the species once at my feeders in Deer Lodge. There occurrence is increasing with sightings in Red Lodge and a possible breeding pair was reported in Bozeman in 2018.

The American Goldfinch is about the size of a house sparrow (five inches) with a slender built. Males in breeding plumage are bright yellow on the back and breast with white wing bars on black wings. The forehead and tail are black as well. The beak and feet are pink. Females are more of a "washed out" yellow and lack the black cap. The non-breeding plumage of the male is similar to the female.

The Lesser Goldfinch is distinguished from an American Goldfinch by a black cap rather than forehead with a green to black back,and black legs.

The American Goldfinch is an active feeder bird and will eat both black oil sunflower seed and thistle seed, preferring the later. They can be found in Deer Lodge year around, but are most abundant in the spring and summer. In fact, as I write this article I saw a male on our feeder. The American Goldfinch is one of our most common feeder birds along with the Pine Siskin and House Finch. American Goldfinch are typically in groups of five to twenty birds.

American Goldfinch breed in the Deer Lodge Valley and I have them breeding regularly in my Caragana hedge. I don't trim my Caragana, but allow it to grow naturally to its 20 foot height. I have discovered that several species breed in the

AMERICAN GOLDFINCH

thick vegetation besides the American Goldfinch.

I do hope that you will try feeding birds in your yard. You can expect 10-12 species a day year around with hours of enjoyment. Dripping water in the warmer month increases the opportunity for more species. My yard list has grown to 105 species over the last 15 years. As I have mentioned before, feed only thistle and black oil sunflower seeds. A thistle sock feeder works well for finches as they seem to prefer feeding by clinging to the sock. They often feed upside down. Avoid millet seed as it tends to attract House Sparrows which can be a real nuisance in large numbers. ♦

BIRDING ON HARRISON LAKE, MONTANA.

Family Calcariidae

Lapland Longspur 215

Lapland Longspur   *Calcarius lapponicus*

LAPLAND LONGSPUR

With the coming of cold winter weather the majority of birds leave our valley for warmer areas with more available food. Of the 442 species in Montana, about 180 species overwinter (Dec. 15 – Feb- 15) and another 43 species have been observed during winter months, but do not overwinter. There are also several birds that summer and breed in Northern Canada and the Arctic that winter locally.

Occasionally, these winter-only residents can be in high numbers such as Common Redpolls. More typically there are a few to single individuals. Examples are Gyrfalcons, Snowy Owls, and Northern Shrikes.

We have a winter-only species in our valley, the Lapland Long-spur, that can be irruptive or in high numbers some winters. The best way to find this species is to wait until we have had a snow storm of several inches and then look for birds in plowed fields that have

LAPLAND LONGSPUR   *Photo by Nate Hohler*

sparse vegetation. We have a lot of these types of fields in our valley, thus a lot of Lapland Longspurs. When looking for Lapland Longspurs they are often mixed in with the more common Horned Lark. The Horned Larks that winter here are most likely not the same birds that we see here in the summer time. As summer ends Horned Larks begin to move south, wintering Horned Larks from Canada move into the area. A third species that often cohabits with the Lapland Longspurs and Horned Larks is the Snow Bunting.

If conditions are right you can find flocks with some Lapland Longspurs on the fence wires as well as in the fields. If you take the time to count you most often will have mixed flocks of all three species.

Lapland Longspurs can be identified by first looking at the tail feathers; they are partly white and partly dark. They also have a reddish patch on the shoulder or greater coverts and tertials. There is also a bold dark triangle outlining a buffy ear patch. The belly and undertail are white.

Occasionally, you get a good view of the name-sake for this family the opposing "longspur" on the leg. Nate Kohler, of Deer Lodge, took this excellent photo of a Lapland Longspur and captured a good view of the "Longspur" on the lower leg.

Horned Larks are distinguished by black hornlike feathers on the forehead, white or yellow under the chin and a black breast plate. Snow Buntings show warm buff brown tones with a lot of white on the wing and belly. Taking a field guide with you such as *National Geographic* or *Sibley* will help you separate the species easily.

This winter, after a good snow, drive the dirt roads in agricultural crop areas and look for flocks of small brown birds in the fields. Often when you drive up to the fence line they will rise and fly off ahead of you which is a group protection behavior. If you sit for a while they typically return and perhaps you can get views of all three species. ♦

BIRDING ALASKA

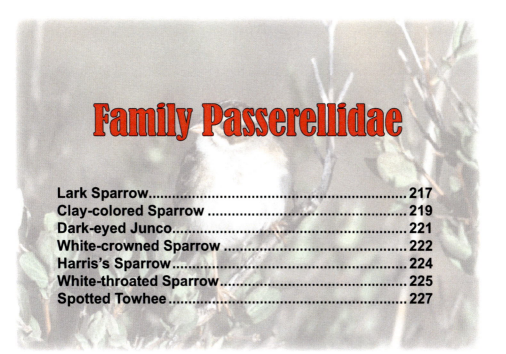

Family Passerellidae

Lark Sparrow	217
Clay-colored Sparrow	219
Dark-eyed Junco	221
White-crowned Sparrow	222
Harris's Sparrow	224
White-throated Sparrow	225
Spotted Towhee	227

Lark Sparrow   *Chondestes grammacus*

LARK SPARROW

This is the first in a series on sparrows. I hope that you will enjoy learning about the seven species I have chosen.

I first observed this species February 7, 1997 on a birding trip to Texas. The next time I saw it was in California in March of 1998, and then in May, 2003 in Uinta Mountains near Salt Lake City. I didn't see this species in Montana until April, 2004 near Wolf Point. Since then I have recorded it 44 times in Montana and ten times in the Upper Clark Fork Watershed. My earliest sighting in our valley was May 17th and the latest August 8th. (You see how handy records are if they are stored in a computer program.)

In Montana they are abundant east

LARK SPARROW

of the Continental Divide and occasional west of the divide. There are no recent records for the species in the extreme northwest corner of the state. If you study the distribution map for this species it is really only found in the valleys of Western Montana and not in the higher elevations coniferous forest. There are few records of the species being found in Montana after September or before May. Perhaps that is why my latest record was in August. They winter along the coast of California, Southern Arizona, Texas and all of Mexico. The species is commonly seen however, as there are 5,286 recorded sightings in Montana according to the Montana Natural Heritage Program.

BIRDING CLARK FORK RIVER, UPPER DEER LODGE VALLEY.

It is a rather large sparrow with a wingspan of 11 inches, in comparison to 7.5 inch wingspan for the Clay-colored. The distinguishing field marks are the bold facial pattern. Some have described the alternating chestnut, white and black streaking of the head as a harlequin or clown pattern. There is also a black central breast spot, but it is often overlooked because of the bold facial pattern. In flight the tail is unique. The tail is long with the gray of the back extending through the middle of the tail. This gray center is bordered in black. The edge of the tail from the rump around the base is boldly white. The tail pattern is often missed when they are feeding or perched but stands out in flight.

Lark Sparrows like to feed on the ground for seeds. They typically feed in a slow methodical walk, but I have seen them hop and run. They are not easily flushed and often allow good views at close distance. Their overall demeanor seems quiet and calm.

Their song is highly variable and loud. It is difficult to describe and consists of warbles, busses and trills. The overall effect seems to be an uplifting bubbly and happy-go-lucky rapid song.

My experience with this species is that I find them in riparian zones feeding under willows. I have also noticed that they are more abundant where the willows intergrade into grassy areas. ♦

CLAY-COLORED SPARROW

The Clay-colored Sparrow is a little known sparrow of the Upper Clark Fork Valley and is truly an LBJ, "Little Brown Job".

In the right habitat, riparian stream zones, I usually hear this bird long before I see it. The song is a series of four to five toneless insect-like buzzes. It sounds something like *"bzzz-bzzz-zeee-zeee"*. Once you learn this song it will stick with you forever.

The sparrow family is a large family in North America with 49 species and 17 genera. In Montana this family is represented by 32 species in 14 genera. The genus Spizella has six species of which, there are five in Montana,

CLAY-COLORED SPARROW

American Tree (Winter only) and in the summer; Field, Brewer's, Chipping, and Clay-colored. The other one, Black-Chinned, is found in California, Arizona, New Mexico, Texas and Mexico.

Clay-coloreds begin to show in April and are abundant by May. My earliest observations in the Upper Clark Fork Valley is May 8, 2013 and May 10, 2007. Both of these were sightings were along the Clark Fork River near Warm Springs.

Clay-colored Sparrows are small, 0.4 ounces. The overall color is brown to buff. The breast is buff above and dull white below. The bill is small for a sparrow and pink with a black tip on the upper mandible. The head pattern is distinctive. There is a bold, buffy "supercilium" or stripe above the eye. Below the eye is a dark "mustache" or line. The throat is white with two distinct lateral throat-stripes. The top of the head is dark brown with a whitish medial crown-stripe. From a side view there is a clean gray nape, and the back is striped. The eye is dark. Wing bars are present but indistinct. When you see this bird, especially in non-breeding plumage, the overall appearance is rather drab.

When you first observe the bird the tendency is to say, "Oh great, another of those hard to identify sparrows". If you hang in there and look for the head pattern and song, you can identify it.

The number of Clay-colored Sparrows in the United States decreased with the loss of habitat with the migration of folks with the Homestead Act and the plowing of the prairies. Forest clearing has again increased its numbers. This species breeds statewide, but total observation records are only 5,799. Compare that to 42,405 for the similar Chipping Sparrow in the same genus. I think the reason for this is that the Chipping Sparrow has a distinct rufous crown. Clay-colored has no

Clay-colored Sparrow   *Spizella pallida*

CLAY-COLORED SPARROW

distinct head markings, thus identification for many is uncertain and they go unreported.

The Upper Clark Fork Valley has abundant numbers of Clay-colored along the Clark Fork River and its tributaries. In spring go into thick willows in the riparian zone and sit and listen. If you hear the insect like *"bzzz-bzzz-zeee-zeee"* song, you have found them. If you have trouble seeing them they are a curious species and will respond to pishing or recordings and will come closer for a look.

A word of caution, don't overdo recordings. Males think your recording is a competitive male invading their breeding territory and it does produce stress. Once you have established identification, stop playing your recording. ♦

DARK-EYED JUNCO

Sparrows at times can be a confusing family of birds to identify. The Passerellidae family or sparrow family is a large family in North America with 49 species and 17 genera. In Montana this family is represented by 32 species in 14 genera. Twenty-two of the 32 species breed in Montana and 16 species have been observed in the winter. Three of the 16 wintering species breed further north in Canada and the Arctic Circle. In the Deer Lodge Valley I have observed 20 species of sparrows which 11 breed, with five overwintering. Of those five, only the Song Sparrow and Dark-eyed Junco are year around residents.

DARK-EYED JUNCO - OREGON

Over the years there has been much debate as to how many species of Juncos exist. Currently only two species are recognized, the Dark-eyed and the Yellow-eyed. The Yellow-eyed Junco is a species of Southern Arizona and Mexico.

The Dark-eyed Junco includes six recognizable populations or subspecies. These populations were once considered separate species. I have a copy of the *1946 Audubon Bird Guide* which says, "There is no general agreement as to the number of juncos. The currently recognized types are assigned to ten full species, many ornithologist believe that only two species are valid the Dark-eyed and Yellow-eyed." Within that field guide they illustrate three species.

There are 15 recognized races or subspecies within the Dark-eyed Junco species today. The most easily identified are Slate-colored, Oregon, White-winged, Pink-sided, Gray-headed or Red-backed. All of these races or subspecies will be illustrated in any up to date field guides. All but the Red-backed have been seen in Montana. The Oregon is most common, followed by Slate-colored and Pink-sided. The White-winged and Gray-headed are very rare with the former seen 78 times and the latter seen only five times in Montana.

The two photographs taken in my yard illustrate the Oregon and the Slate-colored. You can see why early ornithologist thought they were separate species. These two subspecies were feeding together at the time of the photographs.

The main reason that these different races are not recognized as species is that they don't pass the biological test of a valid species. They often interbreed where their ranges overlap and hybrids are common. One will encounter individuals showing combinations of traits from several races if you study junco flocks long enough.

In general juncos are mostly dark gray sparrows with a conspicuous pink bill,

Dark-eyed Junco   *Junco hyemalis*

white belly and white outer tail feathers. In our area they breed at high elevations in coniferous forest and will migrate in the fall to southern states with a few wintering in valleys such as the Upper Clark Fork or Flint Creek Valleys.

Juncos are a highly social species and forage on the ground in flocks near cover. They hop as they feed and are quite tame. When in flight the outer white tail feathers are conspicuous. They respond well to "pishing", that is making squeaking sounds with your lips, or recorded calls.

If you want them to be at your yard feeder in the winter, scatter seed on the ground near cover such as juniper or thick shrubs.

Make a point of noting which races of juncos you see in the future. You will certainly see the Oregon and Slate-colored. If you work at it, you'll find a Pink-sided, and who knows, perhaps you will see all six. ♦

DARK-EYED JUNCO - SLATE COLORED

White-crowned Sparrow   *Zonotrichia leucophrys*

WHITE-CROWNED SPARROW

There are 20 species of sparrows that spend part of their life cycle in the Upper Clark Fork Valley. Two of these species only winter here and ten breed here. Three more may breed locally, but there is no field evidence and the remaining five are spring and/or fall migrants.

Eight of these sparrow species have rather drab plumages and can be difficult to identify. However, they can be separated with good observations and a field guide.

Eight other species have unique plumages that make identification easy. Such is the case with the White-crowned Sparrow. It is a sparrow of the high mountain coniferous forest, but in Spring migration many can be found in backyards and valley fields in April and

WHITE-CROWNED SPARROW

White-crowned Sparrow — *Zonotrichia leucophrys*

WHITE-CROWNED SPARROW

May before they move into to their breeding habitats. They are one of the first signs of spring migration of birds in Western Montana.

This medium sized seven inch sparrow is mostly brown, but both sexes have a distinctive white and black striped crown. They also have a clear gray chest and nape. The bill is pinkish yellow. Their song is a clear plaintive whistle followed by a husky thrilled whistle.

White-crowns are abundant in the western half of the state in proper habitat, but can be found statewide briefly during migration. Fall migration is late and can extend into November. They winter in the southern tier states into Mexico.

Fall migrants can be confusing as the immature of the year have very light brown striped heads and are rather drab in appearance.

White-throated Sparrows superficially look like White-crowned Sparrow as they have similar black and white striped heads. What separates the two species is a white throat and yellow dot above the eye in the White-throated Sparrow. First winter White-throated Sparrows can be difficult to tell from first year White-crowned Sparrows. The best way to distinguish juveniles is the streaking in the upper chest of the White-throated verses the clear gray breast and belly of the White-crowned.

If you visit the coniferous forests of Western Montana, especially near streams with low deciduous bushes, this is a common species. You will often hear the clear whistle long before you see the bird. Take time to see this species as the striped head is a field mark you will notice and not soon forget. ♦

WHITE-CROWNED SPARROW

HARRIS'S SPARROW

We typically think that spring and summer is a better time of year to watch birds than winter. In general that is true. However, there are a few species that are "winter only" species that do not occur in the summer in much of Montana. Typically these species are uncommon and are a little hard to find, the exception being the Rough-legged Hawk.

The list of these annual winter species for Montana includes; Rough-legged Hawk, Gyrfalcon, Snowy Owl, Northern Shrike, Bohemian Waxwing, American Tree Sparrow, Harris's Sparrow, Lapland Longspur, Common Redpoll, and Hoary Redpoll.

To be considered as an "overwinter species", a species must have been observed in a particular county on three separate dates (regular sightings) between December 15 and February 15.

Even less common species have occurred in the winter in Montana, but

HARRIS'S SPARROW

they are so rare that I have not included them in the annual list. Examples are the Northern Cardinal which has occurred 17 times, Vermilion Flycatcher, observed only once, and in the winter, and several species of gulls with infrequent sightings.

Of those that occur as regular winter visitors, the Snowy Owl, Common and Hoary Redpolls, are irruptive species that are seen in small numbers one year, or not at all, and large numbers the next. This cyclic irruption seems to be tied to available food sources in Canada. Snowy Owls are never in large numbers, but I have seen up to 16 at a time in fields near Polson. Gyrfalcons and Hoary Redpolls are typically found yearly, but always in small numbers. The other six species are common regularly occurring species.

All ten common "overwintering" species have been observed in the Upper Clark Fork Valley.

The featured bird in this article is the Harris's Sparrow. This is an annually occurring winter bird in the Upper Clark Fork Valley. I have seen it 19 times in the Upper Clark Fork Valley since 2003 and many of those sightings were in my yard. This species breeds in the Northwest Territories of Canada. Most of the wintering grounds are south and east of

IMMATURE HARRIS'S SPARROW

Montana from South Dakota to Texas.

Harris's are large sparrows weighing 1.3 ounces. This compares to .7 ounces for the common and familiar Savannah Sparrow of Western Montana in the summer.

Harris's have an obviously large head with a pink bill. The tail is long compared to the body. Plumage is contrasting and striking. They have brown backs streaked with black, bright white bellies, black crown and throat. The head and face are ochre-tinged. Their behavior is unique in that they like to forage on the ground and move about by hopping. They tend to be shy and reclusive. When threatened they head for safety quickly in nearby underbrush. They often feed under backyard feeders if there is adequate close cover. ♦

HARRIS'S SPARROW

WHITE-THROATED SPARROW

Fall is always a great time to look for rare and unusual bird species that might come to your yard. This fall was no exception for me with two new yards birds, a Fox Sparrow and a White-throated Sparrow.

The Fox Sparrow was unique in that the *Montana Natural Heritage Program* has only one record for this species for November with a total of 1771 sightings. They breed in Northwest Montana, with indirect breeding records, that is juveniles seen, in most of Western Montana. Unfortunately, the bird was seen the evening of November 24, 2019. It was late in the evening and too dark to get a good photograph. I had hoped to photograph the bird the next morning, but it was gone.

The second rarity in November was a White-throated Sparrow and fortunately it stayed in my yard for nearly a week and I was able to photograph it. This bird is much rarer in Montana with only 359 reported sighting. All sightings for this species in Montana are transient in nature during spring or fall migration. Looking at a distribution map for this species shows that it winters in most of

WHITE-THROATED SPARROW

the southern states, is found year around in the northeast and summers in most of the Canadian providence's with the exception of coastal British Columbia. It can be found as a spring and fall migrant in Eastern Montana, Wyoming, Dakotas and south into Texas. The species is rare west of the Continental Divide in the United States.

So why did I find this species in my yard? The most obvious answer is that this bird spent the summer and early fall in British Columbia or Alberta and instead of migrating in a southeasterly direction, it came directly south. This behavior is typical of juvenile birds who are in migration and simply get off track. I believe that my yard bird was not an adult as the breast is whiter than the gray of an adult, but it is hard to tell from the photos. If the bird was an adult who had migrated before it was probably blown off track by a storm in either Southern Alberta and Eastern Montana that pushed the bird west of the divide. Most fall rarities are juveniles. How it found my feeders to seek refuge and stage for his continued migration is anyone's guess. I simply provide food, water, and protection and the bird found it.

WHITE-THROATED SPARROW

The genus Zonotrichia contains four closely related species in North America: Harris's, White-crowned, Golden-crowned and White-throated Sparrows. White-throated Sparrows superficially look like the more common White-crowned Sparrow that breed in coniferous forest at higher elevations in Western Montana. When White-crowned migrate, I often get several in my yard. In comparison to the White-throated Sparrow that has been observed 359 times the White-crowned has been observed 4,591 in Montana.

Both species have black and white or tan and white stripes on the head. White-throated have both tan and white stripped adults. In White-crowned Sparrows the tan striped individuals are juveniles.

Additional differences are that the White-throated does indeed have a white throat which is lacking in the White-crowned. The bill of White-crowned are yellow, whereas the bill is dark in White-throated. The other main difference is the yellow lores (tiny feathers between the eye and bill) in the White-throated. The lores shows nicely in my frontal picture of the White-throated.

Each spring and fall, if you have feeders in your yard make an effort to identify the less common birds that you see. If you think you have a rare species let someone like myself know. You may be contributing significant information to the eBird database for that species.

One of the things that I like about birding is the challenges that are constantly presenting themselves in both new species and familiar species at the wrong time of year. Good birding and I hope you soon find a rarity! ♦

SPOTTED TOWHEE

The sparrow family is a large family in North America with 49 species and 17 genera. In Montana this family is represented by 32 species in 14 genera. The genus Pipilo, or Towhees, has 6 species of which, there are three in Montana, the Spotted, Eastern, and Green-tailed. The other three; Canyon, California and Albert's are found in Southern California, Arizona, New Mexico and Mexico.

Many sparrows are very bland looking without distinct features and are often called "LBJs", little brown jobs. Not so with the Spotted Towhee, his coloration and traits are unique and bold. In the Upper Clark Fork Valley the Spotted Towhee is not nearly as common as the Dark-eyed Junco, but in proper habitat it can be numerous. The Spotted is the most common of the towhees in Montana having been recorded five times as often at the Green-tailed, 6,563 sightings, compared to 1,213 for the Green-tailed with the Montana Natural Heritage Foundation. The Eastern is rare, having been seen only four times.

SPOTTED TOWHEE

This is a large sparrow, 1.4 ounces compared to the .67 ounce Dark-eyed Junco. This sparrow is stocky and long tailed. The head has a dark hood and red eye. The back and wings are black to dark brown. In flight the tail shows white corners. Wings are dabbled with white spots, thus the name. The flanks are rust red and the "vent" or under tail area is light rust to orange. The white belly contrasts sharply with the rusty flanks. Males and females are basically the same, only males show darker rust to the flanks, much like a male robin has a darker breast than the female. The Eastern Towhee looks superficially the same, but lacks the dabbled white spots on the wing, showing only a small white patch at the base of the primary feathers.

The song of the Spotted once learned is distinctive and consists of eight identical introductory notes followed by a buzzy trill. During spring territorial establishment they are very vocal and respond well to playback.

Towhees spend most of their time foraging in thickets. They feed on the ground and move by several hops, then a pause, and hopping again. They search through leaf litter with a two footed hop/shuffle. Their feeding is so deliberate you can hear them search the leaf litter if you have good ears.

I have found the Spotted to be shy and retreats to nearby cover when confronted by humans. They are curious, and when their song is played and you are not out in the open, they readily fly to your location and perch in a dense bush surprisingly close.

This species breeds statewide. From Garrison to Butte they are not numerous. They are more numerous from Drummond downstream to Missoula. In the Missoula area they are common.

When you are out in the spring spend time searching thickets of brush along streams and look for this colorful sparrow. If you have not seen this species, once you have seen it, you won't regret the time you spent looking for it.

Enjoy spring birding, April is alive with birds in Western Montana. ♦

SPOTTED TOWHEE

STOPPING ON A BIRDING TRIP TO ISREAL

Family Icteridae

Yellow-headed Blackbird	229
Bobolink	231
Western Meadowlark	233
Bullock's Oriole	234
Red-winged Blackbird	236
Brown-headed Cowbird	237
Brewer's Blackbird	239
Common Grackle	239

Yellow-headed Blackbird *Xanthocephalus xanthocephalus*

YELLOW-HEADED BLACKBIRD

Blackbirds are in the family Icteridae of which there are 23 species in North America. You might be surprised at some of the species in this family. They include two meadowlarks, a bobolink, three cowbirds, five blackbirds, three grackles and nine orioles. This is diverse family that have rather slender pointed bills in common.

Four blackbirds occur in our valley. Three are common: Yellow-headed, Red-winged and Brewer's. The Rusty is a rare winter visitor that has only been seen a few times but probably is more common than we realize. I have seen them in small numbers within large flocks of Fall Red-winged Blackbirds and Starlings in feedlots and underfoot

YELLOW-HEADED BLACKBIRD

of livestock being fed in fields.

I want to familiarize you with the Yellow-headed Blackbird. I don't remember seeing Yellow-heads while I was growing up in the Upper Clark Fork Drainage but they are fairly common today. Perhaps they are sensitive to arsenic which was prevalent in the air during the Anaconda Smelter days. The smelter closed in 1981 and I do see a greater variety of species and more individuals within a species than I did while they were in operation.

Yellow-heads are still less common than Red-winged and Brewer's Blackbirds in most habitats. Fall flocks are often a mix of European Starlings, Red-winged and Yellow-headed Blackbirds.

Yellow-head Blackbirds will use backyard feeders but not as often as Red-winged Blackbirds. They winter in extreme Southern Arizona, New Mexico and Mexico. They are basically a Western United States breeder and nest in noisy colonies in cattail marshes.

YELLOW-HEADED BLACKBIRD

Males are considerably larger than females. They average 2.3 ounces compared to females at 1.8 ounces. Males are striking in color. They have a jet black body with white wing patches that are conspicuous in flight. The bright yellow or yellow-orange head and breast contrast with the body in a distinct demarcation of colors. They look like someone dipped a black bird in a can of yellow paint!

Their song is loud and raucous. It is a rasping song which sounds like it takes a great deal of effort to produce. It has been described as "rusty hinges" or someone being strangled.

Females and juveniles are drab brown with most of the yellow on the throat and upper chest. The yellow is often mustard colored and subdued. The lower breast is streaked with white and does not contrast sharply in color as the males do. White wing patches are absent.

Even though the Red-winged and the Yellow-head breed in similar habitats I rarely see them coexist.

This may be due to competition but I have noticed Yellow-heads occupy deeper water marshes than Red-winged.

Yellow-headed Blackbirds rarely overwinter in Montana and flocks show up a few weeks later than Red-winged in the spring.

This is an easy bird to observe in marsh lands and an excellent bird to practice photography skills. They will tolerate human disturbance more than other marsh species and have a tendency to sit high on cattails making good subjects. ♦

BOBOLINK

In this article I want to familiarize you with the Bobolink, one of the more unique members of the Icteridae family. You may have never heard of this species or seen it. It is the least seen of all of the blackbirds and it is a *Species of Concern* (SOC) in Montana. Typically a SOC species is one that is declining in number due to loss of habitat. In this case habitat is not being lost, but the way the habitat is used, endangers the species especially nestlings and juveniles.

Most blackbirds are fairly common and seen and recognized by birders and non-birders alike. The familiar Red-winged Blackbird of marshes, backyards and feeders has been recorded with the *Montana Natural Heritage Program* more than 13,597 times. The Bobolink has only been recorded 1,527 times.

The Bobolink winters in South-central South America which is one of the longest migrations of any songbird. In the Spring they migrate to the northern edge of South America and then fly non-stop across the Gulf of Mexico to the southern tier states of Florida West to Eastern Texas. Some may rest on islands in the gulf such as Cuba on their way. Eventually they make their way north and breed in the northern states which includes all of Montana. Western Montana has more breeding records than Eastern Montana, but that may be a factor of who is sending in records. I have personally seen Bobolinks throughout Montana.

BOBOLINK

Bobolinks are easy to identify with their unique plumage. Males are an all-black bird with a straw colored nape, white rump and scapulars (upper wing when folded). Their call is a rather unique crisp "blink blink". Their song a cheerful, bubbling warble. Even their song contains the *"blink blink"* notes making them easy to identify by song alone. Females look like a large sparrow with a black cap, pale nape and black eye line. Both non-breeding sexes are a yellow-buff color with a boldly striped back.

Bobolinks are a grassland species that prefers wetter rather than drier habitats. I have seen them in dry grasslands in Eastern Montana, but I suspect they were not yet on territory.

In Western Montana they prefer wet hay meadows and therein lies the problem. They are one of the latest arriving songbirds, They show in the Deer Lodge Valley the last week of May into the first week of June. Males arrive before females and territory establishment and nesting does not occur until mid-June. This means birds are just fledged or still in the nest when harvesting of hay begins.

The problem for this species is that most mowing of hay begins on the outside edge of the field and works towards the center. As hay is mowed Bobolinks seek cover in unmowed hay towards the center of the field and they are concentrated there.

Eventually mowers reach the center of the field and unless the species flies up and over the mower back onto mowed hay there is high risk of being killed. I have no idea what the ratio of killed to escaped Bobolinks are when mowing a field, but it is the greatest cause of mortality.

One way to overcome this problem would be for a farmer to travel across unmowed hay and begin mowing from the center of the field back to the outside. I don't know if that is practical, or if it creates problems I am unaware of, but it would reduce mortality. I'd love to have a rancher email me and discuss the practicality of this suggestion (birdmt@charter.net). I know hay that is down is hard to mow and driving to the center of the field would put some hay on the ground.

Another solution would be to hay fields with Bobolinks present as late as possible, mowing other fields first.

If you have never seen a Bobolink the Stuart Field at Grant-Kohrs National Historic Site in Deer Lodge has a number of pairs nesting each year. If you go in late June and early July you will see breeding males and they will be easy to identify. If you go later in August they all look like large sparrows and you will miss the spectacular male breeding plumage.

The picture here is one I took in early June in a hay field near Ovando, Montana. ♦

PELAGIC BIRDING TRIP OFF THE COAST OF ECUADOR.

WESTERN MEADOWLARK

Most people know that the Western Meadowlark is our state bird. It occurs and breeds in every county in the state and is an appropriate state bird. It also winters sporadically across the state but I have not seen it in the Upper Clark Fork Drainage during the winter. In order to be classified as overwintering it must have been seen between Dec 15 and February 15 on at least three separate occasions.

What many casual birders do not realize is that the Western Meadowlark is a member of Icteridae family or Blackbird and Oriole family. In the Upper Clark Fork Basin this family includes Red-winged, Yellow-headed, Brewer's Blackbirds, Common Grackle, Bobolink, Brown-headed Cowbird, and Bullock's Oriole.

Why is this yellow breasted species included with blackbirds? All of these species have a rather slender, pointed bill which is consistent in all species of blackbirds. Other than this trait it is difficult to generalize other physical family traits.

Summer breeding Western Meadowlarks can be found in the Western Canadian Providences and along the Northern Tier States to the Great Lakes. They build dome shaped nests of grass on the ground in grasslands with abundant foliage.

They winter in most western states south of a line below Montana and the Dakotas and are found year around in East Texas to the Mississippi River. Consequently, not only are they the state bird of Montana but also Kansas, Nebraska, North Dakota, Oregon and Wyoming. How disappointing, especially as they sing, "Deer Lodge is a pretty little town" to my ear. The only bird with more state bird status is the Northern Cardinal with seven states. All fifty state birds are represented by only 28 species of birds.

WESTERN MEADOWLARK

Western Meadowlarks are a chunky, brown backed bird. When flushed the short tail shows conspicuous white edges. Typical flight is several quick wing beats alternating with short glides. Most often the flight is short then alighting into tall grass and disappearing. When walking it flicks its tail open and shut. Meadowlarks are most often seen on a perch such as a fence post singing and establishing a territory. In this stance the bright yellow chest shows a black "V" and is the most diagnostic field mark. The song is remarkably variable and consists of 7-10 flutelike notes and gurgles. It is one of the most pleasant songs of early Spring in the Upper Clark Fork Valley.

The eastern counterpart is the Eastern Meadowlark. The two species overlap in

Western Meadowlark *Sturnella neglecta*

WESTERN MEADOWLARK

Texas, Oklahoma and Kansas. The two species are virtually identical with the exception of more yellow in the cheek of the Western. The only way to truly tell them apart is by song. In June of 2009 a college student was doing bird surveys near Ennis and heard an unusual song for a Western Meadowlark. It turned out to be an Eastern Meadowlark. Only one of two sightings Montana has ever had of the Eastern Meadowlark. The bird was on private property and my wife and I along with a few other serious birders were given the opportunity to view this bird and add it to our Montana list. Western Meadowlark is one of Montana's most watchable birds in the grassland habitats of Montana. Take time to become familiar with this species. ♦

Bullock's Oriole *Icterus bullockii*

BULLOCK'S ORIOLE

There are several birds in Montana that are strikingly beautiful. Some that come to mind are the Western Tanager, Lazuli Bunting and Common Yellowthroat.

BULLOCK'S ORIOLE

One that is present in the Upper Clark Fork Valley, though not common, is the Bullock's Oriole. The picture is from my yard on May 21, 2021.

Orioles are members of the Blackbird or Icteridea family. Worldwide this is a large family of birds with 56 species. There are many species in Africa. In Kenya I have seen a single tree with more than 200 oriole nests hanging from the branches.

Orioles are represented with nine species, in North America with four in Montana. Those not found in Montana are found in Southern California, Arizona, New Mexico, Texas and Mexico.

Only the Bullock's is common in Western Montana. Bullock's as well as Baltimore, and Orchard, are found in Eastern Montana with the most concentration in Northeastern Montana. The other species, Hooded, is rare with only three records.

In 1983 Bullock's and Baltimore Orioles were lumped into a single species because they were found to interbreed in the Great Plains. If you have an older field guide both subspecies were called Northern Oriole. Twelve years later in 1995 the American Ornithological Society reversed itself and the Northern Oriole was again split into Baltimore and Bullock's. Basically, Bullock's is a bird of the west and Baltimore a bird of the east. They overlap in range in Montana, Wyoming, Colorado and Texas.

The Bullock's is an orange breasted bird, with black back and shows considerable white in the wings. The orange of the breast extends to the face. The black of the back extends to the top of the head, throat, and forms a black line through the eye. The tail is orange and black tipped. The bill is dark above and the lower mandible is light, unlike any other oriole.

The Baltimore shows less white in the wings, and the black of the back forms a complete hood over the head and neck. The tail is orange with only a black center. First year males are yellow overall, a white belly, dark wings with white wing bars. The throat is black with a black eye line. Females and juveniles show yellow head

BULLOCK'S ORIOLE-MALE - JUVENILE

and tail. Their back and wings are gray with white wing bars and the white of the belly extends onto the breast.

The nest of the Bullock is unique because it is woven from grass strips, lined with hair and plant down, and hangs down from a tree branch. Each oriole species builds a unique nest which identifies the species. The nest is built in 5-14 days by both the male and female working together and is about 12 inches in length.

The *Montana Natural Heritage Database* shows the Bullock's have been reported 2,504 times, Baltimore 318, Orchard 206 and Hooded 3 times.

The best way to attract orioles is to place orange halves in a tree. You will have the most success with attracting orioles early in the spring. As other food becomes available they tend to feed in yards less. My orioles have only fed in the yard for 2-3 weeks most springs. Next spring see if you can attract these beautiful Bullock's Orioles to your yard. They are more common than you think. ♦

RED-WINGED BLACKBIRD

The Red-winged is the one that I remember being in the valley from my childhood as it is such a descriptive name. The glossy black male has red shoulder patches tipped with buffy-yellow medium covert feathers. Occasionally when perched the red is concealed. I have had folks tell me they have seen a Tri-colored Blackbird in our valley. I understand the confusion. In the Tri-colored the medium covert feathers are white. Sometimes in proper light the coverts do look white. However, if you consult a field guide you will notice that the Tri-colored is only found in California and occasionally seen in Nevada and Oregon.

RED-WINGED BLACKBIRD

The other blackbirds in our valley are the Yellow-headed, Brewers and Rusty. The Rusty looks superficially like the Brewers and can be mistaken for it in breeding plumage. However, the Rusty breeds in the far north and is found occasionally in our valley in migration especially in the fall. They are usually found in mixed flocks of blackbirds and starlings. In fall migration the tips of the feathers appear rusty and the eyes are yellow. The Brewer's breeds locally and is more glossy overall.

The Red-winged is the most common of the four, but I have seen Yellow-headed Blackbirds displace Red-winged in cattail marshes as they are larger, 2.3 ounces verses 1.8, and are more aggressive in their behavior. Of the four species the Red-winged is the only one that overwinters locally in small numbers. This is especially true where there are yard feeders providing winter food.

Red-winged are medium-sized stocky birds with a conical bill and short tail. Males are glossy black with red epaulets (wing patch on shoulder) with yellow below. Females are distinctly different and are mostly grayish brown and heavily streaked on the breast and appear sparrow-like in appearance.

This species is very observable in marshes and their behavior is easily noted. Displaying males in spring sit conspicuously atop cattails. They spread their wings, flare their tails and often arch their backs. Females typically sit lower in the marsh grasses. Males are very vocal and there are a variety of gurgles and a high pitched descending whistle. The most common gurgle is a musical "tur-a-leee".

Red-winged Blackbirds are easy to observe and do not take flight quickly.

Red-winged Blackbird   *Agelaius phoeniceus*

When I taught I encouraged students to go to a marsh and spend an hour with this species and write down the behaviors that they saw. Students were always amazed at all the various behaviors they could identify.

Most marshes in our valley contain numerous Red-winged Blackbirds. Fewer marshes contain both Red-winged and Yellow-heads, and some marshes only contain Yellow-heads. As summer turns to colder fall days most Red-winged Blackbirds migrate south or to warm climes within the state. If you feed birds in the winter, occasionally Red-winged will overwinter and become dependent upon your feeder. Red-winged are always counted on our local Christmas Birds Count at Warm Springs Wildlife Management Area. Perhaps the hot springs there provide a micro-habitat for survival.

Red-winged are one of our earliest spring songbirds in large numbers and start showing around the first of May. In spring spend some time at one of our many marshes and observe the difference between males and females and the interaction between them as the males establish territories, mate and rear young. Red-winged Blackbirds are one of the easiest species to study in the Upper Clark Fork Valley. ♦

RED-WINGED BLACKBIRD

Brown-headed Cowbird   *Molothrus ater*

BROWN-HEADED COWBIRD

The Brown-headed cowbird is disliked by many birders as they are brood parasites. This simply means that they lay their eggs in the nest of other species. They typically take one egg out of a nest and replace it with one of their own.

Some host species have learned to distinguish the cowbird egg and remove it from the nest and others simply build another nest over the eggs in the first nest and lay a new clutch. Other species like the Kirkland Warbler of Eastern United States have no defense against this parasitic behavior and have been severely reduced in number. Several eastern states operate Brown-headed Cowbird trapping programs to reduce the stress on Kirkland Warblers and other endangered species. Once the eggs hatch the cowbird chick is larger and more aggressive for food. Cowbird chicks have been known to push genetic chicks out of the nest. Some starve and die because they cannot compete for food with the larger Brown-headed chick. I have seen adult warblers in the Upper Clark Fork Valley frantically feeding a cowbird chick that was much larger than the adult feeding it!

What would cause this odd behavior in cowbirds? Historically, cowbirds fed among grazing bison. As the bison moved across the land their hoofs stirred insects from the ground which the cowbirds then ate. The cowbirds were dependent on the bison, but bison forage on the move and cover large areas in a short period of time. Parasitic brooding was the only mechanism available for the raising of young. There simply wasn't enough time to build a nest, lay eggs, incubate and follow the bison herds across the vast grasslands of North America.

BROWN-HEADED COWBIRD

In Montana cowbirds breed statewide with a few overwintering. Typically they migrate from Southern Tier States and abruptly appear in early May in large numbers with other blackbirds. Fall migration begins in August and stretches into late October.

Free roaming bison are long gone. The cowbirds specialized means of rearing young is no longer necessary, but the genetic DNA code to parasite other species remains and so does the behavior. This is an example of how the environmental conditions in nature can change rapidly, but the genetic adaptation can be very slow.

Brown-headed Cowbirds are rather easy to distinguish from other blackbirds. They are small, 7.5 inches in length compared to 8.75 for Red-winged Blackbirds and 9.5 for Yellow-headed Blackbirds. Males can appear all black, but a closer look will show a dark brown head. Females are overall dull brownish-gray. The bill is short and stout, much like a finch, rather than longer and pointed as in other blackbirds. The tail is short for a blackbird. The only species you might confuse them with is a Brewer's Blackbird which is glossy black with a dark purple head and a yellow eye.

They are gregarious within their species and with other blackbirds. They often have their tail cocked when in a group distinguishing them from other blackbirds. In summary, Brown-headed Cowbirds are a threat to some species but they are a native species whose behavior remains unchanged in a changing environment. ♦

BREWER'S BLACKBIRD

Of the 13 species of blackbirds in Montana I have found nine species in Southwest Montana. For beginning birders this family can be confusing to separate females. Females of all of these species are subdued versions of the males, often with striping on the breast and can require good observations and patience to identify. Males are much less difficult.

Other articles dealt with many of these species. In this article I want to familiarize you with the breeding Brewer's Blackbird and Common Grackle. Both breed in Southwest Montana and can look alike to the novice.

The Common Grackle is the smallest of the grackles at four ounces, but nearly twice as big as a Brewer's at 2.2 ounces. Brewer's have a plumb, bulky body, yellow eye, small bill and stand on short legs. The male is two-toned glossy iridescence purple with a greenish-black head. Females have more brown tones on the head. The tail is long for the plumb body but not as long as the Common Grackles.

MALE BREWER'S BLACKBIRD

The Common Grackle on the other hand has a long heavy bill and pale yellow eye. Its legs are long and the tail is long, straight, and keel shaped. The body is leaner in appearance than the Brewer's. The blue of the head is distinctly separated from the iridescent bronze of the body and wings.

Common Grackles are social and are usually found in mixed flocks of blackbirds. Common Grackles tend to dominate over other blackbirds due to their size and aggressive demeanor. The only other grackle found in Montana is the Great-tailed Grackle, with 25 records. Those records have primarily come from Bozeman with a single bird over several years. That particular Great-tailed was surviving on spilled popcorn from the theater patrons in the mall parking lot. The other location was in Dillon, again at a fast food restau-

MALE COMMON GRACKLE

rant, and this individual had hybridized with local Common Grackles and produced young.

All eight blackbirds I have described in these articles have been observed in the Upper Clark Fork Drainage and common except for the Rusty Blackbird which I did not write about due to a lack of a photo. During summer see how many of these blackbirds you can find and add to your year list. ♦

BIRDING TANZANIA

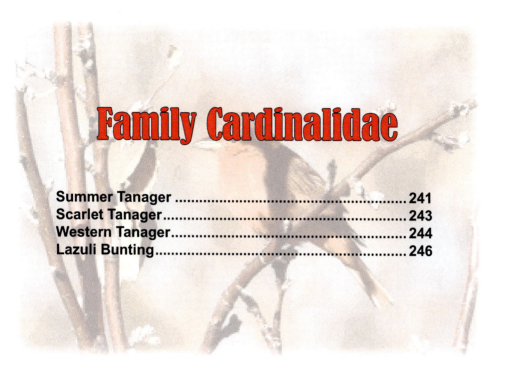

Family Cardinalidae

Summer Tanager 241
Scarlet Tanager.. 243
Western Tanager... 244
Lazuli Bunting... 246

Summer Tanager *Piranga rubra*

SUMMER TANAGER

It might sound like a broken record, but in many articles I start off with "Fall is a great time to find migrants in Montana, especially juveniles which get lost on their first migration."

I got a call from a friend in the Dillon area telling me that he was told of a bright red bird out on a ranch north of Dillon. He went there and stayed for two hours at the feeder and found nothing. They described the bird to him, and he showed them a picture in a field guide of what he thought they were describing; a Summer Tanager. The only problem was they were describing an adult bird, not a juvenile, and distribution maps show the Summer Tanager is rarely this far north.

Looking at the map with this article blue is the winter range of the species.

SUMMER TANAGER

Summer Tanager   *Piranga rubra*

Orange is the breeding range and yellow migration. If you look at the map, Montana is clearly outside the normal range of this species. There have been sightings in Eastern Montana, but never any in Western Montana with the exception of one sighting in Flathead County over 20 years ago. The total sightings, prior to this finding, has only been 19.

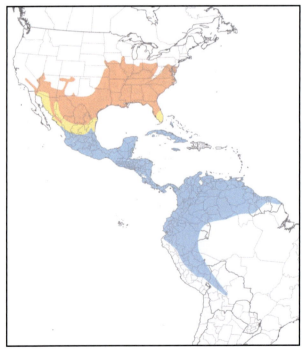

Map from Cornell's "All About Birds" web page

My grandson and I drove down to the ranch north of Dillon on Saturday, October 31 and arrived at 9:30 AM. Our friend was already there having been there since daylight, and had been sitting in the cold for more than two hours on their deck watching their feeder. As we drove into the yard we found the tanager in a tree on the opposite side of the house immediately. It was sort of fun to find our birding friend and announce that we already had the bird! Fortunately for him we had spooked the birding getting photographs and it flew over the house to the feeder just moments before we talked.

I was still baffled as to why the bird was an adult male and not a juvenile.

Talking to the homeowner I soon found out why. The bird had been in their yard since mid-July. It didn't occur to him that the bird might be rare. A bird is a bird – right? WRONG! It had simply stayed in their yard for four months most likely because of the feeder and had just not left. It left permanently four days later with only a few birders able to see it.

A bird is considered rare in Montana if it has only been seen 20 or less times. Our sighting was the 20th!. If seen once more in the future it will be taken off the rare bird list.

There are five species of tanagers found in North America. The Flame-colored and Hepatic Tanagers are basically Mexico/Central American species that have been found along the California to Texas southern border in small numbers. Western Tanager is the familiar tanager of our area with the yellow body, red head and black wings. It is found in large numbers in the western half of the United States with scattered records in the east. *The Montana Natural Heritage Program* (MNHP) records show it has been observed 18,028 times. ♦

SCARLET TANAGER

The counterpart to the Western is the Scarlet Tanager which is found in large numbers in the eastern half of the continental United States with scattered records in the west. The MNHP shows only 22 observations for the Scarlet in Montana. Its field marks are a brilliant red body with black wings and gray bill. Amazingly, one of the 22 sightings was mine on May 31, 2013, and I found the bird in the Dillon area as well!

Field marks for the Summer Tanager male are unmistakable. The species is bright rosy-red overall with a long pale bill and a slight crest to the head.

I feel fortunate to have seen all three of Montana's tanagers with two being

SCARLET TANAGER

so rare. Two things I have learned. If someone calls with a rare sighting go get it immediately. Secondly, encourage people if they think they have an odd looking bird in their yard to call someone knowledgeable. They might just have one of Montana's 103 rare species (20 or less sightings) that others would like to see. I'll be watching my cell phone for your call. ♦

WESTERN TANAGER

There is probably no other common bird in the Upper Clark Fork Valley that is as strikingly beautiful as the Western Tanager. It is a mountain species that migrates through the valley in May. They often congregate in low elevation areas during inclement spring weather. I have seen as many as 50 in a single yard during a spring snow storm. Perhaps you have witnessed this as well. Even though in early spring Western Tanagers are common in yards they nest in coniferous forest above the valley floor from six to eight thousand feet and are seldom seen again during summer unless you are in their habitat.

As the name implies this is a tanager of the Western United States. They are not found in the grasslands east of the Continental Divide in Montana. Their range is from Southern Alaska, British Columbia and the non-prairie portions of Alberta south to Wyoming, Arizona and New Mexico. They winter mainly in Mexico and Central America with a few in Coastal California.

WESTERN TANAGER

There are five tanager species in the United States. The eastern counterpart to the Western Tanager is the Scarlet Tanager. Southeastern US and Texas is home to the Summer Tanager. The Hepatic Tanager, a Mexican species, can be found in Arizona and New Mexico and Western Texas. The rarest of the Tanagers is the Flame-colored Tanager which is a casual visitor to the mountains of Southeast Arizona and abundant in Mexico. I have been fortunate to have seen all five species in the United States.

In my opinion the Western Tanager looks the most like a tropical bird of all of Montana's songbirds. They are a medium sized bird at 7 ¼ inches and the only tanager with bright white wing bars. In breeding plumage the male has a red head, yellow nape, chest, rump and belly. The wings are black with yellow and white bars. The female shows no red and the yellow lacks the brightness of the male. The wings and back are dusky black rather than bold black. The non-breeding fall male looks much like the female with only a hint of red on the forehead and chin. Their song is similar to an American Robin but hoarser.

In late May I received an email from a reader of these articles from Dillon saying that he had a Scarlet Tanager in his yard among a flock of Western Tanagers. I

WESTERN TANAGER

was at his home by 7:00 am the next morning and indeed he did have the eastern counterpart, a male Scarlet Tanager. This was a rare find as the species has been recorded in Montana only 25 times as of 2021. Note the black wings without bars and the scarlet color of the bird in my picture. I appreciate this reader contacting me as it was a new state bird, number 368. (See article on pages 241-243 for more information on the Scarlet Tanager)

If you think you have found a unique or rare bird contact me and I will confirm your finding and perhaps add a Montana life bird to my list.

Birding is so much fun and often full of delightful surprises such as this rare eastern tanager; the Scarlet Tanager. ♦

LAZULI BUNTING

Some birds are just naturally more attractive or beautiful than others. One of these birds that we often see in Southwest Montana is the Lazuli Bunting.

They arrive late in Southwest Montana in the later part of May and June. They breed in the northwest states and are rarely seen further east than Central North Dakota then south to Colorado and Utah to the West Coast. They winter along the West Coast of Mexico to Central America. In Montana by mid-August they have raised their young and migrate south. There are few records in September locally.

LAZULI BUNTING

We see them most often in our yard in early June before migrating to higher elevations in our coniferous forest. The exception is when we get late snow in June which forces them back down into the valley floor in search of insects.

I have seen June days in inclement weather when they seem to be dripping off of the trees around town in large numbers. As soon as the weather clears they are gone again into the mountains. I often have wondered if they have already nested, if they stay with eggs, young or abandon them. Some species are capable of re-nesting in cases like this.

They are rather commonly observed with more than 3,700 observations statewide. When birding in the Garnett Mountains I found no less than six Lazuli's in early July.

About the time that you think you have the life cycle of a species figured out you make an observation that makes no sense. On July 7th we had a Lazuli in our yard on a completely clear and warm day! No explanation for that one.

Sexes are not alike in this species which is an under-statement. As beautiful as the male is, females are just the opposite. She is drab grayish brown, with whitish underparts and a buffy breast. Field guides show a gray-blue rump and a light blue shoulder patch. You can see in the picture I took of a female the blue is barely visible on this

FEMALE LAZULI BUNTING

individual. Juveniles appear much like females only have fine streaking on the breast.

The male of the other hand is bright turquoise above and on the throat with cinnamon across the breast and white belly. Wings are dark with a thick white wing bar. I included two pictures of the male from two angles so you can appreciate all of the field marks.

There are two other bunting species recorded in Montana, the Indigo and Painted. The Indigo has been recorded 54 times and the Painted only five times. Most sightings of this species are from Eastern Montana. I have seen the Indigo in Billings and yet to see the Painted Bunting. The Painted Bunting observations are so few that no distribution pattern has been established. All of the current observations are east of the divide. Even though I have not seen this species in Montana I have seen it in Arizona.

LAZULI BUNTING

In late July it is not too late to find Lazuli Buntings locally. Young of the year are the last to leave and can be seen in proper habitat until late August. ♦

BIRDING IN GREECE

Official List of Montana Birds

APPENDIX A

The official list of Montana Birds printed below was prepared by the Montana Bird Advocacy and Montana Bird Records Committee (MBRC). This list can be downloaded at https://www.montanabirdadvocacy.org/review-list. The list may change as new species are found in Montana. It will also change with lumps and splits by the American Ornithologists Society.

OFFICIAL STATE LIST OF MONTANA BIRDS

According to MBRC 442 species comprise the official list of Montana's birds as of October 4, 2021. Taxonomy and nomenclature follow the 7th edition of the American Ornithologists' Union (Now American Ornithological Society). Species with the label "**R**" are on the *Review List* and require a written report accepted by the MBRC before the record can be added to the Montana Bird Distribution database which is maintained by the *Montana Natural Heritage Program.* We thank them for allowing us to share this information.

Order Anseriformes | Family Anatidae
Snow Goose *(Anser caerulescens)*
Ross's Goose *(Anser rossii)*
Greater White-fronted Goose *(Anser albifrons)*
Brant *(Branta bernicla)* **R**
Cackling Goose *(Branta hutchinsii)*
Canada Goose *(Branta canadensis)*
Mute Swan *(Cygnus olor)*
Trumpeter Swan *(Cygnus buccinator)*
Tundra Swan *(Cygnus columbianus)*
Wood Duck *(Aix sponsa)*
Baikal Teal *(Sibirionetta formosa)* **R**
Garganey *(Spatula querquedula)* **R**
Blue-winged Teal *(Spatula discors)*
Cinnamon Teal *(Spatula cyanoptera)*
Northern Shoveler *(Spatula clypeata)*
Gadwall *(Mareca strepera)*
Eurasian Wigeon *(Mareca penelope)*
American Wigeon *(Mareca americana)*
Mallard *(Anas platyrhynchos)*
Mexican Duck *(Anas diazi)* **R**
American Black Duck *(Anas rubripes)*
Northern Pintail *(Anas acuta)*

Green-winged Teal *(Anas crecca)*
Canvasback *(Aythya valisineria)*
Redhead *(Aythya americana)*
Ring-necked Duck *(Aythya collaris)*
Tufted Duck *(Aythya fuligula)* **R**
Greater Scaup *(Aythya marila)*
Lesser Scaup *(Aythya affinis)*
Harlequin Duck *(Histrionicus histrionicus)*
Surf Scoter *(Melanitta perspicillata)*
White-winged Scoter *(Melanitta deglandi)*
Stejneger's Scoter *(Melanitta stejnegeri)* **R**
Black Scoter *(Melanitta americana)*
Long-tailed Duck *(Clangula hyemalis)*
Bufflehead *(Bucephala albeola)*
Common Goldeneye *(Bucephala clangula)*
Barrow's Goldeneye *(Bucephala islandica)*
Hooded Merganser *(Lophodytes cucullatus)*
Common Merganser *(Mergus merganser)*
Red-breasted Merganser (Mergus serrator)
Ruddy Duck *(Oxyura jamaicensis)*

Order Galliformes | Family Odontophoridae
California Quail *(Callipepla californica)*

Official List of Montana Birds

Family Phasianidae
Wild Turkey *(Meleagris gallopavo)*
Ruffed Grouse *(Bonasa umbellus)*
Spruce Grouse *(Canachites canadensis)*
Willow Ptarmigan *(Lagopus lagopus)* **R**
White-tailed Ptarmigan *(Lagopus leucura)*
Greater Sage-Grouse *(Centrocercus urophasianus)*
Dusky Grouse *(Dendragapus obscurus)*
Sharp-tailed Grouse *(Tympanuchus phasianellus)*
Greater Prairie-Chicken *(Tympanuchus cupido)* **R**
Gray Partridge *(Perdix perdix)*
Ring-necked Pheasant *(Phasianus colchicus)*
Chukar *(Alectoris chukar)*

Order Podicipediformes | Family Podicipedidae
Pied-billed Grebe *(Podilymbus podiceps)*
Horned Grebe *(Podiceps auritus)*
Red-necked Grebe *(Podiceps grisegena)*
Eared Grebe *(Podiceps nigricollis)*
Western Grebe *(Aechmophorus occidentalis)*
Clark's Grebe *(Aechmophorus clarkii)*

Order Columbiformes | Family Columbidae
Rock Pigeon *(Columba livia)*
Band-tailed Pigeon *(Patagioenas fasciata)*
Eurasian Collared-Dove *(Streptopelia decaocto)*
Inca Dove *(Columbina inca)* **R**
White-winged Dove *(Zenaida asiatica)*
Mourning Dove *(Zenaida macroura)*

Order Cuculiformes | Family Cuculidae
Yellow-billed Cuckoo *(Coccyzus americanus)*
Black-billed Cuckoo *(Coccyzus erythropthalmus)*

Order Caprimulgiformes | Family Caprimulgidae
Common Nighthawk *(Chordeiles minor)*
Common Poorwill *(Phalaenoptilus nuttallii)*
Eastern/Mexican Whip-poor-will
  (Antrostomus vociferus/arizonae) **R**

Order Apodiformes | Family Apodidae
Black Swift *(Cypseloides niger)*
Chimney Swift *(Chaetura pelagica)*
Vaux's Swift *(Chaetura vauxi)*
White-throated Swift *(Aeronautes saxatalis)*

Family Trochilidae
Rivoli's Hummingbird *(Eugenes fulgens)* **R**
Ruby-throated Hummingbird *(Archilochus colubris)* **R**
Black-chinned Hummingbird *(Archilochus alexandri)*
Anna's Hummingbird *(Calypte anna)* **R**
Costa's Hummingbird *(Calypte costae)* **R**
Calliope Hummingbird *(Selasphorus calliope)*
Rufous Hummingbird *(Selasphorus rufus)*
Broad-tailed Hummingbird *(Selasphorus platycercus)*

Order Gruiformes | Family Rallidae
Virginia Rail *(Rallus limicola)*
Sora *(Porzana carolina)*
Common Gallinule *(Gallinula galeata)* **R**
American Coot *(Fulica americana)*
Yellow Rail *(Coturnicops noveboracensis)* **R**

Family Gruidae
Sandhill Crane *(Antigone canadensis)*
Whooping Crane *(Grus americana)*

Order Charadriiformes | Family Recurvirostridae
Black-necked Stilt *(Himantopus mexicanus)*
American Avocet *(Recurvirostra americana)*

Family Charadriidae
Black-bellied Plover *(Pluvialis squatarola)*
American Golden-Plover *(Pluvialis dominica)*
Killdeer *(Charadrius vociferus)*
Semipalmated Plover *(Charadrius semipalmatus)*
Piping Plover *(Charadrius melodus)*
Mountain Plover *(Charadrius montanus)*
Snowy Plover *(Charadrius nivosus)* **R**

Family Scolopacidae
Upland Sandpiper *(Bartramia longicauda)*
Whimbrel *(Numenius phaeopus)*
Long-billed Curlew *(Numenius americanus)*
Hudsonian Godwit *(Limosa haemastica)*
Marbled Godwit *(Limosa fedoa)*
Ruddy Turnstone *(Arenaria interpres)*
Black Turnstone *(Arenaria melanocephala)* **R**

Official List of Montana Birds

Red Knot *(Calidris canutus)*
Ruff *(Calidris pugnax)* **R**
Sharp-tailed Sandpiper *(Calidris acuminata)* **R**
Stilt Sandpiper *(Calidris himantopus)*
Curlew Sandpiper *(Calidris ferruginea)* **R**
Sanderling *(Calidris alba)*
Dunlin *(Calidris alpina)*
Purple Sandpiper *(Calidris maritima)* **R**
Baird's Sandpiper *(Calidris bairdii)*
Least Sandpiper *(Calidris minutilla)*
White-rumped Sandpiper *(Calidris fuscicollis)*
Buff-breasted Sandpiper *(Calidris subruficollis)*
Pectoral Sandpiper *(Calidris melanotos)*
Semipalmated Sandpiper *(Calidris pusilla)*
Western Sandpiper *(Calidris mauri)*
Short-billed Dowitcher *(Limnodromus griseus)*
Long-billed Dowitcher *(Limnodromus scolopaceus)*
American Woodcock *(Scolopax minor)* **R**
Wilson's Snipe *(Gallinago delicata)*
Spotted Sandpiper *(Actitis macularius)*
Solitary Sandpiper *(Tringa solitaria)*
Lesser Yellowlegs *(Tringa flavipes)*
Willet *(Tringa semipalmata)*
Greater Yellowlegs *(Tringa melanoleuca)*
Wood Sandpiper *(Tringa glareola)* **R**
Wilson's Phalarope *(Phalaropus tricolor)*
Red-necked Phalarope *(Phalaropus lobatus)*
Red Phalarope *(Phalaropus fulicarius)*

Family Stercorariidae
Pomarine Jaeger *(Stercorarius pomarinus)* **R**
Parasitic Jaeger *(Stercorarius parasiticus)* **R**
Long-tailed Jaeger *(Stercorarius longicaudus)* **R**

Family Alcidae
Long-billed Murrelet *(Brachyramphus perdix)* **R**
Ancient Murrelet *(Synthliboramphus antiquus)* **R**

Family Laridae
Black-legged Kittiwake *(Rissa tridactyla)* **R**
Ivory Gull *(Pagophila eburnea)* **R**
Sabine's Gull *(Xema sabini)*
Bonaparte's Gull *(Chroicocephalus philadelphia)*
Little Gull *(Hydrocoloeus minutus)* **R**
Ross's Gull *(Rhodostethia rosea)* **R**
Laughing Gull *(Leucophaeus atricilla)* **R**
Franklin's Gull *(Leucophaeus pipixcan)*
Heermann's Gull *(Larus heermanni)* **R**
Short-billed Gull *(Larus brachyrhynchus)*
Ring-billed Gull *(Larus delawarensis)*
Western Gull *(Larus occidentalis)* **R**
California Gull *(Larus californicus)*
Herring Gull *(Larus argentatus)*
Iceland Gull *(Larus glaucoides)*
Lesser Black-backed Gull *(Larus fuscus)*
Glaucous-winged Gull *(Larus glaucescens)*
Glaucous Gull *(Larus hyperboreus)*
Great Black-backed Gull *(Larus marinus)* **R**
Least Tern *(Sternula antillarum)*
Caspian Tern *(Hydroprogne caspia)*
Black Tern *(Chlidonias niger)*
Common Tern *(Sterna hirundo)*
Arctic Tern *(Sterna paradisaea)* **R**
Forster's Tern *(Sterna forsteri)*

Order Gaviiformes | Family Gaviidae
Red-throated Loon *(Gavia stellata)*
Pacific Loon *(Gavia pacifica)*
Common Loon *(Gavia immer)*
Yellow-billed Loon *(Gavia adamsii)* **R**

Order Procellariiformes | Family Procellariidae
Manx Shearwater *(Puffinus puffinus)* **R**

Order Ciconiiformes | Family Ciconiidae
Wood Stork *(Mycteria americana)* **R**

Order Suliformes | Family Phalacrocoracidae
Double-crested Cormorant *(Nannopterum auritum)*
Neotropic Cormorant *(Nannopterum brasilianum)* **R**

Order Pelecaniformes | Family Pelecanidae
American White Pelican *(Pelecanus erythrorhynchos)*

Family Ardeidae
American Bittern *(Botaurus lentiginosus)*

Official List of Montana Birds

Least Bittern *(Ixobrychus exilis)* **R**
Great Blue Heron *(Ardea herodias)*
Great Egret *(Ardea alba)*
Snowy Egret *(Egretta thula)*
Little Blue Heron *(Egretta caerulea)* **R**
Tricolored Heron *(Egretta tricolor)* **R**
Cattle Egret *(Bubulcus ibis)*
Green Heron *(Butorides virescens)*
Black-crowned Night-Heron *(Nycticorax nycticorax)*
Yellow-crowned Night-Heron *(Nyctanassa violacea)* **R**

Family Threskiornithidae
Glossy Ibis *(Plegadis falcinellus)* **R**
White-faced Ibis *(Plegadis chihi)*

Order Cathartiformes | Family Cathartidae
Black Vulture *(Coragyps atratus)* **R**
Turkey Vulture *(Cathartes aura)*

Order Accipitriformes | Family Pandionidae
Osprey *(Pandion haliaetus)*

Family Accipitridae
White-tailed Kite *(Elanus leucurus)* **R**
Golden Eagle *(Aquila chrysaetos)*
Northern Harrier *(Circus hudsonius)*
Sharp-shinned Hawk *(Accipiter striatus)*
Cooper's Hawk *(Accipiter cooperii)*
Northern Goshawk *(Accipiter gentilis)*
Bald Eagle *(Haliaeetus leucocephalus)*
Mississippi Kite *(Ictinia mississippiensis)* **R**
Red-shouldered Hawk *(Buteo lineatus)* **R**
Broad-winged Hawk *(Buteo platypterus)*
Swainson's Hawk *(Buteo swainsoni)*
Red-tailed Hawk *(Buteo jamaicensis)*
Rough-legged Hawk *(Buteo lagopus)*
Ferruginous Hawk *(Buteo regalis)*

Order Strigiformes | Family Tytonidae
Barn Owl *(Tyto alba)*

Family Strigidae
Flammulated Owl *(Psiloscops flammeolus)*

Western Screech-Owl *(Megascops kennicottii)*
Eastern Screech-Owl *(Megascops asio)*
Great Horned Owl *(Bubo virginianus)*
Snowy Owl *(Bubo scandiacus)*
Northern Hawk Owl *(Surnia ulula)*
Northern Pygmy-Owl *(Glaucidium gnoma)*
Burrowing Owl *(Athene cunicularia)*
Barred Owl *(Strix varia)*
Great Gray Owl *(Strix nebulosa)*
Long-eared Owl *(Asio otus)*
Short-eared Owl *(Asio flammeus)*
Boreal Owl *(Aegolius funereus)*
Northern Saw-whet Owl *(Aegolius acadicus)*

Order Coraciiformes | Family Alcedinidae
Belted Kingfisher *(Megaceryle alcyon)*

Order Piciformes | Family Picidae
Lewis's Woodpecker *(Melanerpes lewis)*
Red-headed Woodpecker *(Melanerpes erythrocephalus)*
Red-bellied Woodpecker *(Melanerpes carolinus)* **R**
Williamson's Sapsucker *(Sphyrapicus thyroideus)*
Yellow-bellied Sapsucker *(Sphyrapicus varius)* **R**
Red-naped Sapsucker *(Sphyrapicus nuchalis)*
American Three-toed Woodpecker *(Picoides dorsalis)*
Black-backed Woodpecker *(Picoides arcticus)*
Downy Woodpecker *(Dryobates pubescens)*
Hairy Woodpecker *(Dryobates villosus)*
White-headed Woodpecker *(Dryobates albolarvatus)* **R**
Northern Flicker *(Colaptes auratus)*
Pileated Woodpecker *(Dryocopus pileatus)*

Order Falconiformes | Family Falconidae
Crested Caracara *(Caracara plancus)* **R**
American Kestrel *(Falco sparverius)*
Merlin *(Falco columbarius)*
Gyrfalcon *(Falco rusticolus)*
Peregrine Falcon *(Falco peregrinus)*
Prairie Falcon *(Falco mexicanus)*

Order Passeriformes | Family Tyrannidae
Ash-throated Flycatcher *(Myiarchus cinerascens)* **R**
Great Crested Flycatcher *(Myiarchus crinitus)* **R**
Cassin's Kingbird *(Tyrannus vociferans)*

Official List of Montana Birds

Western Kingbird *(Tyrannus verticalis)*
Eastern Kingbird *(Tyrannus tyrannus)*
Scissor-tailed Flycatcher *(Tyrannus forficatus)*
Olive-sided Flycatcher *(Contopus cooperi)*
Western Wood-Pewee *(Contopus sordidulus)*
Eastern Wood-Pewee *(Contopus virens)* **R**
Yellow-bellied Flycatcher *(Empidonax flaviventris)* **R**
Alder Flycatcher *(Empidonax alnorum)*
Willow Flycatcher *(Empidonax traillii)*
Least Flycatcher *(Empidonax minimus)*
Hammond's Flycatcher *(Empidonax hammondii)*
Gray Flycatcher *(Empidonax wrightii)* **R**
Dusky Flycatcher *(Empidonax oberholseri)*
Cordilleran Flycatcher *(Empidonax occidentalis)*
Eastern Phoebe *(Sayornis phoebe)*
Say's Phoebe *(Sayornis saya)*
Vermilion Flycatcher *(Pyrocephalus rubinus)* **R**

Family Vireonidae
White-eyed Vireo *(Vireo griseus)* **R**
Yellow-throated Vireo *(Vireo flavifrons)* **R**
Cassin's Vireo *(Vireo cassinii)*
Blue-headed Vireo *(Vireo solitarius)* **R**
Plumbeous Vireo *(Vireo plumbeus)*
Philadelphia Vireo *(Vireo philadelphicus)* **R**
Warbling Vireo *(Vireo gilvus)*
Red-eyed Vireo *(Vireo olivaceus)*

Family Laniidae
Loggerhead Shrike *(Lanius ludovicianus)*
Northern Shrike *(Lanius borealis)*

Family Corvidae
Canada Jay *(Perisoreus canadensis)*
Pinyon Jay *(Gymnorhinus cyanocephalus)*
Steller's Jay *(Cyanocitta stelleri)*
Blue Jay *(Cyanocitta cristata)*
California Scrub-Jay *(Aphelocoma californica)* **R**
Clark's Nutcracker *(Nucifraga columbiana)*
Black-billed Magpie *(Pica hudsonia)*
American Crow *(Corvus brachyrhynchos)*
Common Raven *(Corvus corax)*

Family Paridae
Black-capped Chickadee *(Poecile atricapillus)*
Mountain Chickadee *(Poecile gambeli)*
Chestnut-backed Chickadee *(Poecile rufescens)*
Boreal Chickadee *(Poecile hudsonicus)*

Family Alaudidae
Horned Lark *(Eremophila alpestris)*

Family Hirundinidae
Bank Swallow *(Riparia riparia)*
Tree Swallow *(Tachycineta bicolor)*
Violet-green Swallow *(Tachycineta thalassina)*
Northern Rough-winged Swallow
  (Stelgidopteryx serripennis)
Purple Martin *(Progne subis)*
Barn Swallow *(Hirundo rustica)*
Cliff Swallow *(Petrochelidon pyrrhonota)*

Family Regulidae
Ruby-crowned Kinglet *(Corthylio calendula)*
Golden-crowned Kinglet *(Regulus satrapa)*

Family Bombycillidae
Bohemian Waxwing *(Bombycilla garrulus)*
Cedar Waxwing *(Bombycilla cedrorum)*

Family Sittidae
Red-breasted Nuthatch *(Sitta canadensis)*
White-breasted Nuthatch *(Sitta carolinensis)*
Pygmy Nuthatch *(Sitta pygmaea)*

Family Certhiidae
Brown Creeper *(Certhia americana)*

Family Polioptilidae
Blue-gray Gnatcatcher *(Polioptila caerulea)* **R**

Family Troglodytidae
Rock Wren *(Salpinctes obsoletus)*
Canyon Wren *(Catherpes mexicanus)*
House Wren *(Troglodytes aedon)*

Official List of Montana Birds

Pacific Wren *(Troglodytes pacificus)*
Winter Wren *(Troglodytes hiemalis)* **R**
Sedge Wren *(Cistothorus stellaris)* **R**
Marsh Wren (Cistothorus palustris)
Carolina Wren (Thryothorus ludovicianus) **R**
Bewick's Wren (Thryomanes bewickii) **R**

Family Mimidae
Gray Catbird *(Dumetella carolinensis)*
Curve-billed Thrasher *(Toxostoma curvirostre)* **R**
Brown Thrasher *(Toxostoma rufum)*
Sage Thrasher *(Oreoscoptes montanus)*
Northern Mockingbird *(Mimus polyglottos)*

Family Sturnidae
European Starling *(Sturnus vulgaris)*

Family Cinclidae
American Dipper *(Cinclus mexicanus)*

Family Turdidae
Eastern Bluebird *(Sialia sialis)*
Western Bluebird *(Sialia mexicana)*
Mountain Bluebird *(Sialia currucoides)*
Townsend's Solitaire *(Myadestes townsendi)*
Veery *(Catharus fuscescens)*
Gray-cheeked Thrush *(Catharus minimus)* **R**
Swainson's Thrush *(Catharus ustulatus)*
Hermit Thrush *(Catharus guttatus)*
Wood Thrush *(Hylocichla mustelina)* **R**
Fieldfare *(Turdus pilaris)* **R**
American Robin *(Turdus migratorius)*
Varied Thrush *(Ixoreus naevius)*

Family Prunellidae
Siberian Accentor *(Prunella montanella)* **R**

Family Passeridae
House Sparrow *(Passer domesticus)*

Family Motacillidae
American Pipit *(Anthus rubescens)*
Sprague's Pipit *(Anthus spragueii)*

Family Fringillidae
Brambling *(Fringilla montifringilla)* **R**
Evening Grosbeak *(Coccothraustes vespertinus)*
Pine Grosbeak *(Pinicola enucleator)*
Gray-crowned Rosy-Finch *(Leucosticte tephrocotis)*
Black Rosy-Finch *(Leucosticte atrata)*
House Finch *(Haemorhous mexicanus)*
Purple Finch *(Haemorhous purpureus)*
Cassin's Finch *(Haemorhous cassinii)*
Common Redpoll *(Acanthis flammea)*
Hoary Redpoll *(Acanthis hornemanni)*
Red Crossbill *(Loxia curvirostra)*
White-winged Crossbill *(Loxia leucoptera)*
Pine Siskin *(Spinus pinus)*
Lesser Goldfinch *(Spinus psaltria)*
American Goldfinch *(Spinus tristis)*

Family Calcariidae
Lapland Longspur *(Calcarius lapponicus)*
Chestnut-collared Longspur *(Calcarius ornatus)*
Smith's Longspur *(Calcarius pictus)* **R**
Thick-billed Longspur *(Rhynchophanes mccownii)*
Snow Bunting *(Plectrophenax nivalis)*

Family Passerellidae
Grasshopper Sparrow *(Ammodramus savannarum)*
Black-throated Sparrow *(Amphispiza bilineata)* **R**
Lark Sparrow *(Chondestes grammacus)*
Lark Bunting *(Calamospiza melanocorys)*
Chipping Sparrow *(Spizella passerina)*
Clay-colored Sparrow *(Spizella pallida)*
Field Sparrow *(Spizella pusilla)*
Brewer's Sparrow *(Spizella breweri)*
Fox Sparrow *(Passerella iliaca)*
American Tree Sparrow *(Spizelloides arborea)*
Dark-eyed Junco *(Junco hyemalis)*
White-crowned Sparrow *(Zonotrichia leucophrys)*
Golden-crowned Sparrow *(Zonotrichia atricapilla)*
Harris's Sparrow *(Zonotrichia querula)*
White-throated Sparrow *(Zonotrichia albicollis)*
Sagebrush Sparrow *(Artemisiospiza nevadensis)* **R**
Vesper Sparrow *(Pooecetes gramineus)*
LeConte's Sparrow *(Ammospiza leconteii)*

Official List of Montana Birds

Nelson's Sparrow *(Ammospiza nelsoni)*
Baird's Sparrow *(Centronyx bairdii)*
Savannah Sparrow *(Passerculus sandwichensis)*
Song Sparrow *(Melospiza melodia)*
Lincoln's Sparrow *(Melospiza lincolnii)*
Swamp Sparrow *(Melospiza georgiana)*
Green-tailed Towhee *(Pipilo chlorurus)*
Spotted Towhee *(Pipilo maculatus)*
Eastern Towhee *(Pipilo erythrophthalmus)* **R**

Family Icteriidae
Yellow-breasted Chat *(Icteria virens)*

Family Icteridae
Yellow-headed Blackbird *(Xanthocephalus xanthocephalus)*
Bobolink *(Dolichonyx oryzivorus)*
Eastern Meadowlark *(Sturnella magna)* **R**
Western Meadowlark *(Sturnella neglecta)*
Orchard Oriole *(Icterus spurius)*
Hooded Oriole *(Icterus cucullatus)* **R**
Bullock's Oriole *(Icterus bullockii)*
Baltimore Oriole *(Icterus galbula)*
Red-winged Blackbird *(Agelaius phoeniceus)*
Brown-headed Cowbird *(Molothrus ater)*
Rusty Blackbird *(Euphagus carolinus)*
Brewer's Blackbird *(Euphagus cyanocephalus)*
Common Grackle *(Quiscalus quiscula)*
Great-tailed Grackle *(Quiscalus mexicanus)* **R**

Family Parulidae
Ovenbird *(Seiurus aurocapilla)*
Northern Waterthrush *(Parkesia noveboracensis)*
Golden-winged Warbler *(Vermivora chrysoptera)* **R**
Blue-winged Warbler (Vermivora cyanoptera) **R**
Black-and-white Warbler *(Mniotilta varia)*
Prothonotary Warbler *(Protonotaria citrea)* **R**
Tennessee Warbler *(Leiothlypis peregrina)*
Orange-crowned Warbler *(Leiothlypis celata)*
Nashville Warbler *(Leiothlypis ruficapilla)*
Virginia's Warbler *(Leiothlypis virginiae)* **R**
Connecticut Warbler *(Oporornis agilis)* **R**
MacGillivray's Warbler *(Geothlypis tolmiei)*
Mourning Warbler *(Geothlypis philadelphia)*
Kentucky Warbler *(Geothlypis formosa)* **R**
Common Yellowthroat *(Geothlypis trichas)*
Hooded Warbler *(Setophaga citrina)* **R**
American Redstart *(Setophaga ruticilla)*
Cape May Warbler *(Setophaga tigrina)*
Northern Parula *(Setophaga americana)*
Magnolia Warbler *(Setophaga magnolia)*
Bay-breasted Warbler *(Setophaga castanea)* **R**
Blackburnian Warbler *(Setophaga fusca)* **R**
Yellow Warbler *(Setophaga petechia)*
Chestnut-sided Warbler *(Setophaga pensylvanica)*
Blackpoll Warbler *(Setophaga striata)*
Black-throated Blue Warbler *(Setophaga caerulescens)*
Palm Warbler *(Setophaga palmarum)*
Pine Warbler *(Setophaga pinus)* **R**
Yellow-rumped Warbler *(Setophaga coronata)*
Yellow-throated Warbler *(Setophaga dominica)* **R**
Prairie Warbler *(Setophaga discolor)* **R**
Black-throated Gray Warbler *(Setophaga nigrescens)* **R**
Townsend's Warbler *(Setophaga townsendi)*
Black-throated Green Warbler *(Setophaga virens)* **R**
Canada Warbler *(Cardellina canadensis)*
Wilson's Warbler *(Cardellina pusilla)*
Painted Redstart *(Myioborus pictus)* **R**

Family Cardinalidae
Summer Tanager *(Piranga rubra)* **R**
Scarlet Tanager (Piranga olivacea)
Western Tanager *(Piranga ludoviciana)*
Northern Cardinal *(Cardinalis cardinalis)* **R**
Pyrrhuloxia *(Cardinalis sinuatus)* **R**
Rose-breasted Grosbeak *(Pheucticus ludovicianus)*
Black-headed Grosbeak *(Pheucticus melanocephalus)*
Blue Grosbeak *(Passerina caerulea)* **R**
Lazuli Bunting *(Passerina amoena)*
Indigo Bunting *(Passerina cyanea)*
Painted Bunting *(Passerina ciris)* **R**
Dickcissel *(Spiza americana)*

Copyright © 2018-2021 | Montana Bird Advocacy

APPENDIX B
Alphabetical Listing of Birds In This Book

To help you find additional information about a bird or birds you see in the wild we have listed all the birds described in the articles in this book alphabetically by first name making it easy to find what you are looking for by including page numbers for each bird.

American Avocet 65	Brown-headed Cowbird 237
American Coot 60	Brown Pelican 92
American Crow 164	Bullock's Oriole 234
American Dipper 195	Burrowing Owl 123
American Golden-Plover 67	California Gull 84
American Goldfinch 214	Calliope Hummingbird 56
American Kestrel 142	Canada Jay 156
American Robin 202	Carolina Wren 187
American White Pelican 91	Cassin's Vireo 152
Anna's Hummingbird 54	Cattle Egret 95
Baikal Teal 30	Cedar Waxwing 176
Bald Eagle 110	Chestnut-sided Chickadee 168
Bared Owl 125	Clark's Nutcracker 160
Barrow's Goldeneye 41	Clay-colored Sparrow 219
Belted Kingfisher 134	Common Goldeneye 40
Black Scoter 39	Common Grackle 239
Black-backed Woodpecker 139	Common Loon 87
Black Vulture 101	Common Nighthawk 52
Black-bellied Plover 66	Common Raven 165
Black-billed Magpie 162	Common Redpoll 209
Black-capped Chickadee 166	Curved-billed Thrasher 191
Black-crowned Night-Heron 96	Dark-eyed Junco 221
Black-necked Stilt 64	Double-crested Cormorant 89
Blue Jay 159	Dunlin 70
Blue-gray Gnatcatcher 181	Dusky Grouse 43
Blue-winged Teal 32	Eared Grebe 49
Bobolink 231	Eastern Bluebird 197
Bohemian Waxwing 175	Eastern Kingbird 150
Bonaparte's Gull 80	Eurasian Collared Dove 50
Boreal Chickadee 169	Eurasian Wigeon 33
Boreal Owl 132	European Starling 193
Brewer's Blackbird 239	Evening Grosbeak 204
Brown Creeper 179	Franklin's Gull 81

255

Alphabetical Listing of Birds

Gray Catbird 189	Red-naped Woodpecker 136
Gray Partridge 44	Red-necked Grebe 47
Gray-crowned Rosy-Finch 206	Red-tailed Hawk 113
Great Blue Heron 93	Ring-billed Gull 84
Great Gray Owl 128	Red-winged Blackbird 236
Great Horned Owl 119	Rock Wren 183
Greater Yellowlegs 74	Ross's Goose 26
Gyrfalcon 145	Rough-legged Hawk 114
Harlequin Duck 33	Rufous Hummingbird 57
Harris's Hawk 115	Sabine's gull 78
Harris's Sparrow 224	Sage Thrasher 192
Heermann's Gull 82	Sandhill Crane 62
Herring Gull 85	Scarlet Tanager 243
Horned Grebe 46	Sharp-shinned Hawk 107
Horned Lark 170	Short-eared Owl 130
House Finch 208	Snow Goose 24
Killdeer 69	Snowy Owl 121
Lapland Longspur 215	Sora 58
Lark Sparrow 217	Spotted Towhee 227
Lazuli Bunting 246	Spruce Grouse 42
Lesser Black-backed Gull 85	Stejneger's Scoter 38
Lesser Goldfinch 213	Steller's Jay 158
Lesser Yellowlegs 73	Summer Tanager 241
Lewis's Woodpecker 138	Surf Scoter 35
Long-tailed Duck 39	Townsend's Solitaire 200
Long-tailed Jaeger 76	Tree Swallow 172
Marsh Wren 185	Trumpeter Swan 27
Merlin 144	Tundra Swan 27
Mountain Bluebird 199	Turkey Vulture 104
Mountain Chickadee 167	Western Kingbird 149
Northern Goshawk 109	Western Meadowlark 233
Northern Shrike 154	Western Screech-Owl 117
Osprey 105	Western Tanager 244
Pacific Loon 86	White-breasted Nuthatch 178
Prairie Falcon 147	White-crowned Sparrow 222
Purple Martin 173	White-faced Ibis 98
Pygmy Nuthatch 178	White-throated Sparrow 225
Red-breasted Nuthatch 177	White-winged Crossbill 212
Red Crossbill 211	White-winged Scoter 37
Red Phalarope 75	Wilson's Snipe 72
Red-eyed Vireo 153	Wood Duck 29
Red-naped Sapsucker 138	Yellow-headed Blackbird 229

Index of Families and Species

APPENDIX C

Index of Families and Species, Within Families, Including Where To Find Species

Avocet
American Avocet 65

Blackbirds
Bobolink 231
Brewer's Blackbird 239
Brown-headed Blackbird 237
Bullock's Oriole 234
Common Grackle 239
Red-winged Blackbird 236
Western Meadowlark 233
Yellow-headed blackbird 229

Chickadees
Black-capped Chickadee 166
Boreal Chickadee 169
Chestnut-sided Chickadee 168
Mountain Chickadee 167

Cormorants
Double-crested Cormorant 89

Corvids
American Crow 164
Blue Jay 159
Black-billed Magpie 162
Canada Jay 156
Clark's Nutcracker 160
Common Raven 165
Steller's Jay 158

Cranes
Sandhill Crane 62

Creepers
Brown Creeper 179

Dipper
American Dipper 195

Dove
Eurasian Collared-Dove 50

Ducks
Baikal Teal 30
Barrow's Goldeneye 41
Black Scoter 39
Blue-Winged Teal 32
Common Goldeneye 40
Eurasian Wigeon 33
Harlequin Duck 33
Long-tailed Duck 39
Stejneger's Scoter 38
Surf Scoter 35
White-winged Scoter 37
Wood Duck 29

Falcons
American Kestrel 142
Merlin 144
Gyrfalcon 145
Prairie 147

Finches
American Goldfinch 214
Common Redpoll 209
Evening Grosbeak 204
Gray-crowned Rosy Finch 206
House Finch 208
Lesser Goldfinch 213
Red Crossbill 211
White-winged Crossbill 212

257

Index of Families and Species

Flycatchers
Eastern Kingbird 150
Western Kingbird 149

Game Birds
Dusky Grouse 43
Gray Partridge 44
Spruce Grouse 42

Geese
Ross's Goose 26
Snow Goose 24

Gnatcatcher
Blue-gray Gnatcatcher 181

Grebes
Eared Grebe 49
Horned Grebe 46
Red-necked Grebe 47

Gulls
Bonaparte's Gull 80
California Gull 84
Franklin's Gull 81
Heermann's Gull 82
Herring Gull 85
Lesser Black-backed Gull 85
Ring-billed Gull 84
Sabine's Gull 78

Hawks
Bald Eagle 110
Harris's Hawk 115
Northern Goshawk 109
Red-tailed Hawk 113
Rough-legged Hawk 114
Sharp-shinned Hawk 107

Herons/Egret
Black-crowned Night-Heron 96
Cattle Egret 95
Great Blue Heron 93

Hummingbirds
Anna's Hummingbird 54
Calliope Hummingbird 56
Rufous Hummingbird 57

Ibis
White-faced Ibis 98

Jaeger
Long-tailed Jaeger 76

Kingfisher
Belted Kingfisher 134

Lark
Horned Lark 170

Longspur
Lapland Longspur 215

Loons
Common Loon 87
Pacific Loon 86

Nighthawk
Common Nighthawk 52

Nuthatches
Pygmy Nuthatch 178
Red-breasted Nuthatch 177
White-breasted Nuthatch 178

Owls
Barred Owl 125
Boreal Owl 132
Burrowing Owl 123
Great Gray Owl 128
Great Horned Owl 119
Snowy Owl 121
Short-eared Owl 130
Western screech-Owl 117

Index of Families and Species

Ospreys
Osprey 105

Plover
American Golden Plover 67
Black-bellied Plover 66
Killdeer 69

Pelican
American White Pelican 91

Rails
American Coot 60
Sora 58

Shrike
Northern Shrike 154

Shorebirds
Dunlin 70
Greater Yellowlegs 74
Lesser Yellowlegs 73
Red Phalarope 75
Wilson's Snipe 72

Starling
European Starling 193

Stilt
Black-Necked Stilt 64

Sparrows
Clay-colored Sparrow 219
Dark-eyed Junco 221
Harris's Sparrow 224
Lark Sparrow 217
Spotted Towhee 227
White-crowned Sparrow 222
White-throated sparrow 225

Swans
Trumpeter Swan 27
Tundra Swan 27

Swallows
Purple Martin 173
Tree Swallow 172

Tanagers
Lazuli Bunting 246
Scarlet Tanager 243
Summer Tanager 241
Western Tanager 244

Thrashers
Curved-billed thrasher 191
Gray Catbird 189
Sage Thrasher 192

Thrushes
American Robin 202
Eastern Bluebird 197
Mountain Bluebird 199
Townsend's Solitaire 200

Vireos
Cassin's Vireo 152
Red-eyed Vireo 153

Vulture
Black Vulture 101
Turkey Vulture 104

Waxwings
Bohemian Waxwing 175
Cedar Waxwing 176

Woodpeckers
Black-backed Woodpecker 139
Lewis's Woodpecker 138
Red-naped Woodpecker 136

Wrens
Carolina Wren 187
Marsh Wren 185
Rock Wren 183

259

APPENDIX D
Checklist of Lewis and Clark Birds 1805 – 1806
Listed in American Ornithological Society (AOS) Order, 2019

No one knows with absolute certainty which bird species Lewis and Clark actually saw. I produced this list from reading Lewis & Clark Journals and doing an extensive web search of what others think they saw. Although many lists contain the same species, there were no two lists completely the same. Like others, I made my best educated assumptions and came up with my list. I believe they saw 131 species, which does not seem like a lot, but remember; they had few field references and poor optics. They were tasked with documenting what they saw, but their main objective was finding a water passage to the Pacific Ocean from St Louis. Their obstacles were gigantic, often pulling boats by rope through ice filled spring flood waters. Not exactly ideal conditions for bird observations. A check space is provided next to each bird of the their *"Voyage of Discovery"*. That space can be used two ways. Check off the birds you have seen in Montana that they saw or, after you finish reading this book, set a goal of seeing all of these species in the next year. Perhaps you would like to set a goal of your own that reflects your personality and birding interest. The line to the right of each bird is for you to make notes.

To make entries more meaningful, bold species were new discoveries to science, italicized questionable species or unclear journal entries, and species in quotation marks have articles in this book.

Waterfowl Notes:
1. ___ "Snow Goose"_____
2. ___ **Greater White-fronted Goose** _____
3. ___ Brant_____
4. ___ **Cackling Goose** _____
5. ___ Canada Goose _____
6. ___ "Trumpeter Swan"_____
7. ___ "Tundra Swan" _____
8. ___ "Wood Duck"_____
9. ___ "Blue-winged Teal" _____
10. ___ Northern Shoveler _____
11. ___ Mallard_____
12. ___ Canvasback_____
13. ___ **Ring-necked Duck** _____
14. ___ Bufflehead _____
15. ___ "Common Goldeneye" _____
16. ___ Common Merganser_____

Lewis and Clark Birds

17. ___ Red-breasted Merganser _____

Grouse, Quail Notes:
18. ___ Wild Turkey_____
19. ___ **Ruffed Grouse**_____
20. ___ **Greater Sage Grouse** _____
21. ___ "Spruce Grouse" _____
22. ___ "Dusky Grouse" _____
23. ___ **Sooty Grouse** *(Not found in Montana)* _____
24. ___ **Sharp-tailed Grouse** _____
25. ___ Greater Prairie Chicken _____
26. ___ **Mountain Quail** *(Not found in Montana)* _____

Grebes:
27. ___ Pied-billed Grebe _____
28. ___ **"Red-necked Grebe"**_____
29. ___ **Western Grebe** _____

Pigeons & Doves:
30. ___ **Mourning Dove** _____
31. ___ Passenger Pigeon *(Extinct)* _____
32. ___ Carolina Parakeet *(Extinct)*_____

Cuckoo:
33. ___ Black-billed Cuckoo _____

Nightjars:
34. ___ **"Common Nighthawk"** _____
35. ___ **Common Poorwill**_____
36. ___ Eastern Whip-poor-will *(Not found in Montana)* _____

Hummingbirds:
37.___ Broad-tailed Hummingbird_____
38.___ "Rufous Hummingbird" _____

Rails:
39. ___ "American Coot" _____

Lewis and Clark Birds

Cranes:
40. ___ "Sandhill Crane" _____
41. ___ Whooping Crane *(Rare in Montana)* _____

Avocets:
42. ___ "American Avocet" _____

Plovers:
43. ___ "Black-bellied Plover" _____
44. ___ "American Golden-Plover" _____
45. ___ "Killdeer" _____
46. ___ **Mountain Plover** _____

Shorebirds:
47. ___ Whimbrel _____
48. ___ **Long-billed Curlew** _____
49. ___ Upland Sandpiper _____
50. ___ **Willet** _____
51. ___ Eskimo Curlew (Extinct) _____

Gulls & Terns:
52. ___ **"Bonaparte's Gull"** _____
53. ___ "Franklin's Gull" _____
54. ___ Mew Gull _____
55. ___ "Ring-billed Gull" _____
56. ___ **Western Gull** _____
57. ___ "California Gull" _____
58. ___ "Herring Gull" _____
59. ___ Glaucous-winged Gull _____
60. ___ Glaucous Gull _____
61. ___ Least Tern _____
62. ___ Common Tern _____
63. ___ **Forster's Tern** _____

Loons:
64. ___ **"Pacific Loon"** _____

Fulmars:
65. ___ **Northern Fulmar** *(Not found in Montana)* _____

Lewis and Clark Birds

Cormorants:
65. ___ **"Double-crested Cormorant"** _____

Pelican:
66. ___ "American White Pelican" _____

Herons & Bitterns:
67. ___ American Bittern _____
68. ___ "Great Blue Heron" _____
69. ___ Great Egret _____

Vultures:
70. ___ "Turkey Vulture" _____
71. ___ California Condor (Not found in Montana) _____

Osprey:
72. ___ "Osprey"" _____

Hawks & Eagles Notes:
73. ___ Golden Eagle _____
74. ___ Northern Harrier _____
75. ___ "Bald Eagle" _____
76. ___ **Swainson's Hawk** _____
77. ___ "Red-tailed Hawk" _____

Owls:
78. ___ **"Great Horned Owl"** _____
79. ___ **"Great Gray Owl"** _____

Woodpeckers:
80. ___ Red-breasted Sapsucker (Not found in Montana) _____
81. ___ **"Lewis's Woodpecker"** _____
82. ___ Red-headed Woodpecker _____
83. ___ Downy Woodpecker _____
84. ___ **Hairy Woodpecker** _____
85. ___ **Northern Flicker** _____
86. ___ **Pileated Woodpecker** _____

Lewis and Clark Birds

Falcons:
87. ___ "American Kestrel" _____

Tyrant Flycatchers:
88. ___ "Western Kingbird" _____
89. ___ "Eastern Kingbird" _____
90. ___ **Western Wood-Pewee** _____
91. ___ Hammond's Flycatcher _____

Shrikes:
92. ___ **Loggerhead Shrike** _____

Vireos:
94. ___ Hutton's Vireo *(Not found in Montana)* _____

Crows, Ravens, & Jays:
95. ___ **"Canada Jay"** _____
96. ___ **Pinyon Jay** _____
97. ___ **"Steller's Jay"** _____
98. ___ Western Scrub Jay *(Rare)* _____
99. ___ **"Clark's Nutcracker"** _____
100. ___ **"Black-billed Magpie"** _____
101. ___ "American Crow" _____
102. ___ "Common Raven" _____

Larks:
103. ___ **"Horned Lark"** _____

Swallows:
104. ___ Bank Swallow _____
105. ___ "Purple Martin" _____
106. ___ Cliff Swallow _____

Wrens:
107. ___ House Wren _____
108. ___ Pacific Wren _____

Kinglets:
109. ___ Ruby-crowned Kinglet _____

Lewis and Clark Birds

Thrushes:
110. ___ "Mountain Bluebird" _____
111. ___ "American Robin" _____
112. ___ Varied Thrush _____

Mockingbirds & Thrashers:
113. ___ "Gray Catbird" _____
114. ___ Brown Thrasher _____
115. ___ Northern Mockingbird _____

Waxwings:
116. ___ "Cedar Waxwing" _____

Longspurs:
117. ___ Chestnut-collared Longspur _____
118. ___ **McCown's Longspur** _____

Sparrows:
119. ___ Lark Bunting _____
120. ___ **Fox Sparrow** _____
121. ___ Golden-crowned Sparrow _____

Finches:
122. ___ Pine Siskin _____
123. ___ **"American Goldfinch"** _____

Blackbirds:
124. ___ **"Western Meadowlark"** _____
125. ___ "Brown-headed Cowbird" _____
126. ___ Rusty Blackbird _____
127. ___ "Brewer's Blackbird" _____
128. ___ "Common Grackle" _____

Tanagers:
129. ___ **"Western Tanager"** _____
130. ___ Northern Cardinal *(Rare)* _____

APPENDIX E
GLOSSARY
Definitions of Terms Used In This Book In Alphabetical Order

ABA: The American Birding Association is a non-profit organization which keeps a list of birds within the ABA Area, that is North America, excluding Mexico.

Accipiter: A genus of hawks characterized by short, rounded wings, long tails and legs.

Adult Plumage: The feather color and characteristics in an adult bird. It is often used to refer to the breeding plumage verses non-breeding plumage.

ALPA Code: A unique four letter code that represents a species such as CANG for Canada Goose and RNDU for Ringed-necked Duck.

Alpine Tundra: A community of low growing plants and grasses that are created by altitude rather than latitude and often begins at timberline above 8,000 feet in Montana mountains.

AOU/AOS: The non-profit American Ornithological Union recently changed to the American Ornithological Society that is responsible for bird taxonomy or classification.

ASA/ISO: The sensitivity of film to light. The term has carried over to the sensitivity of sensors in a digital camera. The higher the number the more sensitivity to light.

Avian: Relating to study of, or derived from a bird.

Barren: Biologically this refers to an area devoid of plant life

Berkeley Pit: The largest open pit mine in Montana that is not in operation. It closed in 1981 and has filled with mine waste water.

Birds of Prey: A general term for hawks, falcons and vultures. In Montana there are 21 recognized birds of prey.

Bluetooth Speaker: A wireless speaker often connected to a cell phone or tablet to play bird songs and calls in the field.

Boreal Forest: A northern latitude forest that is typically comprised of spruce and fir coniferous trees with some broad leaf species such as aspen, poplar and birch.

Boreal Species: Any species that occupies the northern latitude spruce forest of Canada and beyond.

Breeding Plumage: The feather color and on some birds bill and leg color of an adult bird that is able to breed. Males are typically more colorful than females.

Brood Parasite: A chick of a different species that was laid in the nest of another species. These parasitic chicks often kill genetic offspring or out compete them for food.

Calls: Bird calls tend to be unmusi-

Glossary

cal, acoustically simpler and less complex than bird songs. They serve a variety of practical, non-sexual functions.

Caracara: The genus and common name of a bird of prey that is found in the Southeast United States.

Carpal Patches: The bend in a bird's wing is called the carpel. Distinctive plumage markings are found in this area such as the dark patch of a Rough-legged Hawk.

Cere: The fleshy base of the upper mandible in hawks, eagles and falcons through which the nostril opens. The color of the cere is a field mark in some species.

Christmas Bird Count: The longest running citizen science bird count in North America conducted by Cornell University. It is held from Dec 15 to January 5 each year.

Classification: The ordering of birds by family, genus and species according to genetic traits.

Clutch: Refers to the total number of eggs laid in a nest.

Colonial Breeder: A species that breeds in a colony or large group. Examples are gulls, cormorant and some grebes.

Colt: The offspring of a Sandhill Crane.

Coniferous Forest: Forests that are made up predominantly of evergreen trees that have needles rather than leaves, such a pines, firs and spruces.

Corvid: A general name for crows and jays. There are nine corvid species in Montana.

Covert Feathers: The contour feathers that cover the bases of the flight feathers. There can be upper and lower covert feathers and help identify a bird.

Coverts: Flight feathers, known as the secondary coverts, on the outer wing, which overlay the primary flight feathers, the primary coverts. Within each group, the feathers form a number of rows.

Cryptic: Coloration or markings on a bird serving to camouflage it in its natural environment: An example is the Brown Creeper's coloration matching the bark of a tree.

Dabbled: Another term for spotted, but not boldly spotted.

DDT: Synthetic organic compound used as an insecticide, that persist in the environment for a long time and can cause the thinning of egg shells.

Decurved: Typically speaking of the bill which would be curved downward.

Depth of Field: The distance that an image is in focus from the lens of a camera. The higher the f-stop used the greater the depth of field.

"Ear" Tuffs: Feathers in some species of owls that stand upright and appear to be ears. Examples are the Great Horned Owl or Long-eared Owl.

eBird: A national database of bird sightings operated by Cornell University that can be used by birders and researchers to keep life list and study bird

Glossary

trends.

Ecosystem: A biological community of interacting organisms and their physical environment such as the short grass prairie, or the Spruce/Fir forest.

Environmental Lapse Rate: The measurement of air temperature cooling as it rises in elevation. It is equal to 3.5 degrees per 1,000 feet of rise.

Epaulets: Are upper wing feathers that are typically different colored than the rest of the wing, such as the red patch at the top of the black wing of Red-winged Blackbirds.

"Extreme" Flash Card: The term used to denote that a memory card in a camera can download images rapidly.

Facial Disk: The pattern of feathers which creates a disk on the face of some owls and harrier hawks. The shape of the feather directs sound towards the ears.

Falcon: A general term used to describe birds of prey that are fast fliers, have pointed wings, and streamlined bodies. Five species of falcons occur in Montana.

Family: In the classification system family comes before genus and species. A bird family share distinct characteristics but not as many as birds in the same genus.

Flycatcher: A family of birds that are rather drab and difficult to identify, and are best identified by call. The exception within this family are the kingbirds.

F-stop: The F-stop is also called the aperture setting on a camera. The higher the number the less light that comes through the lens.

Gallinaceous: A general term for chicken-like or game birds. Many are exotic and transplanted into North America. We have 11 species in Montana of which four are exotic.

Garget: A term most used with hummingbirds. They are feathers of the throat that can be lifted and show bright coloration.

Genera: Plural of genus. A division of the taxonomic order that usually contains several species.

Genus: Birds that share the same genus share more genetic traits in common than birds that are in the same family. The genus is the first part of the scientific name.

Glossary of Terms: A list of terms used in a book. In this case terms used to describe attributes of birds and Avian studies.

Home Range: A rather loose term that describes the area of a bird that does not migrate such as a Black-capped Chickadee.

Hybridization: It is used to describe a bird that is the offspring of two different species. This often occurs in waterfowl. A hybrid bird is a synonymous term.

Intergrades: A term used in some bird species such as the Northern Flickers. Western individuals have red feath-

Glossary

ers under the wing and eastern individuals are yellow under the wing. Where they interbreed you can get intergrade between these two colors.

Irruptive Species: A species that can be present in large numbers one year and not another year. The Finch and owl families are prone to irruptive species.

Journey of Discovery: The name of the exploration by Lewis and Clark in the Missouri and Columbia river basins from 1803 to 1806. Often called the Corps of Discovery as well.

Juvenile Plumage: This term is applied to first year birds in their fall feathers. The term is also used to describe a non-breeding bird due to its age.

Latilong: An area that is defined as one degree of longitude by one degree of latitude.

Life List: A list of birds that one has seen throughout their life. The list is often stored on eBird or a computer program such as Birder's Diary.

Lores: The lores are the areas of a bird's face on either side from the base of the bill to the front of the eyes.

Mandible: Another name for the two parts of a bird's bill. Bird descriptions often refer to the upper or lower mandible.

Medial Stripe: A stripe in the middle of the crown of the head that is a different color than the crown.

Megapixel: A megapixel is equal to one million pixels. Digital images are made up of thousands of these tiny, tile-like picture elements. The more pixels the higher the image resolution.

Migration: Migration is the annual Spring or Fall movement of many bird species. Spring migration brings birds to the breeding grounds and Fall migration to the wintering grounds.

MNHP: The acronym for the Montana Natural Heritage Program where you can get information on bird species, distribution, and densities.

Montana Bird Distribution: The title of the book that served the same purpose as the MNHP data base. It was put out every five years. The final version was the 7th Edition in 2012.

Morphological: The physical traits of a bird such as weight, wingspan, color of legs and type of beak.

Morphs: A variation of conspicuous plumage coloration. It is thought to be a response to environmental conditions which benefits the bird.

MRBC: The acronym for the Montana Rare Bird Committee, which keeps the official list of birds for Montana. Recently the name was changed to Montana Bird Advocacy .

Murder: A large group of ravens or crows.

Mustachio Line: A vertical black line on the side of the face in falcons.

Nape: The back of the neck. In some species the nape is a different color than the back.

Glossary

National Wildlife Refuge: An area set aside by the federal government for the protection and production of waterfowl. There are 21 NWA areas in Montana. An example is Medicine Lake NWR.

Nestlings: Young chicks that are still in the nest before they take flight.

Nocturnal: A word used to describe animals that are active at night. Typically used to describe night feeding behavior in birds such as owls.

Nomenclature: The devising or choosing of names for things especially in a science or other discipline.

Non-Breeding Plumage: The plumage of a bird that is typically less colorful than the breeding plumage. It is also called winter plumage.

Ochre-Tinged: A word used to describe an orange coloration on a bird.

Omnivores: An animal that can feed on biological material derived from both plant and animal material.

Ornithology: The science of studying and knowing about birds and is full of technical terms to describe the characteristics of birds. I have tried to use as few of the technical terms as possible.

Over-Wintering: The term used to describes birds that are found in a region on a consistent basis between December 15 and February 15.

Passerine: Any bird of the order Passeriformes which includes more than half of all bird species. These birds have the ability to sing and perch.

Passerine: A term used to describe perching songbirds.

Pishing: A sound made with your mouth to imitate bird sounds with the intent of getting the bird to show itself.

Playback: Using any form of electronic bird songs and calls. Typically it involves the use of an App on a phone or tablet with a speaker to locate a bird in the field.

Plumage: A reference to a bird's feathers collectively.

Plumes: Refers to long decorative feathers on some bird such as herons. In the past these feathers were collected for the millinery industry. Collecting plumes is now illegal.

Primary Feather: Primary feathers are the "fingertip" feathers, the longest on a bird's wing and the farthest away from the bird's body when the wings are extended

Rafts: A term used to describe a large number of waterfowl tightly pack on the water.

Raptor: A general term used denoting birds of prey including hawks, eagles, falcons, vultures; but not owls. In Montana there are 22 species of raptors.

Rare Bird Committee: A committee within each state that is responsible for keeping the *State Bird List*. They approve or disapprove rare sightings for inclusion in the state list.

Rarity: In Montana a rarity is any bird that has been seen less that 20 times. It can also refer to a bird that is

Glossary

regionally rare.

Riparian Zone: The area of land next to a river or stream that typically floods and has a high density of deciduous trees. Riparian areas are extensively used by most bird species.

Rufous: A reddish coloration on some birds such as a Rufous Hummingbird.

Rufus: A rust red color of some feathers.

Scapulars: The body of feathers that cover the top of the wing and look like the shoulder.

Scientific Order: The taxonomic order of organisms. In terms of birds we refer most often to Order, Family, Genus and Species.

Sea Gull: A incorrect term used by many. There are only gulls though many are seen along ocean shores.

Sedge Beds: A wet area of dense grass like plant with triangular stems and inconspicuous flowers. Sedges are widely distributed throughout temperate and cold regions.

Sexually-Dimorphic: A term used to describe the male and female of a species having different plumages, particularly in the breeding season.

Shorebird: A general term for species with long legs that occupy shallow waters of lakes, streams and ponds. In Montana there are 41 shorebird species.

Signets: A term used to describe the offspring of swans rather than calling them chicks.

Skulker: A bird that rarely shows itself but is often heard.

Song: Birds songs are different than bird calls. They are melodic extended vocalizations for establishing breeding territories and attraction of a mate.

Species: Two individuals that have the same genetics who can breed and produce a fertile offspring.

Species of Concern: A species that is declining in population numbers or range and/or habitat making it vulnerable to extinction or extirpation.

Species of Interest: A species that is apparently secure, although it may be quite rare in parts of its range and/or suspected to be declining.

Staging Area: These are the stop over areas for resting and feeding of migrant birds. Staging can be as long as three to five days in Spring and Fall migration.

State Bird: A bird that is designated by a state legislature to represent the state. In Montana that bird is the Western Meadow Lark

Sub-Species: A sub-species or "race" of a recognized species that has limited morphological differences. Sub-species are usually caused by geographical separation.

Supercilium: An area of feathers on the side of the head above the eye which is usually white. An eye-stripe runs through the eye.

Taxonomic Order: The classification or genetic order of a species based on sharing similar genetic traits. In bird

Glossary

studies we typically are concerned with Order, Family, Genus and Species.

Territorial Song: A song that can be simple or elaborate that announces and protects a territory for breeding and feeding by a male bird. Most often the song is sung in the early morning.

Tertials: The set of flight feathers situated on the lower portion of a bird's wing.

Ticker: A British word describing someone who lists or keeps records of birds they have seen.

Tundra: An area of low growing arctic plants and permafrost that is caused by latitude. The Arctic Circle is the largest tundra region of the world.

Understories: A description of a plant community that grows low to the ground and is below taller plants in the over story.

Undertail: The bottom of the tail or area of the vent.

Underwing: The bottom side of the wings which may have feathers of a different color.

Vent: The area of a bird under the tail that can be a different color than the rest of the plumage.

Waders: A group of birds that have longer legs than shorebirds and feed and/or nest in shallow to deeper water than shorebirds. In Montana there are 16 wading species

White Geese: Snow and Ross's Geese make up the white geese group in Montana.

Wing Bars: One or often two contrasting lines running across a bird's folded wing.

Wingspan: The distance between the tips of a birds extended wings.

Winter plumage: A term used to describe the plumage of a bird during the non-breeding season.

WMA: A state owned Wildlife Management Area. An example is Warm Springs Wildlife Management Area.

Year List: A list of birds that one has seen in a single year. Many organizations hold informal year list competition for a specific area. ♦

BIRD NOTES:

BIRD NOTES:

BIRD NOTES:

BIRD NOTES:

Made in the USA
Middletown, DE
26 July 2024